THE FOREVER MIND

The
FOREVER
MIND

*Eight Ways to Unleash
the Powers of Your Mature Mind*

Priscilla Donovan

and

Jacquelyn Wonder

Produced by
Alison Brown Cerier Book Development, Inc.

Quill
William Morrow
New York

In certain case histories, names and identifying characteristics of individuals have been changed.

Library of Congress Cataloging-in-Publication Data

Donovan, Priscilla.
   The forever mind : eight ways to unleash the powers of your mature
mind / Priscilla Donovan and Jacquelyn Wonder.
      p. cm.
   Includes bibliographical references and index.
   ISBN 0-688-14623-6
   1. Cognition in old age. 2. Cognition—Age factors. 3. Aged—
Conduct of life. 4. Middle aged persons—Conduct of life.
I. Wonder, Jacquelyn. II. Title.
BF724.85.C64D   1994
155.67—dc20   94-8888
                                                           CIP

Printed in the United States of America

First Quill Edition

1 2 3 4 5 6 7 8 9 10

BOOK DESIGN BY CIRCA 86, INC.

To all the elders
who show us how to stay sharp
and all those younger wise enough
to learn from them

CONTENTS

PREFACE

Medical research shows that we're ready to break the four-minute mile of physical aging—it is now possible to live a full century and still be physically healthy. *Brain research is headed in the same direction and offers the same promising future:* There are many indications that we can grow sharper with age.

In gathering material for this book, we've come across a plethora of research indicating that thinking skills continue to develop throughout the lifespan. Although some physical "accidents" interfere with this continued development, there's virtually no ceiling on how long we can continue to "grow" our brains, except for the limitations we impose upon ourselves and those that the myths of society foist upon us.

The timing for such a breakthrough couldn't be better! Currently, one in four Americans is fifty or older. In twenty years, the ratio will be one in three. While extending life is a great achievement, extending the *quality* of life is what everyone really wants. We've found that it's possible—and the earlier you start, the better.

Since the publication of our book *Whole-Brain Thinking* in 1984, we have compiled a mountain of information about the way the brain develops in adulthood. We've searched for facts and theories on the aging brain and consulted with leaders in the field of medicine and research. We've discussed thinking and living strategies with thousands of our readers and seminar participants. We interviewed a wide cross section of people to discover how adult thinking varies at different times of life.

Throughout the book, we will relate the experiences and wisdom of a group we call the "excellent elders." We found them by asking journalists, lawyers, and counselors in their thirties and forties for names of the sharpest elders they know—people they want to be like when they reach old age. From in-depth interviews with the elders they nominated, we learned much about what it takes to be happy, sharp, secure, and admired in old age. (For details on how these interviews were conducted, see Appendix B.)

Their stories show that you are never too old to change, to learn, to grow; and that, in fact, changing and learning are the keys to an exciting, fulfilling life. Sharp adults *of all ages* are those who take on new challenges in a purposeful way.

The people we interviewed may not have set out intentionally to develop new thinking skills, but were often led to do so when they faced new challenges. For example, Harry Townes, an actor from Alabama, got his first professional role in the road company of *Grapes of Wrath* because the part required a southern accent; but during every spare moment while traveling with the company, he read all kinds of plays aloud in front of the mirror so that he could be cast in roles requiring other accents. It worked! His next role was as a replacement for David Wayne in *Finian's Rainbow*. When he learned that Wayne was leaving the musical, he went to watch how Wayne played the role. Then when he auditioned, Harry read, sang, and danced the part as much like Wayne's portrayal as possible. He won the part and went on to a successful career onstage, in television, and in movies.

This actor was an adult when he changed his way of speaking, a feat equivalent to learning a second language. Such a task is fairly easy in childhood but grows increasingly difficult for adults; yet Harry was able to master it.

You have probably made some equally demanding changes to achieve something important to you. Most of us invent strategies to meet challenging circumstances. We invent ways of remembering, solving problems, making decisions, and organizing our lives. And it is just such strategies that help us end up with better thinking skills in our seventies and eighties than we ever had before.

We found throughout our interviews that those who readily adapted to life and brain changes had not only the most success in life, but also the most fun. When you work on your thinking skills, you can expect more out of life—not only in such practical areas as finances and career, but also in more ephemeral ways such as feeling self-confident and satisfied. *The Forever Mind* was written to help you, too, be more successful and happy your whole life long.

The techniques and skills we will talk about are not only for the whole length of your life, but also for every part of your life—home, work, hobbies, and recreation, and for every role you play. Techniques for organizing your thoughts and your "stuff," for communicating with others, and for learning and remembering are the same at home as on the job. Don't restrict your best thinking to nine to five, or weekends—put your new skills to work in every part of your life.

We first became interested in how the brain ages when we wrote *Whole-Brain Thinking* in the early 1980s. These days, we have a more personal interest in the topic. As Art Carney was told when he was wondering if he'd be able to portray an older person in the movies, "Art, you *are* old." Here are our individual thoughts on the paths that have led us to write this book.

PRISCILLA: Some years ago, I switched from early childhood education to adult education. Teaching kids had been captivating, but working with adults was a dream job. For ten years, I coordinated courses for the Division of Continuing Education at the University of Colorado, creating classes on topics I was curious about. The topic that particularly intrigued me was the human brain. I was able to schedule outstanding researchers and teachers in this field to lecture on the workings of the mind, most notably Robert Bradley, M.D., originator of a mental/physical regimen for painless childbirth; Thomas Budzynski, Ph.D., psychologist and biofeedback researcher; Gerald Jampolsky, M.D., a California psychiatrist known for his work with terminally ill children; and Jerre Levy, Ph.D., brain researcher and professor at the University of Chicago.

I was so fascinated by their work and the many breakthroughs being made in understanding how the brain works that I entered a master's program in adult education, eventually focusing on the applications of brain lateralization research to adult learning.

For the past six years, I've taught classes for a training institute at the university on time and stress management, communication, marketing, and the media, always relating the material to how the mind works.

During the same period, I helped a man in his late seventies named Cecil

Reed write his memoirs and observed how he reclaimed the memories of a lifetime. You'll read more about Cecil later in the book because he became one of our excellent elders. Midway through writing his book, *Fly in the Buttermilk,* he became ill and was hospitalized for the first time in his life. His memory, balance, and energy were affected. He recovered quickly, I believe, because he had been so active physically and mentally all his life. Now in his eighties, Cecil continues his public speaking career nationwide—and he's better than ever.

Cecil proved to me that not only can you keep your mental skills as you age, you can improve them. I now feel I can look forward with genuine optimism to growing old myself. And none too soon. I'm sixty-five and, like Art Carney, ready for the role.

JACQUELYN: Recently, I had an awakening experience about age on a personal level. I'd just turned fifty-five, the age when my local grocery store starts giving a 10 percent "senior's discount." When I gave my proof of age at the checkout counter for the first time, I felt as if I were getting away with something illegal. *Surely,* I thought, *they'll question my age. I can't be old enough to get a senior's discount!* Then I realized, *Hey, I really am!* Age had snuck in while I wasn't looking. And I needed to know how to think about the fifty-five-year-old me.

The subject of aging and the mind had surfaced many times over the years in my career as a management consultant and author. For example, when we were researching our second book—*The Flexibility Factor,* which was about change—we found that the subjects over forty had a much greater capacity for "reflective judgment" than those in their twenties and thirties. I wanted to know whether thinking improves in other ways as we age. And second, I wondered how can one stay alert, clear, and involved at all ages.

When book developer Alison Brown Cerier, who had worked with us on our previous books, approached me with an idea for a new book about the aging mind, I was ready to go!

When *The Forever Mind*'s concept was clarified I discussed it with Priscilla, who was enthusiastic about it. Sometime later, practicing the kind of judgment mentioned above, I reflected on how our thinking styles complemented each other. And when I asked her if she would like to work on the book with me, she happily said yes.

Researching and writing *The Forever Mind* has caused me to reflect on my own experiences. I have recognized many crossroads in my life where learning new thinking skills made all the difference for me. For example, in my twenties I was hired for an incredibly responsible position, mostly because I could remember the names of the forty trustees of the Rocky Mountain Mineral Law Foundation at my first meeting with them. I learned then the importance of having a good memory, and I became committed to having one. Not only did I work hard on my memory in my personal life, but when I became a management consultant, I conducted seminars for lawyers, judges, and businesses on memory skills. When my recall started to slow in my early fifties, I searched for strategies to supplement my lagging abilities, and was thrilled when I found things that really worked!

In my fifty-six years I have experienced many of the types of learning we will talk about in this book. For example, because I've wanted to be more organized, and to make decisions in a more thoughtful way (especially in conjunction with my husband, a left-brained lawyer), I've worked on my left-brain skills. Because I wanted to communicate better with my three sons and one stepson, as well as my three daughters-in-law and three stepdaughters, I worked with both a social worker and a psychoanalyst and learned much about the value of different thinking styles.

A few years ago, I experienced firsthand the power of positive adaption to change, which we will talk about later. When I was in my early fifties, I hit a tree while skiing and broke the first two vertebrae in my neck. I had to wear a twenty-five-pound metal halo screwed into my skull for nine months. I came to empathize with the restrictions of physically challenged people, and was struck by how adaptable we humans are. I learned to wait out this long period, and even to enjoy the time it gave me for reading and reflection. When I could once again participate in hiking, biking, tennis, and exercise classes, I valued these activities so much more.

In a later chapter, we will talk about discovering your passion. My passion is discovering, supporting, and loving all the different ways that people think, learn, and create, especially in their later years. I have enjoyed pursuing my passion through wonderful conversations with productive men and women, by teaching creative problem solving for adults, and by working with such groups as Elderhostel, Active Times, and Explore. I am also pursuing it now through a Ph.D. program in educational psychology and as the director of Denver's Center for Creative Studies.

I hope that you, like me, will come to see life as one opportunity for learning after another.

I also hope that this book will help you, as it's helped me, to look forward eagerly to the years that lie ahead. In my fifties, I befriended ninety-year-old Maud Morgan, a creative, exciting, sensuous artist. She ended a recent conversation with me by saying, "Oh, Jacquelyn, you have so many adventures ahead!" I can't wait!

ACKNOWLEDGMENTS

First and foremost we'd like to acknowledge the invaluable insights shared by the group we came to call excellent elders. Their life stories inspired us, sometimes amused us, and showed us what keeps us all sharp lifelong. They are Chester Alter, Jack Baldwin, Patria Barberry, Jean Barr, Fritz Benedict, Carl Blaurock, Peggy Bliss, David Campbell, Constance Cole, Charlotte Conover, Josephine Taylor Conover, Julian Darst Conover, Harry Dennis, Lady Jean Denton, Babe Denzer, Lillian Echohawk, Betty Fineman, Ruth T. Frazier, Walo von Greyerz, Julie Harris, Ruth Harriet Jacobs, Bob Jones, Edith King, Miles R. Markley, Jack Matson, Maurice Mitchell, Maud Morgan, Toni Morrison, Mrs. Arthur Nielsen, Sr., Nell Noddings, Edna Oliver, Walter Oliver, Elizabeth Paepke, Robert W. Parker, Bea Parnes, Sidney Parnes, Bruce Patton, Russell Randall, Cecil Reed, Ruth Ripley, Ethel Sarkisian, Donald R. Seawell, Jane Silverstein-Ries, Ellio Stacey, Phyllis Stare, Billie Stein, Moe Stein, Meta Stone, Rose Styron, Ken Thompson, Harry Townes, Ida Truscott, Peter Vaill, Houstoun Waring, Mary Welch, Dorothy Wilson, Betty Wonder, and Jean Yancey.

Many thanks to the journalists, consultants, and others who generously helped us find the excellent elders, including Kathy Bradshaw, Carolyn Bushong, Jerry Conover, Ted Conover, Alan Dumas, Polly Gordon, Pat McClearn,

Ken Martin, Arthur Nielsen, Jr., Dave Porter, Annalee Schorr, Wagner Schorr, Hannah Shatz, and John Smedley.

Many other people served as guinea pigs when we were developing and testing interview questions and the memory quiz: Terry Armstrong, Nora Bomasuto, Claude E. Brazzeal, James Breakey, James D. Brown, Clarece Collins, Cheryl Cruz, Laura Lee Cubbison, Betty Dolezal, Eleanor M. Haefner, Maurina Hickman, Ray Hickman, Jean Hoffman, Mrs. Bruce Isaacson, Nancy Johnson, Vic Kammer, Joanna Kincaid, Ron Kincaid, Doug Larson, Gerry McCray, Virginia Nagel, Ellen Padden, William T. Peters, Mary Philcox, Janet Pool, John S. Roberts, Herbert Shatz, Don Weir, and the Friday Morning Breakfast Club.

We are most grateful to the many people who took part in various tests and surveys, or who were interviewed for the book. Those who went above and beyond the call of duty include Connie Brown, Alison Burghardt, Gene Cisneros, Sheila Cleworth, Carol Coppage, Donna Dobrovitz, Katie Dodge, Mary Dominick, Sherry Dorward, Nan Fogel, Jane Gilbert, Neda Graves, Norma Haffenstein, Bob Hickock, Eleanor Katz, Chris Kelley, Karyn Kitchner, Ray Kluever, Dianne Leffly, Linda Lister, Ann Loper, Maro Lorimer, Carol Lynch, Anne Mahoney, Carolyn and Donovan Mahoney, Mary and Daniel Mahoney, Roy Mitchell, Ken Nichol, Dianne Olsen, Lise Olsen, Lynn Parker, Bruce Pennington, Jim Rathel, Karen Rosica, Diane Rowe, Ralph Sorenson, Ruth Thone, Whittaker Wagner, Pam Welch, Vonnie Wheeler, and Edna Wright.

The following institutions were very helpful during our research on the book: Vista Clara Spa and Health Retreat in Galisteo, New Mexico; the Copper Canyon Association for the Tarahumara Nation; Outward Bound; the White Water Institute; Explore; *Active Times* magazine; the Kinetics Fitness Studio; The Denver Athletic Club; the University of Colorado and University of Denver departments of psychology, psychiatry, and educational psychology; the Institute for Developmental Psychology; the Center for the Study of Contemporary Belief, Denver and Boston; and the Denver Center for Creative Studies.

Family and friends endured tests and discussions of half-formed thoughts, went on wild goose chases for and with us, and helped us with tasks we didn't have the time or skills for. Most of all, they soothed us when we were tired, out of sorts, and discouraged. These sainted folks include Jeffrey Blake, Nora Brunner, Jerry Conover, Jeff Donovan, Marty and Mike Donovan, Margo Guralnick, Sandy Johnson, Allison Kempe, Dugan Mahoney, Kobus Neethling, Robert Parker, Sandra Pomeroy, I. Gene Schwarz, Charlotte Sorenson, John Waldrop, and Gregg Winchell.

Thinking About Thinking

1

Reassuring Realities

Man fools himself. He prays for a long life, and he fears an old age.
—CHINESE PROVERB

If you know how the brain works you can set your own directions. If you don't, then someone else will.
—RICHARD BANDLER

Millions of Americans over forty have a secret fear—that their minds aren't what they used to be. As annoying memory problems add up, they begin to worry about their ability to remain in control of their lives. When they forget some minor item, they ask themselves, *Am I starting to lose it?*

The answer is: No! Of course, the brain does change over time, but the changes don't ruin our ability to think. They just alter the *way* we think. Furthermore, these changes complement the physical and emotional development that is normal for young adulthood, middle age, young old age, and very old age. In other words, the natural changes that occur in the brain and body over a lifetime are particularly suited to the stage of life we're experiencing.

The reality is that you can actually be even sharper after forty than you were before—if, as you age, you take conscious steps to make the fullest use of your brain's greatest strengths.

As we talked with people in their forties, fifties, sixties, and beyond, the same fears about the aging brain came up again and again. Do you have some of these same concerns?

THE FEAR: I've heard that brain cells die off as you age. Am I doomed to become senile?

THE REALITY: In our society there is a groundless myth that, sooner or later, we all are stricken with a senile mindlessness. Many people mistakenly believe that as the body ages, the IQ drops, memory weakens, and the ability to learn or change disappears.

The reality is that senility is an outdated term, a misnomer for a variety of conditions sometimes suffered by older people. The myth began before modern medicine when people mistook the effects of diseases such as atherosclerosis, syphilis, cancer, osteoporosis, diabetes, and hearing problems for normal aging. Granted, there are a few serious illnesses, such as Alzheimer's, that disturb mental functions, but even they can be treated. However, as Dr. Robert Butler, founding director of the National Institute of Aging, says, "The belief that if you live long enough you will become senile is just wrong."

You can help your brain perform well at every age through regular exercise, good nutrition, emotional balance, and mental stimulation.

THE FEAR: I'm starting to forget little things. Is this an early sign of Alzheimer's?

THE REALITY: There are some disorders that can affect the brain as people age, but they are much less common than you think, and there are many steps you can take physically and mentally to reduce your risks.

THE FEAR: I don't have the confidence I once had in my mental abilities.

THE REALITY: High self-esteem and feelings of happiness, satisfaction, and security—and their opposites—affect the way the mind works. Low self-esteem, a critical concern because of the way society treats older people, is the true cause of many problems with the mind. A drop in self-esteem is especially troubling for people once recognized as high achievers. There are two things you can do to help: Unmask the myths about aging that can eat into your self-esteem, and seek emotional balance in your attitudes toward hardship and success.

THE FEAR: My memory is not what it once was, and I'm afraid things are going to get even worse.

THE REALITY: Short-term memory does change as we grow older. In most respects, though, it is merely different, not worse. In some ways, memory actually gets better. As we age, our memory's strengths move from the specific to the general—instead of details, we remember the big picture. What you need to do is to discover your best memory skills and learn how to take advantage of them.

THE FEAR: I feel overwhelmed by the routine, day-to-day details of my life. I'm worried I'm getting flaky, out of it.

THE REALITY: Life is more complicated today than ever before, and it is important for people of every age to learn how to manage the details of work or personal life. By using some easy systems to organize the routine details, you can gain control and peace of mind.

THE FEAR: When faced with a decision, large or small, I can't make up my mind as quickly as I used to.

THE REALITY: It does take longer to make decisions as we age, but most older people make better decisions than they did in earlier years. As we age, we become more skilled at "reflective thinking," the ability to see many possible solutions to a problem, and to put them in context using our experience. We can draw on a lifetime of resources in making sound decisions. Instead of the snap decisions of youth, we make the informed decisions of the wise elder.

THE FEAR: Ever since the surgery (or retirement or divorce or move or death of my spouse), I haven't been as sharp as I usually am. I see big changes ahead in my life, too, and I'm afraid they're going to really throw me.

THE REALITY: Many people underestimate the ways that our thought processes can be disrupted by major changes such as surgery, work displacement or retirement, the death of a spouse, illness, or moving, especially as we grow older. The older brain's mental pathways are like deeply rutted roads; changing paths is a difficult, jarring experience. It's natural to feel more "out of it" after a major change. But since life is full of change, with some of the greatest in our later years, it is very comforting to learn ways to manage change. With practice, you may even learn to like change and welcome it.

THE FEAR: I can't remember the last time I felt really passionate about something. Passion is for the young, right?

THE REALITY: Passion is for life—not just youth—because it spurs us to learn and grow. Those who postpone finding and following their passions during youth and middle age rarely enjoy them in old age. Those who wait for retirement to do the things they love rarely have the energy when the time arrives. Six weeks of fishing, reading, or traveling and they're bored and discouraged. Passions should be pursued when they first come to you so that they will flourish—and you will flourish along with them.

In the chapters to come, you will discover how to replace the fears that can limit your success and your happiness with understanding and strategies that will help you have a lifetime of crisp, optimistic, growing mentation. You'll find that you have the potential to live happily ever after!

LATE, GREAT CHANGES

- Your short-term memory isn't as fast, but your long-term recall is stronger.
- You can't do everything at once, but you've got great systems for those things that matter.
- You're not as goal oriented, but you know that progress comes in zigzag ways.
- You're not as strong physically, but you have more mental skills for problem solving.
- You don't feel high as often, and you rarely feel low.
- You say things less emphatically, but your opinions have more authority.
- Learning new information is more difficult, but you know how to apply it.
- Your passions don't burn like the bonfires of youth, they warm with the glowing embers of age.
- Changes are still painful, but you know from past experience that they can bring better days.
- You make decisions more slowly, spending time on front-end information gathering and planning but less time on back-end revamping and redoing.
- You pursue fewer passions, but you're committed body and mind to the chosen few.

The Brainmarkers

Forty is the old age of youth, fifty is the youth of old age.

—VICTOR HUGO

The negative effects of aging on the human brain are minimal in most people. Then how do you account for the differences between people's late-life thinking skills? Why do two people with the same IQ and similar medical histories and social backgrounds have vastly different mental abilities in old age?

There are many paths to being mentally fit, but how and how much you use your brain are the key steps in any path. The sharp elders we've talked with realized early on the importance of "improving their minds." They honed their natural skills and worked hard at those that were not so easy for them. When they experienced a setback or confronted a problem, they'd think it through and try another approach. Instead of losing self-confidence, they learned from their mistakes.

Are you aware of the thinking skills you developed in childhood, and how they affect your thinking today? Are you currently testing and revising any of your thinking skills? Are you adapting to short-term-memory losses or other changes in your mental abilities? Have you actively replaced an old skill with a new one?

People who stay sharp are aware of their brains' potentials. They want to improve their thinking, and always to move forward. And they engage in activities that build mental skills. It is these three areas that make the difference:

- awareness
- attitude
- activities

We've developed a simple set of gauges to help you assess your own awareness, attitude, and level of activity in using natural changes in the brain to improve your thinking skills. Called the Brainmarkers, these gauges measure eight mental skills that we all grow throughout life:

- body wisdom
- emotional balance
- memory
- learning
- systems for control
- decision making
- openness to change
- passion

Before you move forward to realize your brain's potential, you need to see where you are now. So in this chapter, you'll have a chance to evaluate your current awareness, attitude, and activity in each Brainmarker. When you've finished the book, you can check your progress using the follow-up test in Appendix A.

As you'll see, we all grow such thinking skills throughout our lives, beginning at birth.

BRAINMARKER 1—BODY WISDOM

"You are what you eat" and "I move, therefore I am" sum up the latest information on the relationship of your thinking skills to your physical condition. To think clearly and at peak levels, you must eat and exercise properly, because both diet and physical activity influence the amount of nutrients and oxygen that gets to your brain. Conversely, the acts of eating and exercising are influenced by your awareness, attitude, and stage of life.

We are all born with body wisdom, a natural inclination to eat and exercise in a healthful way, but many of us forget by the age of four how to listen to the messages our bodies send us. Think about:

- how aware you are of links between your diet, exercise, and other health habits and the way you think. Do you know which foods contribute to clear thinking and why? (*awareness*)
- how willing you are to change your diet and exercise to improve your thinking skills. Are you interested in learning which exercises best stimulate brain chemicals? (*attitude*)
- how active you are in listening to and practicing your body wisdom. Do you schedule difficult tasks for times when your thinking is apt to be at peak levels? (*activity*)

To help you quantify these estimates of your current body wisdom and physical health, use the scale below.

Gauging Body Wisdom

On a scale from 1 to 10 (with 1 meaning not at all and 10 meaning fully), circle the number that describes how true these statements are for you:

---

awareness: I know a lot about how health affects thinking.
  low 1 2 3 4 5 6 7 8 9 10 high

Since this is your first Brainmarker, we're providing some examples to help gauge your scoring: A 2 score on awareness would be for a person who occasionally reads a newspaper article on nutrition; a 4 knows about the government's new food pyramid and about exercises that produce aerobic results; an 8 knows when he's at the 80 percent level of exertion and which foods appear to counteract cancer.

attitude: I really want to adopt healthful habits.
  low 1 2 3 4 5 6 7 8 9 10 high

A 2 feels that neither food nor exercise contributes to clear thinking; a 4 is intrigued by the brain-body connection; an 8 is determined to find foods and exercises that aid clear thinking.

activity: I practice healthful habits daily.
  low 1 2 3 4 5 6 7 8 9 10 high

A 2 takes no special measures for exercise or diet; a 4 climbs staircases, walks the dog, goes out to get the newspaper, and eats less fatty foods than previously; an 8 does aerobic exercise five times a week and has found that it stimulates clear thinking.

Divide the total number of points you circled by 3 to determine Brainmarker 1: ——

BRAINMARKER 2—EMOTIONAL BALANCE

In order to think with clarity or learn something new, you must have your emotions in balance. When you are very angry, you have limited thinking strategies. You may say or do something foolish or even dangerous. On the other hand, if you exercise *too much* control you may be unable to express your emotions, and sometimes even to feel them. So emotional imbalance can stem from too much or too little control.

Such imbalances occur at all ages; they just look different. You've probably witnessed these examples of too little control: the terrible two who can't handle her anger, so she often screams "No!" and throws a temper tantrum; the teen who gossips about the other person or runs away from home; a middle-ager who argues aggressively or quits her job. Too much control might cause the two-year-old who is angry with his parents to wet his pants or stop eating; the teenager might do poorly in school or start using drugs; the middle-ager might become depressed and withdrawn or develop an ulcer.

While most of us learn some skills for handling our emotions during early childhood, the turbulence of the teen years usually presents a whole new set of challenges to balancing our emotions so that we can think clearly. The same kind of challenge, accompanied by another set of hormonal changes, presents itself to us at midlife when we typically go through an "identity crisis," similar to the ones experienced by the two-year-old and the teenager. The difference is, we have many more thinking skills by this time to help us. However, we also have many more responsibilities and concerns, which make balancing difficult.

But as you'll learn later, middle age is also a time for discovering another side of you; men find themselves becoming more comfortable with their emotions, while women develop confidence in their rational abilities. So hang in there if you're forty and wondering why your moods change so quickly.

To evaluate your present ability to balance emotions, think about:

- how aware you are of your own emotions and others', how fully you have experienced emotional growth at each stage of life, and how much you understand about the effects of emotions on clear thinking (*awareness*)
- how willing you are to make changes in the way you handle emotionally draining situations and how interested you are in finding ways to achieve emotional balance (*attitude*)
- how active you are in improving the way you handle the confrontations and choices you face every day and how successful you are in feeling emotionally balanced (*activity*)

Now, quantify your thoughts about emotional balance below.

Gauging Emotional Balance

On a scale from 1 to 10 (with 1 meaning not at all and 10 meaning fully), circle the number that describes how true these statements are for you:

---

awareness: I am aware of my emotional triggers and how to deal with them.
    low 1 2 3 4 5 6 7 8 9 10 high

attitude: I want to understand my emotions and those of others.
    low 1 2 3 4 5 6 7 8 9 10 high

activity: I express my emotions and try to improve the way I do so.
    low 1 2 3 4 5 6 7 8 9 10 high

Divide the total number of points you circled by 3 to determine Brainmarker 2: ____

BRAINMARKER 3—MEMORY

Your memory is you. Without recall of your name, your loved ones, your work, and the things you learned in school, you are merely a functioning body. Having a good memory in old age depends a great deal on the kind of mental skills you developed earlier and how much you have used them.

Even though short-term memory generally decreases with age, we found that elders who learned *memory strategies* early in life had good short-term memories. Many of those we interviewed had been required to memorize Bible verses, poems, math facts, and lengthy quotations in childhood. They used these skills at home and in church, at spelling and arithmetic bees, and in debates and school plays. So it seems that early training in memory skills has lasting results.

Training in later years—consciously applying tricks, approaches, and strategies for improving recall—can improve memory, too.

To evaluate how well you've made such compensations in mental skills, think about:

- what kinds of memory skills you have already acquired. Are you able to make it through one day without a major omission—such as forgetting the gist of a client's project—and with only one or two minor slips—such as forgetting to buy milk on the way home? (*awareness*)
- how important it is to you that you have good memory skills. Are you willing to be known as the resident "space case" or do you want to be respected for your good memory? (*attitude*)
- how many ways you now actively improve your memory skills. For example, do you prepare yourself for work or social functions by boning up on names and current events? Do you memorize frequently used numbers and bits of information? (*activity*)

Now record your evaluation of these kinds of memory skills below.

Gauging Memory

On a scale from 1 to 10 (with 1 meaning not at all and 10 meaning fully), circle the number that describes how true these statements are for you:

---

awareness: I have a good memory.
 low 1 2 3 4 5 6 7 8 9 10 high

attitude: I want to continue developing my memory skills.
 low 1 2 3 4 5 6 7 8 9 10 high

activity: I use strategies for remembering things.
 low 1 2 3 4 5 6 7 8 9 10 high

Divide the total number of points you circled by 3 to determine Brainmarker 3: ____

BRAINMARKER 4—LEARNING

Another factor that contributes to mental sharpness in old age is a lifelong love of learning. The sharp elders we interviewed had a fondness for learning of all kinds. They learned formally in schools and at work, and informally by observing the world around them.

Studies of adult education have shown that once we've reached maturity, learning becomes easier, mostly because of motivation and experience. When you're in your own start-up business, you really want to learn how to write a business plan. When you're the mother of two preschoolers, it's easier to make sense out of an early-childhood education class. The loss in brain tissue that normally begins around age twenty-five is balanced by the new growth that the thinking person initiates by new learning during adulthood.

Think about:

- what kinds of things you like to learn. When are you a quick study; when are you a fast forgetter? (*awareness*)
- whether you are content to rely on others to work newfangled gadgets, or whether you like to figure things out for yourself. Do you enjoy learning? (*attitude*)
- how many ways (reading, broadcast media, schools and training, discussion with others, hands-on experiences, and so on) you now actively pursue knowledge (*activity*)

Now quantify your evaluation of your learning skills below.

Gauging Learning

On a scale from 1 to 10 (with 1 meaning not at all and 10 meaning fully), circle the number that describes how true these statements are for you:

---

awareness: I learn quickly and comprehensively.
   low 1 2 3 4 5 6 7 8 9 10 high

attitude: Learning enriches my life, and I want to improve my skills continually.

 low 1 2 3 4 5 6 7 8 9 10 high

activity: In the last year, I have consciously tried to add to my store of knowledge through reading, formal and informal classes, discussions, and trying new things.

 low 1 2 3 4 5 6 7 8 9 10 high

Divide the total number of points you circled by 3 to determine Brainmarker 4: ____

BRAINMARKER 5—SYSTEMS FOR CONTROL

Most of us learn in the first few years that there is rhyme and reason to the way things work: If you touch a hot stove you will feel pain; if you flip the light switch, the light goes on or off. Such observations are quite valuable. They save us from reinventing the wheel every time we face a new task. Such simple lessons help us learn that there is order and predictability in life. Once we can identify what is predictable and use it to control our environment and influence others, we rapidly evolve related systems and strategies.

The more you can handle the routine details of life with systems that you follow the same way each time, the more energy and thought you can devote to decisions that require focused attention. A great benefit of older age can be a lifetime's worth of well-learned strategies for handling those details.

Think about the kinds of systematic thinking skills you've developed for planning, estimating, organizing, categorizing, prioritizing, communicating, learning, and relaxing. Do they really work for you? Do you apply them to other areas of your life, other tasks and opportunities? Do you manage your time, money, work, and social life, or do they manage you? What new competencies would help you influence others and have an impact on your environment?

To evaluate how comfortably you control your environment, consider:

- how reliable your current systems are for handling your finances, work, social life, interpersonal relationships, and personal health and growth. Can you perform most routines with minimal hassle? Are you able to meet most deadlines? Is your daily life free from frantic phone calls and schedule changes? (*awareness*)

- how important it is to you to develop new systems. How badly do you want to stop sweating the little things so you have energy for the big ones? (*attitude*)

- how regularly you put new systems in place. How often do you employ a way to organize your closets, coordinate your social schedule, or initiate a timesaving strategy at the office? (*activity*)

Now, record how you assess your control skills.

Gauging Systems for Control

On a scale from 1 to 10 (with 1 meaning not at all and 10 meaning fully), circle the number that describes how true these statements are for you:

---

awareness: I know that I need systems in my life.
    low 1 2 3 4 5 6 7 8 9 10 high

attitude: I know that list making, scheduling, and organizing are worth the effort.
    low 1 2 3 4 5 6 7 8 9 10 high

activity: I reassess old ways of doing things and try to systematize wherever I can.
    low 1 2 3 4 5 6 7 8 9 10 high

Divide the total number of points you circled by 3 to determine Brainmarker 5: ____

BRAINMARKER 6—DECISION MAKING

Children show signs of wisdom early on, by their straightforward statements and their ability to detect fakes. They decide intuitively, because they have little experience to rely on. Their naïveté works for them when they're presented with a situation in which false expectations could lead them astray.

In contrast, adults make decisions about finances, fun, and family based on what has worked in the past, new information they've gathered, and the opinions of people they trust. But today's adults are bombarded by so many choices, concepts, and responsibilities that they often feel overwhelmed. So as we face an ever-more-complex world, we need to find better ways of making decisions.

Ironically, time presents us with the opportunity to develop such an approach. In old age, we grow the ability to use reflective judgment, to see the options for achieving a goal in context with successful past experiences. We see more patterns, themes, and cycles. We take the time to consider all the factors, allowing ourselves to make decisions based on both theory and experience.

As you consider your own ability to make wise decisions, think about:

- how able you are to detect wise decision making in others and yourself. Have you noticed a difference in the ways you made successful decisions and failed ones? (*awareness*)
- whether you feel effective decision making is a learnable skill. Do you like making decisions? (*attitude*)
- how often you base your decisions upon experience or the positive examples of others. Do you search out objective points of view? Do you ever stop yourself midway in "rushing to judgment" and slow down? (*activity*)

To record your decision-making abilities, look below.

Gauging Decision Making

On a scale from 1 to 10 (with 1 meaning not at all and 10 meaning fully), circle the number that describes how true these statements are for you:

---

awareness: I notice when I and others make wise decisions.
low 1 2 3 4 5 6 7 8 9 10 high

attitude: I truly want to be logical, caring, and successful in making decisions.
low 1 2 3 4 5 6 7 8 9 10 high

activity: I review my decisions, analyze why they were good or bad, and seek to improve my skills.
low 1 2 3 4 5 6 7 8 9 10 high

Divide the total number of points you circled by 3 to determine Brainmarker 6: ____

BRAINMARKER 7—OPENNESS TO CHANGE

This Brainmarker deals with your ability to be flexible in the way you relate to people and solve problems, both of which enable you to be resilient and creative.

Physical flexibility is at its height in childhood, but in many ways children are quite inflexible mentally. They become addicted to certain habits: They *must* have a story, a glass of water, and a good-night kiss from Teddy Bear, your spouse, and you—in that exact order. But children's inflexibility in such situations is based upon their need to find and maintain order in their lives. When you think about how flexible they must be to learn language and other basic thinking skills, you can understand how incredibly flexible they really are mentally. When they fasten onto a routine so passionately, it is to get relief from the uncertainty they feel *and* an attempt to build a repertoire of certainties.

Teenagers go through a similar time of testing and needing certainties. They are going out of the comfort of their home life into the big world. They must be flexible to adjust to this new world with all its challenges. To compensate, they want to be just like their peers.

In adulthood, the body grows less flexible, but our reservoir of experiences and accumulated certainties enables us to be more flexible in our thinking. We're able to think of many options in a given situation because we've tested many and had success with a variety of approaches.

During your sixties and early seventies, great flexibility is needed. For many in this age group, it is a time of upheaval: retirement, death of loved ones, failing health, and deterioration of family cohesion. Most of these "young olds" still have plenty of reserve energy, talent, and influence, but they must be flexible in the way they spend these resources. If they cling tightly to expired plans, hopes, and roles, they will descend into "hardening of the attitudes." If they adapt gracefully to the losses and gains typical of this stage of life, they are ready to enjoy the stimulation of the new phase.

To estimate how far you've come in thinking flexibly, consider:

- how clearly you understand that flexibility can help you at your present stage of life; how many times you've found that great rewards can come

from harsh and unsolicited changes; whether you feel stimulated by the prospect of someone or something new in your life (*awareness*)
- how much you are willing to adapt to new styles, ideas, and technology that come on the "winds of change" and how much you appreciate different points of view; whether you want to change some aspects of your life (*attitude*)
- how often you develop numerous options when making plans, welcome changes in your life, and take the initiative in unfamiliar territory (*activity*)

Record your comfort level with change on the scale below.

Gauging Openness to Change

On a scale from 1 to 10 (with 1 meaning not at all and 10 meaning fully), circle the number that describes how true these statements are for you:

---

awareness: I am aware of how differently I feel about change that I initiate versus change that's dumped on me.
    low 1 2 3 4 5 6 7 8 9 10 high

attitude: Doing things in a new way appeals to me.
    low 1 2 3 4 5 6 7 8 9 10 high

activity: I try new approaches when I am faced with change.
    low 1 2 3 4 5 6 7 8 9 10 high

Divide the total number of points you circled by 3 to determine Brainmarker 7: ____

BRAINMARKER 8—PASSION

Passion is not so much a brain ability that develops at a certain age as the natural outgrowth of engagement in life, with ideas and experiences. It operates in tandem with curiosity, open-mindedness, and creativity, and it is expressed differently at different ages.

Children seem to be passionate about everything they choose to do. One day it's dinosaurs; the next, race cars or computer games. Most adults tend to follow one interest for a long time, gradually expanding it into many areas.

We might love dancing in our twenties, expand our interest to folk dance in our thirties, collect folk costumes during midlife vacations, and write about the history of dancing in our fifties and sixties. Such interests develop into passions that keep the brain vital. In neurological terms, the traveling, reading, writing, and discussing that we do in pursuing a passion develop a sizable network of memories in our brains.

You can see that pursuing a passion helps you develop and refine the other characteristics of sharpness. Do you see such passionate pursuits in your own life? What would you do or learn if you had no financial or time constraints? Is there anything you do, any topic you pursue, for the pure pleasure of it?

As you ponder these questions about passionate pursuits, think about:

- whether you find yourself irresistibly drawn to some topic or activity (*awareness*)
- whether you believe you are entitled to and capable of enjoying the pursuit of a passion (*attitude*)
- whether you find the time, money, and opportunity to learn more about or engage in such a topic or activity (*activity*)

Evaluate yourself below regarding your passionate pursuits.

Gauging Passion

On a scale from 1 to 10 (with 1 meaning not at all and 10 meaning fully), circle the number that describes how true these statements are for you:

---

awareness: When I think about a certain idea or project, I'm excited.
   low 1 2 3 4 5 6 7 8 9 10 high

attitude: I believe pursuing a passion is too valuable to be postponed.
   low 1 2 3 4 5 6 7 8 9 10 high

activity: I have a passion that grows stronger with age.
   low 1 2 3 4 5 6 7 8 9 10 high

Divide the total number of points you circled by 3 to determine Brainmarker 8: ____

	1	2	3	4	5	6	7	8	9	10
Body wisdom										
Emotional balance										
Memory										
Learning										
Systems for control										
Decision making										
Openness to change										
Passion										

Was it tough for you to estimate your present levels of awareness, attitude, and activity? Take heart; each one will be dealt with in detail in future chapters and will become clearer with each page that you read.

Now record your self-ratings on the table above. It will help you determine which of the eight thinking skills you have developed most fully.

Do you see a pattern in the kinds of thinking skills you have? Are they fairly equal across the board or stronger in some areas?

Do you have a 10 in one area, meaning that you have that trait well in hand? It's the rare person who scores that high in all areas, or even one. After all, you bought the book to learn about these topics, didn't you? So don't despair if you've got some low spots. We're just trying to establish a baseline that will help you gauge your progress.

Many of us are striving to be 10s in all the areas of this table. *Striving* is the key word here. We have differing strengths and weaknesses. Furthermore, your life may present unique situations that speed up or slow down your development. For example, Thomas Sutherland, a college professor who was an Iranian hostage for five and a half years, developed early wisdom during his captivity. By the time he was released at age fifty-seven, he was the benevolent, resilient, confident, peaceful person we hope to be by our late nineties.

The Brainmarker table helps summarize graphically the skills you have developed so far that will help you stay mentally sharp. If the concepts still seem pretty muddy, don't fret. This chapter is a quick overview, meant merely to alert you to the grand possibilities of your brain.

Breaking Through the Myths About Aging

The meaning or lack of meaning that old age takes on in any given society puts that whole society to the test.

—SIMONE DE BEAUVOIR

We grew up founding our dreams on the infinite promise of American advertising. I still believe that one can learn to play the piano by mail and that mud will give you a perfect complexion.

—ZELDA FITZGERALD

Would you say the following statements are true or false?

1. Better travel while you're young and still healthy.
2. Love and lust are for the young.
3. A poor memory is part of growing old.
4. By fifty, your career just naturally winds down.
5. You can't teach an old dog new tricks.
6. Life, like chewing gum, loses its flavor with age.
7. If you live long enough, you'll be wise.

If you feel any of these statements are true, you are under the influence of some of the most powerful myths of our society. (Yes, number seven is also untrue—wisdom does not come automatically with age.) These widespread myths greatly affect the second part of each Brainmarker—*attitude*— and your ability to forge ahead and grow new thinking skills. There is a strong correlation between your attitude toward aging and how often you challenge your thinking skills. If you believe that you're bound to "lose it" after the fifty mark, then you'll do little or nothing about staying healthy and mentally stimulated. That's why it's important to think about attitude.

Why do so many of us have an "attitude" about aging? Why do so many of us assume we'll lose it by the time we're seventy? It starts in the fairytales of childhood. Little Red Ridinghood treks through the forest to take goodies to her ailing grandmother, the frail, feeble, foolish victim of the Big Bad Wolf. The answer to "Mirror, mirror on the wall, who is the fairest of them all?" is the innocent, flowering Snow White, as opposed to the evil, declining old Queen. Cinderella is treated cruelly by her selfish, ugly older stepmother, who also encourages her daughters to do the same.

Older men aren't given any better treatment. They're portrayed as the Old King who makes young men seeking his daughter's hand go through hell first. Other fairytale fathers are so feebleminded or weak-willed that they barter their daughters' purity away to rich, disgusting men three or four times the girls' age; a young and handsome prince has to come to the rescue. Rumpelstiltskin, the first sweatshop boss, is a conniving, evil, ugly old creature. In "The Emperor's New Clothes," we see an older man in a position of power whose inherent foolishness is magnified by his sycophantic contemporaries.

Fairytales like these reflect the attitudes toward aging that prevailed in eighteenth-century Europe. You can see how little ideas have changed since then by looking at our own art forms—T-shirts, greeting cards, gag gifts, and advertising slogans:

- a T-shirt for past-sixties: CRS—CAN'T REMEMBER SH—
- the cocktail napkins that say: "If I'd known I'd live this long, I'd have taken better care of myself."
- bumper sticker messages: GET EVEN WITH YOUR KIDS. LIVE LONG ENOUGH TO BE A BURDEN TO THEM.
- "over-the-hill" decorations for fortieth- and fiftieth-birthday parties that feature mourning themes and silly-looking dinosaurs

IT'S NOT NATURAL

Why is this negative attitude toward aging so widespread? Aging badly is not genetically coded, and it's not the "natural order" to lose control of your life. To the contrary—in the animal world the elders are often powerful and respected to the end, for some very sensible reasons.

In baboon troops, dominant males first earn their rank by physical force and endurance, but after that, they keep it by virtue of intelligence and experience even as they grow older and weaker. They are important to the troop because they have knowledge of the territory, and because they supervise, educate, and protect the young.

Elder chimps are able to retain the privileges usually restricted to the physically fittest. In the March 1992 issue of *National Geographic,* researchers describe how a wily old male chimpanzee in Tanzania won the power to determine who would succeed him. He first allied himself with the group's alpha male, the only one allowed to mate, and then bonded with the alpha's challenger. The old chimp's reward was access to females in heat without interference from his stronger but less astute juniors.

In other words, experience and wisdom count for something even in the harshest of all worlds, the animal kingdom.

POSITIVE MYTHS OF AGING IN OTHER CULTURES

Human cultures other than our own also have different myths, beliefs, and attitudes about the aged:

- The Inuits of Alaska believe that elders speak the truth. Their word is final. This attitude enables the aged to play positive roles even as they lose physical power. They become the source of wisdom; they are the arbiters of disputes and the trainers for the future. They are paired with children in most tasks, living out a positive myth: "The child is the hands and the elder is the brain."
- A study of a tribe in Zimbabwe, Africa, sponsored by Brown University, found that only elders can practice folk medicine there. The tribe's medicine is so complex that only the old have experienced the many years of apprenticeship needed to learn it, and only they have the sensitivity to apply it wisely.
- The Samoans' myth about aging is "Old age is the best time of life." The most respected member of their community is elected chief (Matai). Occasionally it is someone young, in which case he must act old, walking in slow, measured steps.

  As Samoans age, their occupational roles change: The young do the strenuous work; elders do the complex, skilled work. The elder men are active in the political arena while elder women organize social events and preside over economic matters.

  Even with the changes wrought by a currency economy (employment and education outside the home), the Samoan extended family is still strong. Elders are still respected and their words heeded.

- Even though economic changes have altered daily living in Japan, Korea, Taiwan, and other parts of the Orient, myths about aging continue to show the elder as wise and powerful. The belief there tends to be "If you don't respect your elders and follow their advice, your life gets out of balance and out of harmony with the world. Consequently, life will not run smoothly for you."

    Amy Tan's books about family life of Chinese in America (*The Kitchen God's Wife* and *The Joy Luck Club*) illustrate that even when their mothers seem ignorant and irrational, the American-born daughters fear defying them and respect their passion, courage, and wisdom.

RETHINKING THE "AGING ATTITUDE"

Armed with these examples of how aging has its advantages in other cultures and the animal kingdom, let's rethink and rewrite the attitudes toward aging that opened this chapter.

1. Better Travel While You're Young and Still Healthy

The implication of this myth is that once you're past sixty the old rocking chair's got you, that it takes too much out of you to travel.

The reality is that, according to the American Association of Retired Persons (AARP), 88 percent of Americans past sixty travel worldwide every year. These elders constitute the largest group of travelers in any age group, and many of them say they get more out of traveling now than in their youth.

And think of the physical-fitness elders who are more than active: Jack LaLanne, the TV exercise host who towed a tugboat around San Francisco Harbor with his teeth on his seventy-fifth birthday; Joseph Olsen, the eighty-year-old who water-skies barefoot in competitions; the seven hundred thousand elders who are square dancers; the fifty thousand-plus past seventy who run in marathons every year (statistics from *Modern Maturity,* January 1992).

2. Love and Lust Are for the Young

This myth probably has roots in our childhood reluctance to think of our parents as sexual human beings. We can't bear the thought of Mom and Dad having sex. They perpetuate this myth by refraining from showing affection "in front of the children" and by referring to each other as "Mom" or "Daddy," thereby giving the idea that "We are parents, not lovers." (Obviously, if this myth were true, there'd be no children at all!)

The truth is that the old are quite interested in sex and making love. Research at Duke University shows that 70 percent of the seventy-year-old couples studied have sex about once a week. And it seems that lovemaking gets better with age. A study of eight hundred elderly couples conducted by the Human Sexuality Program at Mount Sinai School of Medicine found that 75 percent of those still sexually active in their eighties said that their lovemaking had improved with age.

3. A Poor Memory Is Part of Growing Old

Show business is replete with examples of people who keep their memories sharp throughout life. A case in point is Johnny Carson, host of *The Tonight Show* for thirty years. During his remarkable career, the nation watched Johnny's hair turn silver and his mind appear to grow more agile. It's possible that television prompters and his sidekick, Ed McMahon, helped cue Johnny's memory, but no amount of sideline coaching could have produced the clever quips and free-flowing interviews that made him as entertaining in his sixties as in his thirties. McMahon himself is two years older than Johnny and still hosts several memory-demanding television shows.

It's our belief that the rigor of constantly memorizing new monologues, playing new roles, reading new scripts, and presenting new material is a key factor in so many actors' and comedians' ability to "keep their wits about them" in old age.

4. By Fifty, Your Career Just Naturally Winds Down

Both statistics and experience dispute this myth. Terry Rohe, seventy-three, is a perfect example. At seventy, she launched into a new role at ABC Television. She is the correspondent who presents features for *Good Morning America* about older people with new or more fulfilling careers late in life. Her guests range from the famous (two-time Nobel Prize winner Linus Pauling and composer Gian Carlo Menotti) to the just discovered (Beatrice Woods, a ninety-four-year-old sculptor and potter who works barefoot and wears Indian saris). Terry finds that what older people lack in competitiveness and drive, they make up with experience and passion.

Even when physical disabilities overtake them, people of fifty-plus are still valuable in the workplace. They are interesting, vital people—usually with some kind of passion for life, some interest or curiosity that gives them a special energy.

5. You Can't Teach an Old Dog New Tricks

Many younger people don't realize that George Burns did not begin his career as "God." Originally he was a song-and-dance man who teamed up with his wife, Gracie Allen, in a comedy duo onstage and in the movies.

Gracie's death when he was sixty-eight left him bereft. But instead of replacing Gracie in the act and continuing the same type of humor, George learned a whole new style of comedy as a single. He won an Academy Award for his role in *The Sunshine Boys,* made in 1976 when he was eighty, and now in his nineties he continues to perform onstage and in movies.

Thousands of people learn new career skills, graduate from college, start businesses, and take up new hobbies after sixty.

Besides, the American Kennel Association assures us that "with patience and three days, you absolutely *can* teach an old dog new tricks!"

6. Life, Like Chewing Gum, Loses Its Flavor with Age

Studs Terkel, the writer, is only one of the countless young olds who find life more flavorful with age. Now in his early eighties, he is at the pinnacle of his career. His 1992 book, *Race: How Blacks and Whites Think and Feel About the American Obsession,* received immense critical acclaim. His radio interview program, in its fourth decade, is more popular than ever. And he's begun work on another book—about elderly people who still make a difference in their communities.

In Asheville, North Carolina, at the Center for Creative Retirement, fifteen hundred older people participate each year in such programs as the Senior Academy for Intergenerational Learning, where they pass on their knowledge to young people. Through Leadership Asheville Seniors, they work in the schools, hospitals, and prisons of the community. In the College for Seniors, they study poetry, physics, or arms control. A seventy-three-year-old man we interviewed told us, "I never knew life could have such variety. It's like I've suddenly discovered Baskin-Robbins options to aging."

7. If You Live Long Enough, You'll Be Wise

In our research, we found a number of past-seventies who weren't wise—weren't even beginning to develop wisdom. Living long is only half the equation for gaining wisdom. Developing thinking skills and the ability to reflect and see things in context is the other half. The sharpest elders we interviewed *were* wise, did make wise decisions, and were able to be in charge of their lives.

This myth, although it appears at first glance to be positive, can be damaging if it causes people just to sit back and wait for wisdom to descend on them, rather than energetically working to develop their mental abilities.

SELF-FULFILLING PROPHECIES

As we repeat negative myths about aging and fail to counter them, they become real to us. What we believe will happen powerfully affects how we behave.

A Harvard study of elementary-school teachers' attitudes toward their students illustrates how this works. When teachers were given the roster of their new classes, each child's *alleged* IQ was listed. In fact, the numbers given the teachers were the students' locker numbers. At the end of the semester, the students with high locker numbers had high grades and were described in glowing terms by their teachers, while students with low locker numbers had middle to low grades and their behavior was described as nondescript to troublesome.

These teachers were set up by psychologists, but often we set up ourselves to fulfill negative expectations. For example, Kathryn had always had a good memory, but shortly after her forty-first birthday she forgot scheduled appointments two days in a row. She told several friends about this lapse with the postscript "I can't remember anything since I turned forty." Sure enough, the more she repeated this, the more forgetful she became. Eventually, her performance rating at work dropped. From then on she was passed over for bonuses and promotions.

Just as negative programming is powerful, so, too, is positive prophecy. Change a belief and you change reality.

REWRITING THE MYTHS

In the business world, turnaround specialists frequently change reality by rewriting the myths of an ailing company. They do this by establishing new rituals, creating new symbols, and then telling new, positive "fairytales" about the company.

When AT&T wanted to change its emphasis from manufacturing to service, it created stories about the history and personnel of the company that made it much more customer-friendly. The company's ads changed from promoting worldwide leadership and technology to "reach out and touch someone," an emphasis on the personal, emotional value of telephone service.

Another example is Sam Walton. When he started his gigantic Wal-Mart chain, the myth prevailed that discount stores offered only bargains—never efficient, caring service. Walton changed this myth in numerous symbolic ways. He was a hands-on, down-to-earth owner who regularly visited all of his outlets and occasionally rang up purchases in the checkout lines. He hired retirees to greet customers at the front door of every store, and he created country-style entertainment at sidewalk sales and other promotions. The fairytale worked. When he died in 1992, Walton's stores constituted the largest retail operation in the country.

There are many other real-life fairytale endings, not in terms of dollars or fame, but in terms of people who have built their own myths for a satisfying, secure, and happy old age.

Josephine is a slender, attractive Idaho native living in Florida, a pioneer who, at eighty-five, still wears high-heeled shoes and designer clothes. She plays duplicate bridge daily, coordinates the local symphony membership, coaches piano duets, and is open and available to her six grandchildren. She knits stylish sports and evening wear that is sold at a trendy boutique in West Palm Beach. Jo's phone rings frequently, in part because of her business success, but mostly because she is so popular with friends and family. They were concerned a year ago when her ninety-seven-year-old husband needed to move to a residential nursing home. Would Jo be able to leave their big, comfortable home and adjust to living in a retirement-village apartment? The answer was a resounding yes. The myth in our society is that a nursing home environment means the end of participation in the wider society. But Josephine says that now, without the responsibility of maintaining a large house, she has even more time for creating new designs and enjoying her active social life.

Just as corporations and wise elders have effectively rewritten their myths, so, too, can you. Write a new myth about yourself that "accentuates the positive, eliminates the negative."

For example, here's one way to rewrite the myths that opened this chapter:

1. I can enjoy traveling, exploring, and adventures throughout my life.
2. Love and lust get better with age.
3. A good memory is part of growing old.
4. By fifty, my career can just be starting, if I want it to be.
5. You *can* teach an old dog new tricks, and he can teach you some, too.
6. Life, like fine wine, gets more flavorful with age.
7. If I cultivate my mental skills, I will be wise in old age.

RX: New myths = a new attitude = a multitude of new possibilities your whole life long.

How Your Brain
Works

4

What Happens When the Brain Ages

I would go without shirt or shoe,
    Friend, tobacco or bread,
Sooner than lose for a minute the two
    Separate sides of my head!

—RUDYARD KIPLING

To think is to practice brain chemistry.

—DEEPAK CHOPRA

It's been a hectic day at the office and a frustrating drive home on the freeway. As you pull into your driveway, you recall that you were supposed to pick up your dry cleaning.

Well, I'll check in at home first and then go get the cleaning, you say to yourself as you swing out of the car, leaving it in the driveway, and hurry up to the porch. There's a large package in front of the door. *Oh, a present for my fortieth birthday,* you think as you bend down quickly to pick it up. You feel a wrench in your back, then a stabbing pain.

You drop the package and grasp the small of your back, groaning. You are unable to stand up straight.

(Your spinal column has just extruded slightly between vertebrae 4 and 5 in your spine, sending pain signals over the nerves in your spinal column to your brain's pain center in your parietal lobes, buried deep in your brain under the crown section of your skull.)

As the pain subsides, you gingerly straighten up from your crouched position. You reach for the doorknob and notice that the door is ajar. There have been several daytime burglaries in your neighborhood recently, and you suddenly feel hyperalert. Unconsciously surveying the entire porch, driveway, and yard, you visually recall an unfamiliar car that was parked down the block as you drove into your subdivision. The hair stands up on the back of your neck.

(The nerves in your brain stem are excited by the dangerous possibilities raised by the open door. This primitive, Reptilian part of your brain, located atop the brain stem, is responsible for processing automatic responses that broaden your vision and quicken your self-protective reactions.)

You feel a rush of fear and anger as you imagine your children inside the house with a burglar menacing them. Your heart begins to pound, and you take a deep breath.

(As the irritating stimulus moves upward in your nervous system, it next reaches the Limbic layer located deep within your brain, which serves as a sending and receiving center between your emotions and conscious thought. The Limbic Brain enables you to identify and care about loved ones as well as devise strategies for protecting hearth and home. It sets off signals that stimulate "mind pictures," which in turn increase your heartbeat and respiration so that you can gird yourself to run or defend, the "fight or flight" response.)

You look at your watch and notice that it is 5:40 P.M. *No, the baby-sitter never brings the kids home until six* P.M. You got off early today because of the meeting you're attending tonight.

(The Limbic Brain, which wraps around the Reptilian Brain, contains two important switchboard mechanisms, the thalamus and hypothalamus. The thalamus receives information from the senses, while the hypothalamus receives emotions. These two kinds of signals are integrated and then sent to the cortical area of your brain, the outer layer called the cerebral cortex in which conscious thinking is conducted. The left side of the cortex converts feelings into language, is aware of time, and analyzes information.)

You calm down a little and take another look at the package. *Wouldn't a burglar have taken it?* you think. You look at the address. *It's from Mom. She's probably sending my birthday present before she visits next week. Good old Mom.* As you see her face and feel a glow of happiness, you suddenly remember that your friend Nora is wallpapering the guest bedroom today, so that it will be ready for Mom's visit.

Then it dawns on you that you'd given Nora a house key so she could come and go as she needed. *She must have left the door ajar,* you say to yourself with relief.

You open the door and go in.

(Once your left brain figured out that your children weren't home from school yet and that the package is from your mother, your right brain takes over, seeing Mom's face, then Mom in your newly redecorated guest room. Then the left brain takes over again and determines that it is Nora, not a burglar, who has left your front door open.)

This story describes an event—the whole thing taking place in seconds—in which the four major sections of your nervous system were activated:

1. The spinal column (wrenching your back)
2. The brain stem within the Reptilian Brain (broadening your vision and calling up your survival instincts)
3. The thalamus and hypothalamus within the Limbic Brain (connecting what you see and feel and then sending it on to the part of your brain that thinks new thoughts, the cerebral cortex)
4. The cerebral cortex or the "New Brain" (shifting back and forth between the left and right hemispheres and thereby reaching a whole-brain understanding of the situation)

From this story, you can see how the brain serves as a central clearinghouse for all the messages that are communicated in your nervous system.

We hope that this story has stimulated *your* brain—to want to learn more about the way it operates. For if you want to get the most from your brain during every stage of life, it is useful to understand how the brain works, and how these workings will change over your lifetime.

When we first began compiling information on how the brain changes during the eighty-odd years that most of us expect to live, we were dismayed. Frankly, we wondered about the wisdom of sharing such facts as these: The brain is 40 percent smaller at seventy-five than at twenty, and short-term memory is the first thing to go. However, as we learned more about brain physiology from our readings and the medical experts with whom we consulted, we found that such brain changes don't ruin our ability to think, but instead merely alter the *way* we think. Furthermore, we found that these changes are congruent with the physical and emotional changes that are normal for young adulthood, middle age, young old age, and very old age. *In other words, the natural changes that occur in the brain over a lifetime are suited to the stage of life we're experiencing.*

These two exciting realizations enabled us to suggest mental strategies to you for every stage of life. These revelations also made us aware of how important it is that you understand as much as possible about your brain.

For that reason we offer here an overview of the human nervous system and its most important component, the brain. If you hate to read technical material, you can skip forward to the section called "A Whole-Brain Affair," and just rely on the information you got in the story that began this chapter. But if you are even slightly taken with the topic, we recommend that you read the next few pages, which provide more details about the brain and its operation.

THE NERVOUS SYSTEM: ONE CORD AND FOUR BRAINS

There are five major parts to the nervous system, with these basic functions:

The Spinal Cord

This long fiber lies within the spinal vertebrae. It transmits and receives messages passing between the brain and all other parts of the body—skin, joints, muscles, ligaments, and so on. When it is cut, all the functions below the cut are in jeopardy.

The Reptilian Brain

This is the innermost and oldest layer of the brain. It is responsible for the automatic, programmed actions we perform to fulfill our basic needs and the way we respond when our survival is threatened.

The main component of the Reptilian system, the **brain stem,** rests atop the spinal cord and has three parts. The **medulla** is next to the cord and controls such tasks as breathing, talking, singing, swallowing, vomiting, and heart rate and blood pressure maintenance. The **pons** is next; it links primitive urges and body movement to the part of your brain where new thoughts are formed, thereby making the pons important in such intentional activities as sports and dancing. The third section of the brain stem is the **midbrain,** which enables some forms of seeing and hearing.

The Limbic Brain

This layer is a system of nerve centers deep within the brain. Sometimes called the old mammalian brain, it is more primitive than the New Brain but more sophisticated than the Reptilian. It is a link between your brain's thinking parts and its feeling and sensory parts. The Limbic's **hypothalamus** is responsible for your moods and motivation, since it regulates endocrine levels, water balance, sexual rhythms, food intake, and the autonomic nervous system. In other words, it is the hypothalamus that tells you when you are angry or placid, tired or hungry.

Another Limbic part, the **thalamus,** gathers information from your senses and connects it to the cortex. This enables you to identify familiar faces, tastes, sounds, and touches. From this function, you see that the Limbic Brain operates on a higher level than the Reptilian Brain, with its automatic response for survival.

So the main contribution of the Limbic system is to allow your emotions and senses to be used by the outer layer of your brain to remember and devise survival schemes. In contrast, the Reptilian Brain, described earlier, produces merely an instinctive survival response.

The Cerebral Cortex

The cerebral cortex is sometimes called the New Brain because it evolved most recently. It has left and right hemispheres and is the largest part of the human brain. This wrinkled outer layer of the brain controls what we call conscious thought. Each hemisphere is divided into areas with different functions: the frontal, parietal, temporal, and occipital lobes.

Researchers have found that the two sides have distinctive thinking processes: one that's analytical and verbal, housed in the left half; and another that's intuitive and visual, seated in the right hemisphere. We shift back and forth between these hemispheres as we change activities. Most of us prefer to use one side more than the other and are, therefore, said to be left- or right-brain dominant. This preference affects the way you work, have fun, communicate, and choose your friends. The left-dominant person is logical and organized in thinking, talks in specifics and detail, and likes to plan ahead—even for a romantic interlude.

The right-dominant is emotional and artistic, sees the big picture rather than the details, and likes to "go with the flow." Life experiences often force right-dominants to develop left-brain skills and vice versa. That's why, as you age, you tend to become more whole-brained!

While there's a lot of overlap, physically and functionally, among the lobes, it's helpful to describe their locations and roles in general terms. To get a feel for the importance and locations of these lobes, first put your hands on your forehead, where the wrinkles are. Behind that area lie the **frontal**

lobes. They are protected by the bone in your forehead. The newest parts of the cerebral cortex in evolutionary terms, these lobes control your highest mental functions, such as the ability to plan ahead, learn from experience, be socially sensitive, and behave altruistically.

Now move your hands back from your hairline about two inches (assuming you don't have a greatly receding hairline!) to the area where you would wear headphones. Situated here are the **parietal lobes,** the parts of your brain's cortex that receive sensory impulses from all over your body, process pain and pleasure, and integrate your sensory skills. The surface area of the parietal lobes dedicated to each part of the body is in direct proportion to the part's importance and sophistication. For example, the hand area is much larger than the area for your ankle because the functions of your hands are so much more complex and vital to your well-being.

The **temporal lobes** are located, appropriately enough, under your temples—the areas slightly above and in front of the top of your ears. These lobes are involved in memory and hearing, as well as your sense of self and time. Because they are connected to the Limbic system, the second most primitive part of your brain, they're also important in your emotions.

Next, clasp your hands behind your head and lean back. Your hands are cupping the area of your skull under which lie the **occipital lobes,** in the bulge of your head that is poised over the back of your neck. This is the visual center of your brain.

The Cerebellum

The cerebellum lies just below the occipital area. Unlike the other lobes we've described, it is not covered by the cerebral cortex, the wrinkled outer layer of the brain. It is located where your thumbs would be if your hands were clasped behind your head.

The cerebellum looks like a small brain but its exterior is pleated rather than wrinkled. It controls movement and balance and the ability to experience pleasure. It develops early in the womb and is the only part of the brain that continues to produce new brain cells after birth. (Don't let this alarm you; later you'll learn that the role you play in growing endless connections between brain cells is much more important than how many you have.) When it is injured or undersized (as in the case of autistic people), the abilities to learn from experience and to control movement and emotions are adversely affected.

All Together

To understand how all these ''brains'' operate in tandem, picture a scene described in *The Brain* by Richard M. Restak, M.D. You're at a weekend ski lodge with your spouse and kids. While they're in the room getting ready for dinner, you encounter an old sweetheart in the bar. Your cerebral cortex rambles on with pleasant chitchat, but your Limbic system is another matter. It remembers old drives and feelings that move on down into the Reptilian brain stem, and soon your heart is racing, palms sweating, stomach churning—and perhaps you even feel the beginnings of sexual arousal.

We've described the involvement of three of the brains. The fourth brain that may come into play here is the cerebellum, the miniature brain that processes physical movement and communicates emotions between the old brains and the New Brain. If you have a lot to drink in Restak's ski lodge scene, your cerebral cortex (the new, thinking brain) will become drunk first, leaving you without the inhibitions that help you ''just say no'' through its left-brain judgment and right-brain values.

When this higher thinking center is depressed by alcohol, the Limbic Brain (the second one) takes over, and you experience the warm fuzzy feelings of moderate drinking. As the Reptilian Brain (your most primitive one) is affected, your body language will become exaggerated, your speech slurred, and your language coarse or at least ungrammatical. It will be more difficult now for the Limbic Brain to control your behavior.

Continued drinking will put you completely at the mercy of your most primitive emotions. If you have a strong sexual urge or a penchant for violence, it may come into play. If you have a normal cerebellum and your emotional life is in order, you may do nothing more than be charmingly flirtatious or effusively sentimental in this situation. But if you are already depressed or in emotional conflict, your Limbic Brain may not be able to control the knee-jerk reactions of the Reptilian Brain.

A WHOLE-BRAIN AFFAIR

While the lobes and areas of the brain we've just described are only a fraction of the total brain, they are the most important ones for understanding the effects of aging on the brain. They are the parts of the brain that will be most affected by your strategies for staying sharp.

In truth, almost every part of the brain is involved in every activity. For example, sipping a cup of coffee certainly requires the planning of the frontal lobes to decide if it's cool enough to drink, as well as an emotional memory from the Limbic system that says you *like* coffee. Without the cerebellum, you might raise the coffee cup past your mouth to the top of your head or drop it on the floor!

All the lobes of the cerebral cortex that we've discussed (the frontal, parietal, temporal, and occipital) are divided into two sections, the right and left. Although the two halves resemble each other, they function differently. For example, the ability to speak in a sequential, accurate way lies in the left parietal lobe. But it is the right parietal that enables you to speak with passion and to gesture appropriately. The left lobe, considered the verbal, logical side, has two speech areas: Broca's, for accessing your vocabulary, and Wernicke's, for understanding language. The right lobe is the emotional, visualizing half of your brain. It sees matters in a global way and is in charge when you're behaving spontaneously and intuitively.

The two halves of the cortex are connected by the corpus callosum and the anterior commissure. The corpus callosum, larger from birth in most females than in males, helps integrate the thoughts and actions of the two sides of the brain. Yes, that means women have more opportunity to integrate right- and left-brain skills. For example, women connect what they see, hear, and feel about what is going on, giving them a broader picture of the situation. Males have a different advantage. They tend to focus on one aspect of a conversation—emotion or content. If it is content, they'll have better understanding and recall than women. If they're engaged by the emotions of the situation, they'll recall that aspect vividly but have difficulty connecting it to the content. Even though these are broad generalizations, there is compelling evidence that men and women do indeed think differently.

Another phenomenon of brain operation related to hemispheric differences is **contralaterality,** which means that your left hemisphere controls the actions, hearing, seeing, and sensations of the right side of the body, and vice versa. As a result of this factor, someone who's had a severe injury to the left side of the brain will suffer paralysis on the right side of the body.

You now know more about the brain than 99 percent of Americans. Congratulations! (If you opted to skip the section with details on the brain's operation the first time around, you may want to go back to it now that you're more comfortable with the topic. It's one of the dynamics of learning that when you have established a network of memories related to a subject, you usually want to know more about it and can more easily add the new information to a broad pattern of understanding. On the emotional side, learning more becomes fun and your curiosity about the topic grows.)

To sum up, your brain is the most important part of your body's nervous system. (1) It thinks the abstract thoughts that give you a unique personality. (2) It processes the signals that start and stop your physical functions such as walking, talking, seeing, and hearing. The spinal cord, Reptilian Brain, Limbic Brain, cerebellum, and cerebral cortex are the structures for your ability to think and act.

THE COUPLING THAT NEVER HAPPENS

Now, just when you thought we were finished with brain physiology, we ask you to hang in there for a few more paragraphs about the workings of the brain. You've been good about learning its structure—but you still don't know what makes it work. Aren't you just dying to know what happens when you think a thought? Can you really face life without understanding how your brain cells connect with each other? Just in case your answers to these two questions are no and yes, respectively, we're going to load this description with romantic innuendos to keep you interested.

Just like your body, the cord and four brains in your nervous system need exercise and nutrition to stay healthy, to function efficiently, and to develop to their greatest potential. Brain cells (also called **neurons**) do not reproduce as do body cells, but they expand in volume because of the growth of connections between cells. An electrochemical process forms and nourishes these connections. And it all starts with what you're thinking.

Every thought you think sets off a stream of chemicals called **neurotransmitters** that flows from the brain cell's **axon,** a slender fiber that reaches out toward another cell's receptor device, called a **dendrite.**

This excited axon is discriminating in its pursuit of a dendrite. It is attracted to a cell with which it has something in common, one whose interests are consistent with the thought impulse that flooded your mind. For that reason, the object of its affections may be close by or far away. For instance, if your thought was *I'm going to jump over this six-foot fence,* the axon would have to search far and wide to find a cell with welcoming dendrites, unless you are an Olympic high jumper. But if you were thinking of a new adjective to describe your sweetheart and merely added *generous* to the long list you'd already accumulated, your axon would need only to find a dendrite of a neighboring brain cell. Since this latter thought path about your love is one you've trodden many times before, it would be well established and easily traversed.

The dendrite will have numerous fingerlike extensions, each with a concave end that is saturated with an inviting chemical receptor. The axon's end bulges outward and is thus a perfect fit for the dendrite's end. Separating these two meant-for-each-other ends is a minute space called the **synapse.**

With all this closeness and bulging and receiving, you'd think these two extensions of brain cells would get pretty tight with each other. But no! They're always a synapse away. Alas, the coupling is never completed. In spite of the strong attraction between the axon and dendrite, the romance is never consummated.

Then how does your thought bridge the gap? Electrically and chemically. A spark jumps from the axon's bulbous ending, across the synaptic breach, and into the dendrite's welcoming receptor. Be still, my heart.

Perhaps this is not your idea of a tender coupling, but it works. It works, in part, because of the brain's support system, called the **glial cells.** They are like matchmaking friends who introduce the couple, have them to dinner, and keep the conversation going during the early stages of the romance. The brain's glial cells nourish and insulate the brain cells and connections. They take up 95 percent of the brain's cellular volume at birth and outnumber brain cells ten to fifty times in adulthood—an indication of their biological importance to brain function. Wouldn't it be wonderful if people had the same ratio of glials to support unattached and yearning males and females?

Now that you've learned about how the brain's cells operate within its many parts and structures, we'll focus on you and your particular brain.

How You Become Uniquely You

It takes a long time to become a person. The older you get, the more individual you become—and the more individual your brain becomes. Which is why aging is so exciting! All through your life, your thoughts and actions have a direct impact upon your brain's shape. That's why each brain has its own look. It is as if each of us were the sculptor of her own brain. We are given a block of marble at birth, and we chisel and pound away at it, discarding the unneeded portions, refining and polishing the areas we use the most.

During your first few months of life, the number of axon-dendrite connections between your brain cells increased dramatically as you looked around and tried to make sense out of your environment. You learned to distinguish a face from a round pillow, a toy from the ceiling light fixture, your hand from another's, Mom's voice from Dad's. Because you were experimenting indiscriminately, most of these connections were wild goose chases that produced an excess of connections. Many of these extras were eliminated in the first wave of streamlining, which occurred during the first two years of your life.

Still, there was so much experiencing and thinking going on in your brain that the overall area of its outer layer increased tremendously. This would have been a problem were it not for two factors. First, at birth, you had a "soft spot" on top of your head, a membrane-filled space between your skull's two halves. It is just one of four such spots called **fontanels** that makes it easier for big-headed humans to pass through the birth canal. These gaps close gradually during the first eighteen months of life. The fontanels also give the brain some much-needed growing space. A baby's cerebral cortex increases in size rapidly during the first few years of life because of the tremendous growth in brain connections produced by its learning brain.

Also, the cortex accommodates this growth by folding within itself and becoming wrinkled. Some brains wrinkle more in one place than another because of the kinds of stimulation they receive. For example, if you're in a family that verbalizes a great deal, the language lobes (in the parietals— remember?) of your brain will grow earlier and be better defined than if you had a less verbal upbringing.

In some cases, specific areas of the brain have optimal times for development. When these opportune moments are missed, the skill itself might not ever develop fully. In an extreme case of this, newborn kittens kept in total darkness during their first weeks, when sight is normally developed, never "learn to see" and are blind for life.

Extra stimulation and deprivation are only two reasons why each brain is different and why each of us is different. Another is that brain changes occur at different rates from person to person, although the changes do tend to follow a certain order. The rate is influenced by your genes and their interaction with the life you lead. So next we'll describe those normal changes that occur throughout life—and explain how these changes seem ideally suited to each stage.

How Normal Brain Changes Relate to Your Stage of Life

When you were born, your brain had approximately 100 billion cells distributed throughout its layers and lobes. During your lifetime, it will lose about 10 percent of its weight, partly because of the actual death of cells.

Such losses have some positive aspects. In fact, many losses merely streamline your vehicle for thinking. Furthermore, you have the ability to continue to develop brain connections until the day you die. So, while cell losses hurt, they are not necessarily debilitating. And though some loss is inevitable, you are always capable of building new brain power.

From young adulthood on, it is normal to experience a gradual erosion in brain matter and some alterations in functions. Six of the most significant changes are:

1. Brain cells die and brain connections slough away.
2. Brain connections lessen in number, complexity, and size.
3. The amount and strength of neurotransmitters decrease.
4. Brain tissues thin.
5. Some brain functions change with age.
6. Losses in brain lobes occur at different rates, producing differences in the way thinking changes in individuals.

These six changes in the way our brains operate may seem negative, but each complements one's stage of life:

1. Brain cells die by the thousands every day from the time we're born, and the loss picks up momentum after the age of twenty. Concomitantly, cell connectors die at an even greater rate. However, this loss is offset by constant growth of new connections between the still-vital cells. The overall effect is that our brains shrink, losing about one gram per year.

This gradual attrition has little affect on overall abilities, partly because we have many more cells than we need. But the truly mitigating factor about this attrition is the number of new cell connections most of us are constantly building. These are high-quality additions to our brains because they reflect the new information we are assimilating. You can continue this kind of brain building until the day you die.

Most brain cell deaths occur in the cerebral cortex, the outer layer of the brain where new information is processed. This explains why the short-term memory of a ninety-year-old is not as good as it was at thirty or forty. But there are many more associated memories stored in the older brain, so that once recall *is* established, it is a fuller, richer remembrance.

2. With age, our brains have fewer dendritic connections, in part because brain cells sometimes metabolize protein abnormally, and the resulting debris builds up in the brain. This debris not only slows down reaction time but can also interrupt the thought process, just as trash on the tracks slows or derails a train.

If you frequently stop in midsentence and can't complete your thought, you may be worrying now that you've got brain debris. Spare yourself such concerns. You may simply have a lot on your mind and be interrupting yourself with other thoughts. Brain debris accumulates gradually over a long period of time, and most of us unconsciously make compensations as we go along.

On the plus side, slower thinking and broken thoughts often prevent us from jumping to false conclusions or from saying something hurtful. It is more than coincidence that older people often have a nicer way of dealing with sticky situations than the blunt twenty-five-year-old. This may be why they so often provide emotional ballast to children and teenagers. The elders we interviewed were sought out by friends and family to mediate communication problems, often because youngsters said they could be counted on to ''really listen'' (and they could be entrusted with the youngsters' secrets).

3. Neurotransmitters are chemicals that enhance the electrical charge that forms connections between brain cells. When neurotransmitters diminish in quantity and quality, the thought process slows down. However, there are many kinds of neurotransmitters, each making a different contribution to overall thought, somewhat like the various parts in a choral group. When the soprano can no longer hit the high notes, the alto's role becomes stronger. The song is still performed, but not in the same way. It may or may not be more pleasing to the ear.

Like brain debris, the loss of neurotransmitters slows thinking, reaction time, and such activities as copying words and adding figures. However, by the time this happens, most people have developed a pretty good organizational system that reduces the need for a lot of busy work. In other words, older people know how to work smarter instead of harder.

Many of the elders we interviewed were quite enthusiastic about the systems they'd devised over the years to stay on top of their responsibilities. For example, Houstoun Waring, former editor of a small-town newspaper, needed to stay abreast of local issues, and so he began inviting seven "interesting" people to breakfast every Thursday morning. He constantly added new names to his list and altered the mix of guests. At ninety-two he has a card file of 350 names and still continues to network with intellectually challenging people on Thursday mornings. (He also still writes a column for the paper.)

4. As we age, both body and brain tissues become thinner and lose their elasticity. When this happens in the walls of the circulatory and nervous systems, the brain becomes more susceptible to strokes and, consequently, **cascading.** When blood pressure builds, the dendrites and axons sometimes rupture, creating a cascade of tears that spread through a wide area and damage many brain cells. This is one reason high blood pressure is called the silent killer; without showing advance symptoms, it can set off a chain reaction that causes strokes and death.

One advantage elders have in controlling high blood pressure is that they generally cope better with life's upsets. As you mature, you tend not to sweat the big things—*or* the little ones—the way you did when you were young. Also, the healthy elders we interviewed were more aware of their physical needs than most younger people. Their "body wisdom" prompted them to exercise, watch their salt intake, and get their blood pressure checked. When medicine was prescribed, they took it, rather than forgetting it as many younger people do.

5. Functions of some parts of the brain change with age. For example, the role of glial cells (which nourish and insulate the brain cells and connectors) changes from childhood to maturity. Early in life, they play an important role in organizing the connections between various parts of the brain to the body, obviously a much-needed function. Later in life, they shift to playing the supportive role of *attracting nutrients* to established neurons or brain cells. As the body loses some of its ability to process nutrients, the glial cells take on the responsibility of attracting more of them to the vital brain cells.

Interestingly, when Dr. Marion Diamond, a professor of neuroanatomy at the University of California, Berkeley, studied a slice of Einstein's brain, she found that it had 73 percent more glial cells for every neuron than the average brain. Not that we're equating Einstein with a rat, but she also found that rats that had toys to play with had more glial cells than rats without such stimulation. The human toys that keep our brains vigorous are the challenges of working and creating.

Perhaps it is this shift in the role of the glial cells that leads healthy older people into the passionate pursuit of knowledge about topics ranging from genealogy to wildlife in the Himalayas. It is as if the body signals a need for mental stimulation of the glial cells so they can provide nutrients to the aging brain cells.

6. An individual's specific genetic/environmental interaction results in different rates of cellular losses in the brain's lobes, which produce a variety of changes in behavior. For example, the locus ceruleus, located in the brain stem, generally loses about 40 percent of its cells with aging, which upsets sleeping and waking cycles and occasionally emotions and memory. Furthermore, levels of the neurotransmitter melatonin decrease with age, which means we sleep fewer hours and less deeply. Lack of "good sleep" leads to poor concentration and memory deficits. Elders without sleeping problems may not have experienced such brain changes, or they may have unconsciously devised ways to overcome them. It's important that you notice such changes as altered sleep patterns in yourself and address them early on. We'll discuss sleep further in Chapter 6, "Physical Health and Mental Sharpness."

OTHER CHANGES WITH AGE

Some areas of the brain are particularly susceptible to brain cell damage as we age, with special, characteristic effects. For example, many of the brain cells in the motor regions of your frontal lobes send out axons to the spinal cord, which in turn is connected with your outlying muscles and nerves. When you lose cells in these lobes, the messages they send to your muscles are not as strong and clear. Consequently, your balance is affected; you're not as surefooted as you used to be.

At thirty, you could easily stand on one foot with your eyes closed, but at eighty, even if you are in good health, you will have trouble keeping your balance. (Of course, at eighty, do you care about standing on one foot with your eyes closed?)

While brain cell loss is inevitable, muscle loss is not—and furthermore is reversible. Even though balance is affected, you can compensate for it through good muscle control; you can continue to enjoy sports, dancing, and exercise forever. Witness dancers Fred Astaire and Martha Graham, who were erect, bright, and active throughout their long lives.

Many elders attribute their good health to continued physical activity. They participate in some kind of regular exercise such as stretching and exercise classes, walking and hiking, bicycling, or even "pumping iron." One ninety-five-year-old walks half a mile daily to his favorite bar—for a glass of beer.

Other parts of the brain particularly affected by age are those related to our senses. Losses in vision, hearing, taste, smell, and touch are a natural part of aging. Probably the most damaging are diminished hearing or sight. If you are hard of hearing and repeatedly ask "Huh?" others may think you're not mentally alert. Fumbling for your reading glasses, or squinting to read without them, gives the impression that you are inept, if not incompetent. So it is vital that you have your hearing and eyesight tested regularly from the age of forty onward. Most of us resist examinations *and* corrective devices because "it's such a nuisance." But it seems a small price to pay for the social benefits.

The good news is that corrective measures are improving daily. Hearing aids grow smaller and more tailored to individual auditory losses; eyeglasses and contact lenses continue to become more comfortable and less expensive; bloodless laser surgery is nearly foolproof in restoring sight to victims of cataracts and other eyesight problems; developmental ophthalmology is discovering ways to avoid and/or mitigate the effects of aging on vision, such as farsightedness.

The Same Story—Redux

Let's revisit the scene that began this chapter, but now an older but wiser person confronts the same situation:

It's been a busy but productive day. You completed the Turner project on schedule and wrote a letter to Dianne commending her work on it. Of course, you sent a copy of the letter to her supervisor.

You had lunch with Ted and Jim and mediated their dispute. In the afternoon, you outlined a five-year plan for your department.

Since the freeway was full, you noodled home through some old, established neighborhoods you hadn't seen in a while. You lost a little time, but still arrived at 5:55, early enough to catch Nora before she left the house. She was wallpapering the guest room today in preparation for your granddaughter's visit next week.

As you pull into the driveway, you feel the joy of being home and look forward to being in its cool, comfortable rooms. You walk up to the porch and notice that the yellow rosebuds of this morning are now in full bloom.

In front of the door is a rather large package wrapped in brown paper. You squat down and read the label. *Oh yes, it's the new tetherball we ordered for Nikki's visit. We'll have to get that up after dinner tonight,* you say to yourself. *I'll leave it out here on the porch.* Then you notice that the front door is ajar and your curiosity is piqued. Bemused, you wonder if Nora left it open by accident or if there might be an intruder. You step back, look around, and finally call inside: "Nora. Is that you?"

"Yes," she replies. "I'm just bringing the ladder out. I'm all finished."

You recognize her Irish brogue and open the door wide for her exit.

In this version, you are older and slower, but your frustration level is lower. Physical changes in the brain seem to contribute to a general mellowing process. Columbia University psychiatrist Steven P. Roose reports that the brain's alarm system, the center involved in arousal, anxiety, and hearing, begins to shrink around forty. And isn't it wonderful! You avoid stressful situations and physical strains. You enjoy the small things in life and don't jump to conclusions.

In short, you are older, but wiser—and you're getting more out of life than you did when your brain had more cells and branches, more and stronger neurotransmitters and blood vessels, larger and more vital lobes. Instead, your brain has more potential to give you the blessings of perspective, peace, and joy.

CHAPTER

Good News

The human brain is a wonderful organ. It starts to work as soon as you are born and doesn't stop until you get up to deliver a speech.

—GEORGE JESSEL

Most people say that as you get old, you have to give up things. I think you get old because you give up things.

—SENATOR THEODORE FRANCIS GREEN

Polls have shown that most of us fear public speaking more than pain, snakes, elevators, even death. Why do you suppose we're so afraid to speak in public? Because we know that public speaking is a perfect opportunity to humiliate ourselves in front of a number of our fellow human beings.

In a similar way, we fear aging because it makes us vulnerable to losing our dignity. We fear that the physical and mental losses of old age may cost us the esteem of others. We worry every time we show any sign of diminishing mental faculties. Is it any wonder, then, that growing old is a dreadful prospect for most of us?

When we forget little things, we're sure we're showing early signs of Alzheimer's disease. We learn we have high blood pressure, and "just know" that soon a stroke will damage our brains. One of our parents develops a disease that affects the brain, and we resign ourselves to having that same problem someday.

It is true that there are some diseases, physical traumas, and genetic disorders that affect the brain as we age. But it is also true that these problems are not as widespread or as immutable as many believe. In this chapter, we'll give you the plain, unvarnished facts about them, because they will help you gauge the authenticity of your concerns. We'll also give you the other side of the story—lots of good news about the bad news.

Many of the most dreaded problems of the aging brain are abnormal—most people do not experience them. For example, Alzheimer's is common only in advanced old age, beyond the life expectancy of most of us.

Also, there is much you can do physically and mentally to avoid many of these problems. Just as you can avoid ridicule in public speaking through proper preparation and training, you can prepare for the changes that come with aging and train yourself to compensate for losses. In most cases, you have some control over your brain's destiny.

Finally, medical and biological research is daily discovering new ways to reverse and prevent many of the losses that threaten our dignity in old age. As you learn about the latest research in treatments and remedies for brain disorders, you'll see that your chances of a long, vital life improve each day.

In the meantime, understanding what is currently known about the problems that can affect thinking will help calm the fear that you're "losing it."

WHAT ALZHEIMER'S IS AND ISN'T

No word frightens people more when they think about aging than **Alzheimer's.** You're forty-five and you start forgetting names or appointments. *Uh oh,* you think—*is this the beginning of Alzheimer's?*

Alzheimer's disease is the cause of 80 percent of cases of senile dementia, the medical term for a disorder of the brain in which there is a progressive loss of memory and intellectual functions. With this affliction, the person becomes increasingly confused and unaware of surroundings.

It is true that short-term memory loss *is* one early indication of Alzheimer's, but there are many other causes of forgetfulness: stress, lack of sleep, inattention, information overload, malnutrition, depression, and various medical conditions such as chest infections, urinary tract infections, stroke, heart attack, brain tumor, and hypothyroidism. Confusion can be caused by a low blood-sugar level, hypothermia, drug or alcohol use, or a vitamin deficiency. Very often the mental confusion or loss of memory will improve when the medical or psychological condition is properly treated.

The early signs of Alzheimer's may be very subtle—a lack of initiative, irritability, and, most commonly, loss of memory of recent events. If you are worried about such signs in you, or in a relative or friend, it's time to visit your doctor. The physician will take a personal history, do a physical exam, test your memory and reasoning power, then conduct tests for diseases and conditions with symptoms similar to yours. If no other diagnosis is apparent, a CAT scan can be done to detect signs of Alzheimer's within the brain.

Unfortunately, an absolute diagnosis of Alzheimer's is currently possible only through autopsy. However, University of Minnesota researchers have developed a ten-word memory test to help identify Alzheimer's early on. Dr. Soren Ryber and Dr. David Knopman found that Alzheimer's patients could not store words for easy retrieval and so forgot them five minutes after exposure. Normal elderly people forget at a much slower rate and are helped appreciably by memory strategies.

The ten-word memory test is a reliable diagnostic tool that can help doctors avoid the misdiagnosis. Too many times when older people are depressed or confused because of poor diet, strong medication, or lack of social contact, they are mistakenly identified as having some form of senile dementia, such as Alzheimer's. Once they have this label, their relatives and friends often treat them in a condescending, worried way that worsens their condition.

COMMON HEALTH PROBLEMS THAT CAUSE MENTAL CONFUSION

The side effects of many common health problems are often mistaken for mental deterioration. Lawrence E. Lamb, M.D., a syndicated medical columnist, estimates that one in five persons labeled "senile" has a misunderstood underlying medical condition. Such health problems could include an underactive thyroid, a disturbance in salt and water balance, and changes in blood circulation to the brain. Medications such as tranquilizers and muscle relaxants, insulin, anti-inflammatory drugs, diet pills, and sleeping pills—or too much alcohol—can also give the appearance of mental deterioration.

How likely is it, though, that you will contract Alzheimer's? Today's forty- and fifty-year-olds have a minimal chance of developing Alzheimer's at their age or later. A study by Dennis A. Evans of Harvard Medical School and his colleagues indicates that, as a group, more than 89 percent of all people older than sixty-five are free of dementia. The researchers found that less than 5 percent of their subjects, aged sixty-five to seventy-four, exhibited such symptoms. That figure rose to 20 percent between seventy-five and eighty-four. At greater ages, the percentage jumped to 50 percent, higher than most other research estimates, which usually put the rate at 25 to 30 percent for those over eighty-five. In other words, Alzheimer's is a disease of advanced old age. With the current life expectancy of seventy-eight for females and seventy-six for males, most of today's middle-agers will not live long enough to get Alzheimer's. And breakthroughs in science may rescue the young olds, those now in their sixties, from developing it.

The amount and quality of research under way promise a cure by the turn of the century. Although we don't yet know the underlying cause of Alzheimer's, we do know its physical effects on brain tissue. Autopsies show that the dendritic connections between cells turn black and become tangled, which explains why behaviors change so drastically as the disease progresses. It's as though your brain's railroad tracks, over which ideas are carried, turn into spur tracks or sometimes go to the wrong station entirely.

Many causes for Alzheimer's have been suggested and are being researched:

1. Some researchers believe it is caused by a *slow virus* that takes many years to develop or lies in wait until the resistance of the brain is low.
2. Other researchers think it may be caused by an *immune system gone awry*. The factors that formerly prevented brain deterioration are no longer working, or the immune system itself may be actively contributing to the deterioration.
3. Some people believe it is caused by *environmental trauma,* such as water, air, and food pollutants. For example, there's a long-standing belief that aluminum cooking pans cause Alzheimer's, because unusual amounts of aluminum have been found in the brains of its victims. No direct connection has yet been found, but why take a chance? Why not replace your aluminum pans with stainless steel and monitor the amount of aluminum foil you bring in contact with your food?

   More substantive research is being conducted on the effects of air, water, and food pollution. And some people are taking action in such areas as controlling air particulates, eliminating sources of lead poisoning, and avoiding further deterioration of the ozone layer.

   (With all of society's concern about the effects of pollution, it's ironic that we overlook an avoidable way the environment can directly harm our brains: head injuries from motorcycles, cars, boating, biking, and skiing. Rehabilitation centers treat many more people with these trauma injuries than patients suffering from brain disorders.)

4. A large area of brain research is based on the belief that *neurotransmitters* play a significant role in Alzheimer's. It's been shown that with age the brain cells in the locus ceruleus, which controls moods, lose half of their neurotransmitters, the chemicals that make the connection between brain cells. This loss could account for the depression and emotional outbursts associated with Alzheimer's. Researchers are investigating how to increase the amounts of neurotransmitters in the existing cells through growth induction and transplants of "engineer cells," those that control neurotransmitter levels.

Also incriminating neurotransmitters is the fact that Alzheimer's patients have only 60 to 90 percent of normal amounts of the enzyme that synthesizes acetylcholine, a neurotransmitter that is known to be important in such Limbic Brain functions as memory and emotions. While attempts to remedy this lack by administering soybean extract rich in choline did not help, other approaches might. For example, scientists researching AIDS have found that diet, nutrition, and vitamin therapies seem to improve the performance of neurotransmitters.

Exercise has been found to increase the production of neurotransmitters in the brain and may help Alzheimer's patients. For example, Rita Friedman of the nursing school of Barry University in Miami and Ruth M. Tappen of the University of Miami's nursing school found that a daily half-hour walk improved the communication skills of Alzheimer's patients. Compared with patients whom nurses engaged in one-on-one conversation as a form of therapy, "walkers" did much better in a test that gauges communication abilities of the mentally impaired. The communication scores of the "conversational" group actually declined 1 percent after their therapy, whereas those who walked regularly showed a 25 percent increase.

5. Other research into the cause of Alzheimer's is focusing on identifying the presence of *substances that damage the brain,* in somewhat the same way that cancer cells assault healthy cells in the body. One is an abnormal protein called beta amyloid. It is a suspected cause of Alzheimer's because it is present in Alzheimer's victims' brains. Another study showed that beta amyloid causes cell destruction in rats' brains. Encouragingly, the same study found that "Substance P," a natural brain hormone that is in short supply in Alzheimer's victims, blocks beta amyloid when injected into rats' brains.

6. Some believe that Alzheimer's is *inherited,* a part of one's genetic makeup. Although there is no proof that the condition is hereditary, this possibility adds to the misery of the children of Alzheimer's patients. Not only are they stretched financially, physically, and emotionally from caring for the parent, but they fear they see the script for their own future unfolding.

Many who hold that Alzheimer's is inherited say it is a natural part of aging that we experience at different rates. Others believe the Alzheimer's gene doesn't kick in until the seventies and eighties, and that we are only now living long enough for sizable numbers of people to develop it.

We can take some heart from the fact that no genetic characteristic linked to Alzheimer's has yet been identified, in spite of the high state of genetic research. Furthermore, genetic engineering is making such strides in transplanting and cloning that if it turns out that Alzheimer's *is* inherited, a process to alter this gene at the cellular level may be developed soon.

The search for a cure for Alzheimer's disease continues. For example, in supervised medical tests, Hydergine and Centrophenoxine have had some benefits. Similar small discoveries are made daily in a vast range of research, so the eventual possibility of treating and even reversing the course of Alzheimer's is good. But in the meantime, many fads and false alarms appeal to a vulnerable public. "Smart cocktails" and "smart drugs" (mixes of nutrients, herbs, and nonadditive pills) are dispensed in "smart bars" across the country. While they harm nothing but your pocketbook, a smarter approach is to incorporate into your life-style the activities we know are good for your brain: physical exercise, memory training and mental stimulation, social contact, rest and recreation, proper nutrition, and avoidance of harmful substances.

STROKES AND HOW TO REDUCE YOUR RISK

After Alzheimer's, the most common cause of senile dementia is the stroke-induced problem called **multi-infarct dementia** (once called arteriosclerotic dementia). Strokes in turn are caused by hardening of the arteries, high blood pressure, and circulatory problems. Strokes occur more frequently as blood vessels narrow and lose their elasticity. While this can occur at any time in life, strokes do increase in frequency and intensity with age.

Some strokes affect the brain so little that they go unnoticed. Others affect a broad area and significantly change thinking and behavior. For example, a stroke in the left hemisphere of the brain may leave the person paralyzed on the right side of the body and unable to speak. If the damage is limited to the speech area in the left hemisphere, the person may have no paralysis but may be unable to speak in a logical way and use words appropriately. When asked to name pizza, this person might say "house" or "car." If you showed this person pictures of all three (house, car, and pizza), he would be able to *select* the correct one but not *say* the correct one. This shows that the memory for vocabulary is intact, but cannot be accessed verbally—only visually. This is because most of us (particularly right-handers) access vocabulary through the left side of the cerebral cortex.

Therapists sometimes teach these patients to perform the affected abilities in *another part of the brain.* The person who knows what pizza looks like but can't say the word may be able to relearn it by singing it, a right-brain mode of expression.

When the damage affects a large area, the individual is often unable to learn alternative ways of doing things. Cues will not help as they do in ordinary memory lapses. For example, for a normal older person who's trying to recall the word *buggy,* the cue "horse and . . ." would immediately prompt the correct word. But instead of helping people with dementia, such a cue might prompt a story about a pony they owned in childhood.

There are several comforting thoughts about multi-infarct dementia. Reliable medication is readily available for those who have a natural predisposition for high blood pressure or arteriosclerosis.

Another piece of good news is that many strokes affect a small area of the brain, and the effects are *reversible.* In fact, some small cerebral strokes clear out clogged blood vessels, thereby preventing a major stroke and sometimes enabling the person to think more quickly!

But don't allow this to lull you into complacency about the value of good health habits. Unlike the causes of Alzheimer's, those of multi-infarct dementia are well understood. You have a great deal of control in warding off this type of dementia. Following *good health habits* reduces your chances of suffering a stroke, since high blood pressure and arteriosclerosis are contributing factors. By controlling your diet, exercising regularly, not smoking, and avoiding substance and alcohol abuse, you can minimize your chances of having strokes.

Besides making life-style changes, you can also help protect yourself by developing both right- and left-brain skills. Research shows that individuals with skills on both sides of the brain are better able to recover from strokes to one side of the brain. For example, the ambidextrous person is often not only able to shift physical movement to the unaffected side, but can also regain speech skills. Presumably, this occurs because the ambidextrous person has developed speech skills on both sides of the brain.

COMPENSATORY SKILLS

You can offset the effects of a future stroke by developing certain brain skills ahead of time. For example:

- Learn new words in conjunction with music. We call this the advertising jingle method. It involves both hemispheres and makes the recovery of vocabulary easier in the event of damage to the left-side speech center.
- Take a lesson from left-handers who are forced by the right-handed world to develop opposite-hand skills. Using your left hand develops backup handwriting skills and increases your general dexterity. Besides, it helps you get more in touch with your feelings. Therapists use it as a way of enabling people to understand and express their emotions; writers use it as a way of adding insight to their compositions.
- Whether you currently *need* computer skills or not, think about learning some. They can be invaluable in the event you develop paralysis or loss of vision and speech. There are constant developments in software programs and hardware systems that help disabled people to communicate and perform useful work. The computer becomes their connection with the outside world.

Besides Alzheimer's and multi-infarct dementia, there are at least 5 percent of dementias with simply unknown causes. Another 5 percent (and perhaps even more) of dementias after the age of sixty-five result from Korsakoff's syndrome, Huntington's chorea, and Parkinson's disease, about which quite a bit *is* known.

A DISEASE OF ALCOHOL ABUSE

Korsakoff's syndrome is not a disease just of old age. Although it often shows up in late middle age, its primary cause is alcoholism, a problem increasingly common among older people.

Drinking alcoholics (as opposed to recovering alcoholics who aren't drinking) past sixty-five are divided into two groups: About two thirds have abused alcohol most of their lives and are in poor health as a result. The remaining one third, whose problem is more recent, are not as impaired physically, mentally, or emotionally at present. But after just two years of heavy drinking, they can harm their brains and bodies as much as alcoholics who have been drinking for twenty to forty years.

In Korsakoff's, brain cell losses from alcohol abuse deprive the person of short-term memory. Such people are unable to recall what day it is or what you said to them three minutes ago. While there are other brain disorders that produce these same symptoms, alcoholism leaves telltale signs in the brain: an actual change in the texture of certain brain cells.

The good news is that with just three weeks' abstention, the former health of the cells will return, at least to those in the early stages of alcoholism. Research at the University of Colorado at Boulder showed that tissue in the brains of alcoholics that had "gone soft" regained its healthful texture less than a month after patients stopped drinking.

For more about alcoholism in later life, see Chapter 6, "Physical Health and Mental Sharpness."

TWO MORE DISEASES OF THE BRAIN

Huntington's chorea is a form of cerebral degeneration that occurs in middle age. While it is rare, it is invariably fatal. At first, the person just seems clumsy and fidgety, but then movements become jerky and writhing, especially in the face and tongue and in the upper body. There is an increasing loss of nerve tissue in the cerebellum's basal ganglia, causing the cerebral cortex to atrophy and shrink. The brain's ventricles enlarge and harden. The individual becomes depressed and inattentive. About 25,000 Americans have Huntington's, and 125,000 others are at risk. Its best-known victim was Woody Guthrie, who died in 1967.

Although there is no known cure for Huntington's, drugs can slow its progress. Furthermore, its cause, a renegade gene, was discovered early in 1993. The Huntington's Disease Collaborative Research Group, which tracked down the gene, was organized by Dr. James Gusella of Massachusetts General Hospital and Nancy Wexler and Allan Tobin of the Hereditary Disease Foundation. Identifying the cause of Huntington's is a significant step toward finding a cure. Other promising research is being done by a team of American and Swedish scientists that is studying the possibility of transplanting a tiny section of the human brain as a treatment for both Huntington's and Parkinson's.

Parkinson's disease is another disease of the basal ganglia that overlay the cerebellum. It particularly damages the dark cells in the substantia nigra ("black substance") located at the crest of the brain stem. Parkinson's causes a progressive depletion of the neurotransmitter called dopamine, thereby interfering with perception and movement. First symptoms are difficulty in swallowing or speech and with such hand tasks as fastening buttons or writing. The person develops involuntary tremors and problems with initiating and controlling such voluntary movements as walking, sitting down, or getting up. While the disease is progressive, some patients are affected only slightly for many years. Parkinson's disease usually attacks people aged fifty to seventy-five, and affects twice as many men as women.

There's no pain and no loss of sensation, awareness, or mental abilities. But patients sometimes freeze in midstep or midair, suffer from trembling and impaired speech, lose their voice strength and modulation, and develop increased rigidity—even to the extent of having a "frozen face." Related symptoms include excessive sweating, digestive trouble, slowed thinking, depression, lethargy, and irritability. The disease is not considered hereditary, but rather a naturally occurring degenerative disease.

Recent research indicates that transplanting fetal brain tissue into Parkinson's patients is a successful treatment. Other research is focusing on stimulating the body to make dopamine.

The Speedy Progress of Medicine Today

There are other brain disorders, such as epilepsy and tumors, that can occur at any time of life but affect and are affected by aging. Research and treatments for these two conditions have been extremely important in extending our understanding of the brain.

For example, in an effort to help patients with life-threatening **epilepsy,** Dr. Roger Sperry severed the bundle of nerves that connects the brain's two hemispheres (the corpus callosum). In studying the side effects of this operation, he was able to identify skills specific to each hemisphere. This line of research led to the Split Brain Theory, for which he won the Nobel Prize for Medicine in 1981. From his discoveries in the 1950s a host of research and therapies sprang. (Our first book, *Whole-Brain Thinking,* used this research as a starting point.)

Before the fifties, there was little treatment for persons with epilepsy. But because of the understanding that developed from Dr. Sperry's work, there are now medications and therapies to treat almost every kind. And many of these treatments have spread serendipitously to other brain and health problems.

Research on **brain tumors** has led to an understanding of how the plasticity of human intelligence changes with age. It was found that the earlier brain tumors occur, the more easily we adapt to the loss of brain tissue and its function. For example, in small children who have lost one entire brain hemisphere, through surgery or accident, the remaining hemisphere usually grows to fill the brain cavity.

Furthermore, they develop many or most of the skills of the missing hemisphere. However, such compensatory skills may not be as sophisticated as the natural ones. A case in point is the little girl whose right hemisphere was removed at three years of age because of a tumor. By eight, she could dance, but not in the natural way that most children can. Since the ability to coordinate movement with music is in the right hemisphere, she used a left-brain way of learning to dance: She memorized the steps and practiced them until she could perform the dance steps, albeit rather awkwardly. An adult with a similar operation would probably not be able to dance or even walk.

But who knows what lies ahead? Research in biology and psychology may find ways to make the adult brain just as flexible as the young brain. After all, it's possible that adults *could* compensate for loss of brain tissue if they didn't believe "it's impossible"—and if they had the curiosity and enthusiasm of a young child.

Even now, physical therapists are having remarkable success with adults whose spinal injuries have always been considered irreversible. By using therapy that includes visualization, self-esteem building, and enthusiastic coaching, these physical therapists find that adults with spinal injuries *can* recover partially—and sometimes totally. So perhaps a change in attitude can produce a change in the physical.

Besides these bits of good news about the bad news about the aging brain, there's one other heartening thought: The very complexity of brain disorders has freed researchers to test all kinds of treatments. For example, the very stubbornness of Alzheimer's has produced a go-for-broke attitude that sets the stage for creative breakthroughs. People no longer make fun of studies about Native American remedies, extracts from trees and shrubs, or music and art therapy. Along with this freedom to search creatively, advances in computers have speeded data gathering and analysis, which adds momentum to progress in research.

For example, studies at Thomas Jefferson University in Philadelphia identified a renegade protein formed by two genes that swap positions and trigger acute leukemia in children. This was announced just a month after research at the Salk Institute located the site where "breaks" occur in the chromosomes of leukemia patients. These breaks are the sites where the swapping takes place!

When findings about the brain reach a critical mass, a breakthrough will undoubtedly happen. Suddenly a big, clear pattern will emerge. Then, as with Thomas Edison's progression from inventing an electric vote counter and the ticker tape to the phonograph and the electric light bulb, all sorts of related improvements will follow.

This dynamic process will surely lead to "silver bullets" that will treat or cure most of the brain maladies we have discussed. In the meantime, support brain research with your energy and your money. And for you personally, commit yourself to following the recommendations for brain and body health you'll discover as you continue to read this book. They'll help you become a whole-brain thinker for life!

Physical Health and Mental Sharpness

The only reason I would take up jogging is so that I could hear heavy breathing again.

—ERMA BOMBECK

When I have trouble writing, I step outside my studio into the garden and pull weeds until my mind clears.

—IRVING STONE

Over the years our bodies become walking autobiographies.

—MARILYN FERGUSON

You've probably heard many times that a healthful diet, regular exercise, and avoiding cigarettes and excessive alcohol greatly improve the health of your body now and for the future years. What you probably haven't heard is that a healthful life-style makes a great difference in how sharp your thinking is—again, both now and for future years.

In this chapter, you'll learn why this is so, and how you can gain these benefits. We'll also share strategies and tips to make the changes a little easier.

BODY WISDOM

First, and most essential, you have to develop a kind of wisdom that's different from the kind measured by an IQ test or an SAT test. We call it body wisdom—the ability to listen to the messages your body is sending you, and use them to your advantage.

Humans seem to be born with body wisdom, a natural inclination to eat and exercise in a healthful way. Tests with infants who've not had snacks or sweets for rewards indicate that they will eat a well-balanced diet. When allowed to select their own food, they reject foods loaded with salt, sugar, and additives. Furthermore, their overall daily intake includes the proper amounts of needed nutrients, even though they may binge on one food at a time.

They have a similar wisdom about exercise. You've never seen a lazy baby, have you? Infants and toddlers are constantly on the move. Unfortunately, as we move through life, most of us get more and more out of touch with our body's wisdom. Start now to listen in.

Most of the sharp elders we interviewed knew intuitively which foods were right for them. They could feel when they needed exercise, and they knew when they needed rest. They knew when the noise or music level disrupted their thinking and when it was soothing. They had wisdom about their own bodies. They knew what they needed to do to stay healthy, and they did it.

For example, Russell Randall, eighty-six-year-old champion in the Senior Olympics, commented, "I noticed in my twenties that my days just went smoother if I went for a brisk walk, rowed, or bicycled in the mornings. I just naturally want vegetables and fruit; they look so desirable to me, even more so as I age. I still have an occasional alcoholic drink to be sociable, but I prefer fruit juice!"

The latest and most substantial research today confirms what your body wisdom tells you are the causes of poor aging: lack of exercise, poor eating habits, and harmful environmental factors such as cigarette smoke. These life-style decisions affect your body, and they affect that part of the body known as the brain.

If a person who starts to listen to her body is at the "1" level of body wisdom, the champion athlete is at the "20" level. Tennis champion Martina Navratilova's reaction time was fast, her sensory skills strong. In milliseconds, she used her body to anticipate, to communicate, and to solve problems. Michael Jordan's command of the basketball court was amazing. He jumped; he turned, shifting his weight from one foot to the other. He was completely blocked, surrounded. He glanced down, looking defeated—then suddenly he faked to the right and drove left. He was in the clear. What a move!

Such individuals are the intellectuals of the body wisdom world, with a kind of intelligence that's no less impressive than that measured by an IQ test or an SAT.

As Harvard Medical School's Dr. Herbert Benson has said, there is no greater sign of intelligence than that of persons who treat their bodies well.

The Body Wisdom Tests

Here are a few simple tests that will help you develop body wisdom. In fifteen minutes, with the help of a friend, these tests will give you a rough reading of your physical age, which may be different from your chronological age. Some of your readings may surprise you.

1. For as long as possible, stand on one foot (the right foot if you are right-handed, and vice versa), with your other foot bent at the knee and with your eyes closed. Have someone keep track of the number of seconds you can maintain your balance each time. Do this three times. Add the scores together and divide by three. Write down the average number of seconds.
2. Hold a newspaper at a distance where you are able to read the print. Wear your glasses or contacts if you wish, but not bifocals. Then move the paper toward you until the print blurs. How many inches was the paper from your face when it blurred?
3. Have a friend dangle an eighteen-inch ruler vertically in front of you, holding it from the top, with the number 1 at the top. Hold the thumb and middle finger of your writing hand three and a half inches apart at the bottom end of the ruler. When your friend drops the ruler, catch it between your thumb and finger as quickly as you can. Look at the inch mark where you caught the ruler—that's your score.
4. Grasp your midriff skin above the waist between your thumb and forefinger. Each knuckle's depth indicates ten pounds of excess weight. How many pounds overweight are you?

What Your Answers Meant

1. Standing on one foot with eyes closed is a test of static balance. Four seconds means your functional age is between sixty and seventy; 10 seconds, between fifty and sixty; 18 seconds, between forty and fifty; 22 seconds, between thirty and forty; and 28 seconds, between twenty and thirty.
2. Reading the newspaper at a comfortable distance is a test of visual acuity.

At about 39 inches, you've got a functional age of sixty. Fifteen inches brings the functional age down to fifty; 9 inches, to forty, 5½ inches, to thirty; and 4 inches, to about twenty-one.

3. Catching a dropped ruler is a test of reaction time. If you averaged 11 inches or more, that gives you a functional age of twenty. At 9¾ inches, you're around thirty; 8½ inches, about forty; 7¼ inches, fifty; and 6 inches or less, sixty or more.

4. Grasping the loose skin at your waistline measures weight gain. While the dangers of moderate weight gain have been overemphasized in recent years, doctors have found that excess body weight in the waist does increase the risk of many diseases, including heart disease. It takes fewer calories as you age—500 fewer at seventy than at twenty-five—to maintain body weight. Too much body fat around the waist probably indicates that you aren't exercising enough, and also that your arteries may be clogging up with cholesterol.

While these tests are no replacement for a thorough medical examination, they do give you an idea of how far along you are in certain areas of the aging process. Use your scores to heighten your awareness of your body's needs and abilities. One fifty-four-year-old woman was shocked that her balance score for her left foot and leg showed a physical age of sixty-five! Then she realized that in recent years she *had* become slightly less graceful on the dance floor, a bit more tenuous on stairways, and less agile while gardening. So she began to focus her attention on balance in everyday activities and practiced calisthenics that used both legs equally and required balance. Six months later her score was that of a forty-year-old.

Visualize yourself performing the actions involved in these four tests. How do you look? Is your gait beginning to wobble, your stomach sagging, your speech slowing down? Whether you're above or below your chronological age is not as important as realizing that what you do makes a difference in how well you age. If you're losing ground in flexibility, strength, and vitality, you need to discover how to regain and improve your body health so that your thinking will stay sharp in years to come.

If you're doing fine in all areas of the tests, congratulations! You may already have discovered how to keep your body healthy and, therefore, your thinking vital. But don't get smug; you might have great genes that have kept you above average—so far—but that doesn't mean you haven't or won't lose ground.

The bottom line is that your genes and your experiences so far in life have determined how old your body is today, but from this point forward, it's up to you. Medicine and you can push the limits way beyond what we usually think of as "normal aging."

EXERCISE AND THE BRAIN

In 1980, the U.S. Bureau of Statistics reported 77,717 scientific studies confirming the direct positive relationship between physical exercise and mental performance. You can imagine how many more studies have been made since then. Physical exercise improves health. Exercise helps relieve stress, increases energy, and reduces the risk of disease. Most people know about these physical benefits, but they don't realize that daily physical exercise benefits mental performance as well. In fact, exercise is the single most important thing you can to do keep your brain sharp all your life.

Chess champion Bobby Fischer knew this, and used it to his advantage. When he was training for the world chess championship in 1972, he followed a demanding physical regimen. He began each day with an hour of tennis lessons and a three-mile run. He then went to the gym to lift weights, jump rope, pedal the exercise bike, and punch a three-hundred-pound bag. To build his wind, he jumped into the pool and swam lap after lap under water.

After he rested from his workout, he practiced for his upcoming world championship match. Fischer was known for his eccentric ideas, but this regimen wasn't one of them. Intelligent mental performance for any endeavor requires physical support from the body.

"Chess appears to be as cerebral and sedentary as a human pursuit can get," Fischer told *Life* magazine. "But when grand masters battle, it's physical. No matter how well the master knows chess, he cannot deploy his mental skills unless he has physical stamina. Mental work is physical work. Intelligent performance requires energy. And with every year that goes by, I have greater appreciation of the importance of exercise to my performance."

Exercise has been shown to improve concentration, creativity, mood, and alertness.

THE POWER OF LIFTING

Weight lifting and other muscle builders are powerfully helpful in warding off the losses of aging, both physical and emotional. For example, many men are troubled when, as they age, they lose some physical strength, making it hard to open a jar or hike ten miles. And of course, nicely toned muscles lift the spirits of both sexes. So lift your way to better health and self-image with muscle-building exercise.

Why Exercise Benefits the Brain

Exercise Promotes General Health. First, exercise is important for the brain because it is important for the body as a whole. Regular aerobic exercise reduces the risk of heart disease by widening the arteries, reducing cholesterol levels, and strengthening the heart. For women, weight-bearing exercises such as walking, jogging, aerobic dancing, stair climbing, weight lifting, and calisthenics help the bones retain calcium, lowering the risk of osteoporosis. Muscle strength is lost with age, so strengthening exercises such as weight lifting are important, too.

While many people over fifty believe that exercise is dangerous for them, the truth is that it is dangerous for them *not* to exercise. Not only is exercise a good idea for older people, it is probably more important for this age group than for any other. Unfortunately, over fifty is exactly when most people slow down and do less physical activity.

Exercise Increases the Amount of Oxygen Reaching the Brain. Clear thinking is impossible without abundant oxygen. Think about situations in which people are deprived of oxygen. For example, when mountain climbers ascend suddenly to high altitudes they experience light-headedness, difficulty in concentrating, loss of comprehension, and sometimes even collapse.

The brain accounts for only 2 percent of the body's mass, yet it uses 25 percent of the body's energy. To generate all that energy, it burns glucose, and to burn glucose, it needs lots of oxygen. The way to increase the supply of oxygen, and thus enhance thinking, is through aerobic exercise, which makes you breathe more deeply and makes your heart pump more blood through the body.

Exercise Improves Your Mood. Exercise improves people's moods immediately, and in some cases helps lift depression and reduce anxiety as well. As we'll see in the following chapter, your emotional balance greatly influences the working of the brain.

In a study at Loma Linda University, thirty-five overweight and sedentary women were assigned either to walk briskly for forty-five minutes five times a week or to remain inactive. After fifteen weeks, the group that had exercised regularly showed significant improvement on tests measuring freedom from health concerns, sense of satisfaction with life, relaxation, and emotional stability.

Aerobic exercise improves mood by causing the body to produce endorphins, chemicals that act on the brain to reduce pain and elevate mood. The release of endorphins causes the "runner's high." You may not get a runner's high when you exercise, but you can expect to feel calm, relaxed, and happy after exercise. Endorphins are thought to be at least partly responsible for the reduced stress and anxiety experienced by many people who exercise regularly.

THE TALKING TEST

To gauge your level of exertion during aerobic exercise, try the talking test. Say out loud, in a measured way, two stanzas of "Mary had a little lamb whose fleece was white as snow." If you can make it through the sentence before needing a breath, you are working at the best level for getting oxygen to your brain (about 80 percent of your aerobic capacity). If you had to take a breath in the middle of the phrase, slow down the intensity of your exercise. If it was easy and you didn't need to take a breath at the end of the phrase, then up the intensity.

Exercise Increases Vigor and Stamina by Changing the Brain's Chemistry. At any moment, a fourth of the body's blood supply is coursing through the brain, so whatever affects the chemistry of the bloodstream will have immediate mental consequences. A few minutes of vigorous activity stimulates production of the neurotransmitter called norepinephrine, making you feel more alert and energetic.

Exercise enables the brain to work more efficiently and allows the neurotransmitters to scan further areas.

Exercise Sharpens the Senses. Walter M. Bortz II, in the *American Medical Association Journal,* reported that three weeks of regular aerobic exercise increased the ability to hear and see of sixty-seven out of seventy-eight men over seventy-five years of age. He wrote, "I was amazed to discover that regular physical exercise sharpened eyesight and hearing. It was almost as if we had put new lubricating fluid in a car. The increase in hearing was especially significant."

Age and Exercise

When tuned in to their needs, our bodies crave physical activity. Remember when you were young? You ran and played all day. We don't have to tell kids to exercise (unless they're TV or computer addicts). As a teen you biked for hours, and in your twenties your energy still seemed boundless. Take the twenty-six-year-old mother of three who water-skied all day, then fixed dinner for six that evening because of some unexpected out-of-state guests. At that age, exercising was never something you *had* to do. It was part of life—a fun part.

Sometime in your mid-thirties, exercising may turn into recreation. You take a slow walk, garden, or watch your sons play baseball and soccer. While this is a way of moving your body, the lack of intensity fails to get your heart pumping, muscles flexing, and endorphins flowing.

Then in your forties, as your responsibilities increase, you may find you have little time for athletics and, furthermore, you don't care. Your tastes change to music and reading. Once always on the move, you are now content to flop on the couch.

The fact of the matter is that at each stage in life, different needs and realizations motivate us to exercise. The type of activity we choose or are able to participate in also changes as we grow older. Here are reasons people commonly exercise at each age:

2–9:   Development of psychomotor skills, release of energy, having fun

10–19: Development of relationship and competency skills, release of energy

20–29: Weight control, competition, networking, relief of stress

30–39: Appearance, relief of stress, competition, health awareness (wanting to avoid illness because of the pain, cost, and inconvenience)

40–49: Improving concentration, stamina, companionship, health awareness, relief of stress, appearance

50–59: Health awareness (at this age, health awareness is related to wanting to avoid injury or disease—often provoked by the problems of friends or self)

60–69: All the previous reasons, but now the motivation is to stay healthy to enjoy "the golden years" through travel, continuing to work, shifting into new, more satisfying work, generating new kinds of relationships, and mentoring others

70-plus: Continuing passionate pursuits, retaining mobility and intellect, being healthy and in charge of yourself

---

EXERCISE SAFETY

- If you are over forty-five or are sedentary now, check with your doctor before starting an exercise program.
- Build up your exercise program gradually to avoid injury.
- Always warm up and cool down.
- If you experience light-headedness, chest pain, or excessive shortness of breath during exercise, stop exercising and see a doctor.
- Always stop if you experience pain.

Easy Ways to Smart Moves

How much do you need to exercise to get these benefits? How hard, how often? You can experience some mental benefits at lower levels of exercise than you might think. This is true of physical fitness, too—while cardiovascular fitness does require reaching 60 to 90 percent of your maximum heart rate for at least twenty minutes three to five times a week, doctors are finding that all physical activity brings physical benefits—even daily chores like gardening or lifting children. Even a little exercise or daily activity is much better than none at all. You'll know you're exercising enough to gain mental benefits when the exercise is relieving stress, changing your perspective, elevating your mood, and stimulating new ideas.

IT'S EASIER TO GET INTO THE ZONE

As you get older, you don't have to exercise as hard to get your pulse into the target zone in which you experience the cardiovascular benefit of aerobic exercise. To find the target zone, subtract your age from 220. Sixty percent of that number is the minimum heart rate in your target zone, and 90 percent is the maximum rate. For example, if you are forty, your heart should be beating between 108 and 162 times per minute during aerobic exercise.

What does it take to motivate you to move? Must you see flames engulfing the living room before you'll get off the couch and run outside? Or are you the type who leaps up eagerly at the mere mention of the word *walk,* like the poor pet poodle who never gets to go anywhere? You're probably somewhere between those two extremes. But even the "eager for action" need motivation and guidance. Even if you love exercise, you need variety to keep you inspired and to make sure your muscles develop evenly. Try these tips:

- **Write your exercise schedule on your calendar** just as you write your social and work appointments, but highlight your exercise plans so you won't miss them and to remind yourself that they're important.
- **Have an exercise partner.** It greatly increases the chances that you'll stick with it.
- **Build exercise into your favorite pastimes.** If you love novels, listen to them on cassette tapes while you walk, bike, and so on. Watch television or listen to the radio while you're using your workout equipment. Do stretches while chatting on the phone.
- **Associate exercise and sociability.** Instead of having dessert when you're dining with a friend, go for a walk. When you're entertaining, include walks, bike rides, and active games in your plans.
- **Do it your way.** Covert Bailey, the author of *Fit or Fat,* says, "The best exercise is the one you'll do." So figure out what you really enjoy and start there. Even if it's something pretty low-level like strolling three blocks to the park, it's a start. Build on that until you can go farther, faster. Then search for related activities that you'll look forward to.

- **Build variety into your activities,** especially if you hate routine. Try some different ones like Tai Chi, yoga, or tap dancing. When exercise becomes too predictable, boredom sets in and your commitment dwindles. Besides, varied activities produce greater results physically.

- **Keep your exercise environment pleasant.** Make sure you have decent equipment and cheerful surroundings. If you hate your swimming instructor or the overly chlorinated water, you're not apt to swim long or often. Allowing adverse or stressful conditions to complicate your exercise is a form of self-sabotage.

- **Aerobic dance classes may be a good bet for you.** Many participants find the companionship of the classes inspires them to stick with it. Exercises like aerobic dancing are particularly good because they require both movement and thinking. They've been shown to speed reaction times in men and women over forty.

- **Follow the dictates of the weather and the seasons.** On cold, windy days, walk in the mall instead of outdoors. Or how about jumping rope? Have a sport or exercise for every season so that you don't hibernate all winter or dodge the heat all summer.

- **Take the exercises of your choice seriously.** Take lessons, practice them, schedule them. The more skillful and informed you are about your exercises, the more interesting and stimulating they will become. There are books and special-interest magazines and newsletters about every sport imaginable. Find out why other people are so hooked on a certain form of exercise, and you'll be hooked, too.

- **Perceive a lapse in your exercise regimen for what it is**—a momentary interruption. Don't let a minor setback throw you. Just get right back up on that horse as fast as possible!

- **Become an exercise mentor** to someone who can benefit from exercise the way you have. This is a surefire way to renew your own commitment.

- **Take part in sports competitions.** They will become a source of pride and achievement. In the beginning, just compete with yourself, especially if you're starting out cold in a new sport. Once you're established, you can enjoy working your way up through the ranks.

- **Go on record saying that exercise is important to you.** Sign a contract with yourself. State your reason for going on the program in writing. List quantifiable goals and when they'll be achieved. Example: "I am exercising to reduce stress and feel more relaxed, so I'll do at least one 20-minute exercise today." To keep your commitment-fever high, record minor and major breakthroughs as you move toward your goal.

Persistence is absolutely vital because *you can't store up the benefits of exercise* the way you can hoard money in a bank. Moderate exercise or a high degree of daily activity has to be ongoing. Interruptions in your usual mobility pattern will cause your fitness to plummet almost immediately.

One seventy-five-year-old woman said, "When I was in my forties, my life was so busy, I was often too tired to stay with a diet and exercise plan. Now, I have the time and energy but find it takes planning to stay motivated." She took a course in "elder aerobics" at the Y, and then found a friend to exercise with three times a week. She discovered that, like most of us, she initially needed some expert guidance to find the best exercises for her, and then someone to exercise with until it became a habit.

NUTRITION AND THE BRAIN

It is not news that eating well can help keep the body healthy, but it may be news to you that what you eat affects the way you think. What you eat, how much you eat, and when you eat it influence your emotional state and mental performance.

For example, a 1991 study at MIT by nutritionist Judith Wurtman and her neurobiologist husband, Richard, showed that when you want to be on your toes, you should eat protein. Protein-rich foods are high in the amino acid tyrosine, which stimulates the brain to produce the neurotransmitters dopamine and norepinephrine. When these neurotransmitters are present in the brain, you think more quickly, react more rapidly, and are more attentive. Solving problems, even difficult ones, is easier because of heightened brainpower.

For overall physical health, follow the guidelines of the new USDA Food Pyramid, which emphasizes grains, vegetables, and fruits, with lesser amounts of fats, sugars, meats, and dairy products. Most Americans need to reduce fat and increase fiber in their diets.

Within these general guidelines, you can make use of the different ways the different nutrients in food affect mental performance:

- If you need to be alert in the afternoon, eat a high-protein lunch.
- Eat simple carbohydrates for quick energy. If you have to write a memo in fifteen minutes, simple carbs are just right. But beware if your task requires much longer: The spurt of energy and quick thinking you get

from a candy bar or even a piece of fruit quickly fizzles and will hit you as hard as a wrestler's body slam.

- For endurance, eat lots of complex carbohydrates, found in grains and vegetables. They convert slowly into energy, giving you staying power. That's why runners stoke up on pasta before a marathon.
- Carbohydrates also trigger the release of tryptophan, which relaxes the body and makes you sleepy.
- Make sure that you continue to eat well as the years pass. There are startling statistics on the number of older people who, after checking into the hospital for treatment of a disease or injury, are found to be malnourished, and many cases of mental confusion and long-term fatigue can be traced to poor diet.

Listen to Your Body

More important than how much you eat, or even what you eat, is getting in touch with the way different foods affect you. Each of us reacts to foods differently. Sarah F. Leibowitz, Ph.D., of the Rockefeller University has located the epicenter of eating behavior deep in the brain's hypothalamus, a structure toward the base of the brain already known to control sexuality and reproduction. The neurons that affect eating are part of the body's elaborate mechanism for regulating energy balance, ensuring that we take in sufficient food to meet day-to-day internal and external energy demands.

Potatoes promote clear thinking for one person; an orange or a bagel or a jelly bean or a piece of chicken does it for another. Reflect on what works for you. Ask yourself: *What was I eating just before I couldn't sleep? What did I have for lunch that day when I felt so dull?*

You might find that listening to what your body says about food can free you from fat fighting and mood swings. It's hard to believe from looking at our slender friend Rosalyn at age sixty-one that she weighed 145 when she was in her twenties. "One day I simply decided that being overweight was a burden I would no longer carry. I didn't go on a diet; I just stopped eating in an automatic way. I started eating those foods I really liked and that made me feel good. The pounds just fell away. I am mindful of my weight. When I go two pounds over a hundred ten, I eat a little less until they're gone." Rosalyn learned many years ago to pay attention to her body wisdom.

So look within yourself and see what your body likes in terms of food.

You also need to look outside yourself and see what elements in your environment are helping or hindering your ability to think clearly.

THINKING THIN

Rosalyn's example illustrates that your mental attitude has a great deal to do with how your body processes nutrients. Here are some other ways you can think thin:

- Give yourself mind treats instead of food treats. When you have the urge to snack, treat yourself to reading an article on your favorite topic.
- Keep your life full of fascinating activities. When you have many interests and friends, you don't have time to eat between meals or anticipate the next meal.
- Avoid talking or fantasizing about food. Food fantasizing releases enzymes, increasing your appetite and nutrient absorption.
- Eat to live, not the opposite. Spend as little time planning meals as possible.
- Think before each meal about how uncomfortable overeating can make you. Stop eating the minute you feel satisfied.
- Tell yourself and others that you prefer to eat light meals. Biofeedback tapes for dieters implant this message subliminally.
- Avoid television commercials for burgers, pizza, and such. The visuals go directly to your right brain, arousing your emotions and then your desire to eat.
- Don't linger over menu decisions when you're eating out. Instead, choose and move quickly to a fascinating discussion with your dinner partner.

ALCOHOL AND THE BRAIN

The obvious mental effect of alcohol is that it blurs the ability to think straight. Excessive levels of alcohol speed up arteriosclerosis, which slows down the flow of blood to the brain. Furthermore, the eating habits of excessive drinkers deteriorate, sometimes leading to malnutrition, which in turn affects the brain. In Chapter 5, "Good News," we talked about another effect of excessive alcohol, the brain disease known as Korsakoff's syndrome.

In spring of 1992, *Modern Maturity,* the magazine of the American Association of Retired Persons, reported that 10 to 15 percent of people over sixty suffer from alcoholism, the same percentage as in the general population. A gene called A1 is suspected of being responsible for most alcoholism, but alcohol is an addictive substance. If you drink enough of it for a long enough time, you will become an alcoholic. And your chances of becoming addicted increase with age because aging lowers your tolerance for alcohol.

Medical opinions on what is an acceptable level of drinking vary: Some say no drinking at all; some say four ounces of wine, three times a week; some say a glass or two of wine per day. And there are studies to support each opinion. The point is, tolerances are individual and change with age. Alcoholics Anonymous offers this guideline in *Time to Start Living,* a pamphlet for older people:

> The true test . . . for alcoholism . . . is the answer to this question: What has alcohol done to you? If it has affected . . . the way you schedule your days, . . . your health, . . . if you are in any way preoccupied with alcohol—then the likelihood is that you have a problem.

Overt signs of alcoholism in elders differ from signs in younger people because elders are less likely to be involved in traffic accidents and public frays. Here are some more subtle indications:

- abrupt or significant changes in behavior, such as sudden hostility, forgetfulness, unsteady gait, slurred speech, or trembling hands
- a flare-up of diseases such as diabetes or hypertension that were controlled with medication before
- complaints of insomnia or restless sleep; frequent napping
- deterioration of grooming, housekeeping, and eating habits
- falls, broken bones, bruises, or burns
- stashed bottles

Free information on alcoholism, as well as other forms of substance abuse, is available upon request from the AARP, Dept. MH, 601 E St. NW, Washington, DC 20049.

Caffeine and the Brain

Studies suggest that people who drink two cups of coffee or other caffeinated beverages a day are not harming their physical health. However, caffeine can cause irritability, nervousness, and sleeplessness in some people. If you suspect that caffeine is causing difficulties for you, try cutting back, or even stopping for a month. You may experience withdrawal symptoms such as a headache at first, but these problems will taper off in a few days.

SLEEP AND THE BRAIN

As we found in Chapter 4, "What Happens When the Brain Ages," the locus ceruleus, located in the brain stem, loses about 40 percent of its cells with aging, which upsets sleeping and waking cycles. Furthermore, levels of the neurotransmitter melatonin decrease with age, which means we sleep fewer hours and less deeply.

Many older people adjust easily to such changes in their sleep patterns. "I love getting up with the chickens," one retired farmer commented. "It's the best time of day—when the world is quiet and fresh. Besides, I rest midmorning and nap in the afternoon. That way I don't have any times when I feel down," she continued.

Ernest Lawrence Rossi, Ph.D., and David Nimmons, authors of *The Twenty-Minute Break,* would agree. They recommend restful exercises and naps for all ages so that we can take advantage of the brain's natural 90- to 120-minute cycle of arousal, peak performance, stress, and rest.

It's important to get the sleep you need, because lack of sleep can cause problems with concentration and memory. REM sleep (with rapid eye movement), which is related to emotions and dreaming, occupies 20 percent of your sleeping time, while non-REM, thinking-related sleep occupies 80 percent of the time. Both are important because of their restorative value. Without REM we become delusional and paranoid. Without non-REM, we become inattentive and dull.

In addition to losses in the locus ceruleus, sleeplessness can be caused by depression, a medication you're taking for some other condition, too much alcohol, caffeine, or being excited by a project or upcoming event, to name a few possibilities. A major cause of sleeplessness is stress. Forty percent of adults can sleep no more than six hours a night because of stress, according to *Prevention* magazine. Stanford University's sleep center researchers claim that "most Americans no longer know what it feels like to be fully alert." Because your brain is different from every other brain, you are the best monitor for its proper functioning. Pay attention to what helps you sleep, and what causes problems.

To encourage restorative sleep:

- Don't exercise before bedtime, because it stimulates endorphins that keep you awake.
- Focus on a boring book rather than exciting or worrisome thoughts.
- When you're restless, get up and read or finish some tasks rather than getting frustrated with yourself.
- Snack on tryptophan-loaded foods such as turkey.
- Visualize yourself pushing the hold button on your worries and the access button on your "inner peace" thoughts.
- To avoid fretful sleeping, go to bed *before* you are exhausted. You don't have to wear yourself out to earn the right to sleep.
- Be patient. It takes four to six weeks to change sleep habits and to catch up on lost sleep.

THE ENVIRONMENT AND THE BRAIN

Some people find that their thinking is influenced by environmental factors such as sound, wind, water, and darkness. For example, studies show that many people feel irritated by wind. They become crotchety and unable to focus mentally. But sailors and hardy outdoorsmen or -women seem to love the power of the wind. People who grow up in windswept Patagonia feel off balance when there is no wind.

Many people find water soothes them and makes their minds sharper, too. Painter Maud Morgan observed, "When I'm stuck or stymied on how to proceed with my present project, I no longer try to push it through as I once did. I just get warm and wet. That soothes my body and my mind, and as the water flows over me, whether in a stream, a pool or a bath, the paint begins to flow in my mind, and I jump up, excited to get back to my art." She continued, "Some years ago, I noticed the connection between times of good health and the amount of time I spent in the sea or water. My particular body craves soaking, so I respond to that body need.'' Studies show water is extremely conducive to creative thinking and to finding a focus when overwhelmed.

Tune in to which elements in your environment affect you. Are there times when sounds keep you from ''thinking straight'': the CD player's background music, the TV's racket, children's playing, the air conditioner's hum? Does sunlight make you feel irritable and headachy, or cheerful and relaxed? Does water help your thinking? What kind and where?

Learn to listen to your body's messages about exercise, nutrition, alcohol, sleep, and your environment. Your body is wise, and it will teach you what you need to do for peak performance of your body and your mind.

Emotional Balance and Mental Sharpness

The advantage of the emotions is that they lead us astray—OSCAR WILDE

He who laughs, lasts.   —MARY PETTIBONE POOLE

Have you ever said, "I'm so mad I can't think straight!"? You were right! A brain flooded with strong emotions doesn't work well for you. It's less able to be creative or flexible, organized or in control. Besides being affected by sudden, crisis-driven emotions, thinking is also affected by low levels of persistently draining emotions such as anxiety. The aftermath of both these emotional assaults on your thinking is diminished energy and self-confidence.

Finding emotional balance starts with understanding the emotions you feel. Too often, people hide or ignore their emotions. You need to think about the powerful emotions that we all feel, and understand how these feelings affect your brain and your body. Then you can learn ways to achieve balance.

We live in a stressful world that can evoke strong emotions. By using your brain to bring balance to your emotions, you can reduce these stresses and strains. That frees you to let your brain work better for you.

HOW DOES IT FEEL?

He stomped into the hospital, chewing on a cigar, loudly complaining to his wife that everything was stupid: the hospital procedures, the rule against smoking, the idea that he could be having a heart attack. Moments later, he was strapped on a gurney, on his way to the emergency room, leaving his wife sitting in the hospital reception area. Next to her was a fiftyish woman, slumped sideways, her head drooping, her eyes listlessly gazing at the chipped floor tiles. Her eyes gave not a flicker when a young man walked through the room, exuberantly describing the eight-pound nine-ounce boy his wife had just given birth to.

All of these people were experiencing different strong emotions, each having a distinctive effect on the brain. Anger is a deep red, depression a royal blue, and happiness is yellow or pale red. Over the past five years, using positron emission tomography (PET), biomedical researchers have photographed thousands of colored images of the human brain and identified configurations of colors that appear when individuals are angry, sad, or happy. They've also discovered that there are "picture profiles" of mental illnesses such as schizophrenia and brain diseases such as Alzheimer's.

This ability to "see" emotions and brain disorders has been a tremendous boon to scientists who are trying to understand how your thinking effects the way you feel and vice versa. The benefits to medical science are obvious. To the layperson, it's heartening to know that hope lies ahead for understanding and treating emotional problems. Besides, it's comforting to know that your feelings are real and that others experience the same feelings in many of the ways you do.

Emotions are wispy phenomena. You can't touch them or see them. They come and go. But emotions are real. You can measure them in the biofeedback lab, and PET scans give us pictures of emotions. You can see the effects of negative emotions on the faces of people who are always angry or anxious or fearful. Likewise, you can see the effects of positive emotions in faces with laugh wrinkles and loving eyes. Emotions leave a legacy in the face and personality.

Let's think about the effects of eight primary emotions on your brain and body: fear and anxiety, anger and hate, sadness and shame, pleasure and love. We've divided them into four easy-to-remember categories: Scared, Mad, Sad, and Glad.

See if our portrayal of each emotion *feels* right to you. Do you feel it in the same place? If not, pause for a moment and imagine a scene that would provoke that emotion. Then write on a sheet of paper how you felt. Add a cue word or two to remind you later of the scene you saw. Keep the paper available to make notes about the remaining emotions on the list.

Scared

Fear. Fear is a quaking feeling in your stomach, accompanied by trembling voice and hands. A cold, stiff feeling sometimes overtakes you. If it's profound physical fear, you may either feel frozen in place or have a strong urge to run. In either case, your mind goes blank.

Psychological fear is just as powerful as physical fear. Remember the scene in the film *An Unmarried Woman* when Jill Clayburgh first realizes her long marriage has ended? Her fear of facing life on her own is so intense, she vomits.

Fear sends a rush of adrenaline to your brain, which can cause you to be hyperalert and so energized that some people can perform superhuman feats such as lifting a car off a trapped child. With training, you can use the same kind of fear reaction to make dynamic speeches and public presentations.

Anxiety. This is a feeling of tension that can be general or specific. When you experience tension throughout your whole body, it is often accompanied by nausea and a jittery, nervous feeling that makes it difficult to think clearly. When you tense up in one specific place, it becomes painful. For instance, you might tighten the trapezius muscle above your shoulder blade every time you think you're going to be late. If you worry daily about being late, eventually the muscle will knot in constant pain, it will atrophy, and your posture will be affected.

Like fear, anxiety produces extra energy, but at a persistent low level. When anxious, emotives—those who readily express their emotions—often can't sit still and involve themselves in unproductive activity such as repeatedly pushing an elevator button or dialing the same telephone number. Nonemotives—emotionally self-contained individuals—often eat, hum, or get diarrhea when they're anxious.

Anxiety causes speech to come in short, choppy sentences. If you've brooded over what you'll say, you feel like your "heart is in your mouth." You may be on the verge of tears, with your throat aching, heart palpitating, and mind darting from one thought to another. Anxiety produces rumination, chewing over the same problem or grievance again and again until you and others are exhausted and exasperated.

Mad

Anger. Anger often begins with a tight feeling in your throat and stomach. Sometimes you have such a hot feeling in your head, it seems ready to explode. Your eyes may look searing, like lasers that could burn a hole in the object of your fury.

Sometimes anger produces a sour taste in your mouth and churning in your stomach. You often have a surge of energy that makes you feel that you'll burst if you don't do something NOW! You'd really like to punch someone out, but you will probably settle for slamming a door or stepping on your car's accelerator.

Anger affects the speech centers of your brain strongly; some of us can't speak or can only babble incoherently when in a rage, while others can't stop talking. The latter slash and burn with their words, taking no prisoners, giving no quarter. Emotives cry and curse, while nonemotives lapse into a smoldering, deadly calm.

Hate. Hate is related to anger but is an ongoing feeling rather than an automatic response. Hating involves more mental skills than anger because carrying a grudge requires both long-term memory and planning skills to "get even." It uses both sides of the brain—the left rationalizes why something is hateful and verbalizes it, while the right feels and acts upon it.

Hate burns fiercely in the chest and throat. It thwarts clear thinking because every new piece of information, rather than bringing insight and change, merely adds fuel to the fire. Although hate exercises higher thinking skills, its power harms us emotionally, physically, and mentally.

Sad

Sadness. There is a heavy feeling in your chest. Your whole body sags and facial features droop. Your throat may feel tight, even to the point of hurting. This "lump in your throat" sometimes seems to be your only defense against a flood of tears. Sadness discolors your perception of everything: A song will sound plaintive rather than happy; a holiday will be torture instead of fun.

It's difficult to concentrate when you're sad because everything reminds you of your sadness. Furthermore, the effort it takes to "put on a happy face" for the outside world leaves you feeling drained and sluggish.

Emotives talk and cry about their sadness, while nonemotives sigh and shrug their shoulders repeatedly or sleep a lot.

Sadness is a normal feeling when you've experienced a loss, but prolonged sadness or feeling sad for no apparent reason is often related to depression, which we'll talk about later.

Shame. Shame is a feeling of self-disgust that erodes your confidence. If it is intense, you might feel as though you have a "black hole" of negativity in your chest so strong that it forces you to slump forward and avoid eye contact with others. Your body also advertises milder forms of shame—for example when you blush or glance about furtively to see who might have noticed that you stumbled.

Shame can run rampant through your mind, making concentration difficult. Instead of staying on a logical train of thought, you concoct ways to excuse or cover up your perceived failings, or try to place the blame elsewhere.

When you are filled with self-doubt that comes from excessive shame, you may come across to others as aloof, devious, and just plain nerdy. This sets off another cycle of assaults on your self-confidence.

Emotives talk constantly about the inadequacies they see in themselves, hoping that others will disagree with them. Nonemotives suffer their shame in silence.

Shame is not all bad; it is the germ of conscience. The shame we experience in childhood can help make us aware that we are not perfect, that what we do affects others. Sociopaths feel no shame or regret, and therefore cannot put the needs of others ahead of their own.

Glad

Pleasure. This is a feeling of excitement and freedom that stimulates your mind and body. Time seems to fly by; laughter and joking come easily; your mind and body become totally involved in what you're doing. Pleasure is in the eyes of the beholder: Sports, attending an entertainment, being with friends or loved ones, learning, creating, work, and even mowing the lawn can be pleasurable.

Having fun improves your mental functioning. You say clever things, come up with new ideas and solutions; you see the bright side of life and the advantage in every situation.

You can feel pleasure as you anticipate, experience, or recall a pleasant event. While pleasure is a helpful emotion to experience at every stage, focusing on the pleasures of the past or future keeps you from fully enjoying the present. Also, it's difficult to be realistic about the pleasures you look backward or forward to, because all are colored by memory and imagination.

Love. Love is deeper and lasts longer than pleasure. It affects your general attitude toward life and others, rather than precise events and activities. You seem to walk taller, feel freer, and dream bigger when you're in this joyous state.

You feel this many-splendored emotion in your heart, chest, and throat. Physically, feelings of love can range from a warm flutter to a prolonged, intense contraction that leaves you breathless. Your "love thoughts" can encompass everything from admiration and tenderness to good humor and comfortable closeness.

These are feelings and attitudes you experience with sweethearts, friends, relatives, children, and pets. In romantic love, you typically and ideally have all these feelings and attitudes, plus physical passion.

Love heightens your mental awareness and tunes you in to the positive side of life. The comfort of loving and being loved aids creativity. You are more able to see many options, be more accepting of your own ideas and those of others, and in general feel more mentally energetic.

We could fill this book with derivatives of and variations on these eight primary emotions. There may be other terms for feelings that are important to you. Feel free to add them to your list. Describe where and how you experience them and then project what behavior they lead to.

The Evolution of Emotions

The four categories of emotion—Scared, Mad, Sad, and Glad—represent the refining of human emotions from their primitive beginnings to present levels.

Dogs can have fun retrieving a stick. Cats enjoy grooming themselves. Chimpanzees get pleasure from eating a banana. But only humans experience joy and the other higher emotions. What's the difference? Why can't brown cows be sensitive?

The answer is, they just don't have the brain for it. Long ago, humans developed the ability to translate their feelings into language. When they saw a woolly mammoth approach, a thought meaning *danger* provoked a signal to the adrenal gland, which secreted adrenaline. Eventually, they came to associate the physical effects of the adrenaline (fluttering in the stomach and heart palpitations) with their version of the word *fear*.

These early humans had a brain structure that allowed them to devise a sound that signified the specific feelings they had when they were scared, mad, sad, or glad. The more they thought about these emotions and expressed them in words (which eventually were written), the more complex their brains became. In turn, their emotions became richer, full of subtleties and nuances.

Fear and anxiety are the most primitive emotions and come from the Reptilian and Limbic Brains. The Reptilian expresses fear in a very crude manner—by provoking the body to strike out or run. The Limbic Brain, which developed later, deals with fear in a more sophisticated way because it has primitive abilities to remember and strategize. The snake and the bird provide an informative contrast: The mother snake abandons her progeny as soon as she lays an egg, but the mother killdeer broods the eggs and feeds the babies. She can even fake a broken wing to distract the fox from her babies in their ground nest. Mommy snake is operating from a Reptilian point of view, while mother bird uses both the Reptilian and Limbic.

Neither of them feels emotions that we would connect with such experiences. The mother bird is not mad at the fox; she is responding automatically to danger. She reacts this way to any animal or thing that seems to threaten the survival of her babies (and, therefore, the survival of her species). Her decoy strategy represents a much more sophisticated level of response than the snake's, but it is doubtful that she has any feelings connected to it. Cats and dogs, being mammals with a cerebral cortex, often seem to feel emotions.

The human mother uses both these primitive layers plus both sides of the New Brain: She feels fear when she looks down the supermarket aisle and sees two oddly dressed people lifting her son out of the grocery cart. The mother, who looked away from her child momentarily to price a can of ripe olives, now grips the can tightly, as though it were a weapon she might use to fend off these strangers. But as she sprints down the aisle, she notices that these people are both small, graying, and frail looking. They're smiling benignly and talking to each other excitedly in a foreign language. When they notice her, the woman says in broken English: "He is so beautiful . . . such a nice boy . . . just like our little Karl, our grandson. It's such a long time since we've seen him."

The mother sets the can of olives in the basket, takes a deep breath, and manages a smile. She reaches out for her baby, and says, "You have a grandson?'' They both tell her their story: They came to the United States six weeks ago to visit an ill relative. They've been unable to return home and miss their only grandson very much. Tears well up in their eyes as they talk about their joy in seeing this child who looks so much like Karl.

As the young mother feels her fear ebbing, she realizes that they are not aware of how inappropriate it was for them to pick up her child. They do not live in a big city. When their children were babies, people did not abduct babies from grocery stores. This analysis by her left brain quells the anger she felt. A moment later, she experiences a rush of sympathy for this elderly couple as she thinks of her own parents, who live five states away and can see their grandchild only once a year. The mother's frontal lobes enable her to understand the elderly couple's state of mind, and consequently she experiences emotions of the highest order: sympathy and caring for total strangers.

This scenario shows how the progress of the human brain in monitoring and controlling emotions parallels the progressive nature of emotions from base, almost automatic ones to the higher, more refined feelings. As you review the eight emotions, notice how they advance from simple and negative to complex and positive, and that this progress is matched by the part the brain used—i.e., from the oldest, most primitive to the most recent and altruistic. It looks like this:

Reptilian	→	Limbic	→	New Brain	→	Frontal
2. anxiety		4. hate		6. shame		8. love
↑		↑		↑		↑
1. fear		3. anger		5. sadness		7. pleasure
SCARED		MAD		SAD		GLAD

The progress shown on this table is driven by the need to survive. As the environment changes, methods for adapting to it must change. The "fight or flight" response, which is provoked by feelings of fear, was adequate in primitive times, but no longer. In adapting, humans "grew" new parts to their brains. The new brain structures accommodated new thinking skills that fostered more refined emotions.

YOUR EVOLUTION

Just as emotions evolved in the whole race of human beings, they evolve in individuals, too. We begin life at a very primitive thought/emotion level. Newborns do not cry because someone hurt their feelings; they cry for food and for release from physical pain. However, you may have noticed that they soon grow accustomed to having food and diapering on demand and will add anger to their crying repertoire when service is not instantaneous.

By the end of the first year, a child has felt, in a rudimentary way, most of the primary emotions:

Fear—of falling, strangers, abandonment
Anxiety—when a big, shaggy dog approaches
Anger—at not getting Fluffy *now*
Sadness—when Mommy leaves the child with a sitter
Pleasure—when playing in water
Love—when Mommy comes home

Notice that hate is missing from the child's repertoire, because the brain skills needed for hating have not yet developed. Remember the song from *South Pacific* explaining so poignantly that hate must be carefully taught? Also, shame is not there yet, but it can be added soon.

As we reach the terrible twos, an unnerving thought sneaks up on us: We are not the center of the universe! Parents, siblings, and friends occasionally expect us to conform to *their* needs. At two we also often feel anxious because we like our independence but also fear it.

This same ambivalence strikes teens, who are victims of hormones that send their thoughts hurtling from one side of their brain to the other. These poor creatures have little control over moods and attitudes. It may be some small comfort to parents of teens that most of them master these mood swings and grow into balanced adults.

Besides, parents, the same kind of unsettled feelings can overtake you in your forties due to hormone changes and social factors. But the dynamics are different at midlife. The teen's brain needs relief from the raging hormones (testosterone, adrenaline) that produce the physical feelings we associate with fear, anger, love, hate, and other strong emotions. However, testosterone and adrenaline levels are decreasing in males at midlife. They need greater stimulation to get a rush of adrenaline or sexual drive. All of this can be dispiriting to the male, and he often searches for new stimulants (a new hobby, career, or wife) or lapses into inertia.

Females' estrogen levels also drop at midlife, but their testosterone often increases, accounting in part for the power surge and increased aggressiveness often experienced at this time.

The fifties and sixties are a time for a transition from the strong emotions of youth to the quieter ones of old age. The waning in strength and volume of hormones and enzymes is partially responsible. Changing roles and attitudes of the "thinking person" help the maturing process along. However, even the most thoughtful people can become sidetracked at this juncture by what they perceive as failure or a significant loss of ability. Those who have been high achievers all their lives are especially prone to feel disappointed in themselves or life in general when they experience declines in their physical and social power.

BATTLING FATIGUE

Medical doctors report that one in four people who visit the doctor have fatigue as one of their major complaints. While there are legitimate physical reasons for constant weariness, more often the causes are boredom, loneliness, and physical inactivity. Research shows that the best prescription for fighting fatigue is a life-style that includes:

- regular contact with a variety of friends and loved ones
- setting goals and accomplishing them
- broadening your interests and activities
- regular physical exercise

Being aware of the natural body changes that occur at this juncture in life can be an immense relief, but there is no substitute for self-confidence in keeping your emotional balance. Even the most confident adults may feel a sense of failure when their powers are threatened. It's like being a three-year-old again, struggling to master the tasks of living: You want to pour your own cup of milk; it spills and your parents yell at you, or your siblings laugh at you. Such experiences are a normal part of growing up but can tug at your ego with great force when you hit upon hard times. That's why careful maintenance of your self-esteem is valuable. Here are a few techniques that will help:

Act Self-confident. Sit straight, stand tall, smile, and walk with a firm stride. The way you act has a direct effect on your brain. Good posture and a positive attitude release neurotransmitters that enhance your feelings of well-being.

Quell Negative Self-talk. You can't feel good about yourself if you're under constant assault from within. Convert negative statements into positive ones. If you deserve the negatives you're thinking, then correct the behavior rather than wallowing in guilt and regrets.

Look Your Best. Dress and groom yourself in a manner that helps you feel as attractive as possible. If dyeing your hair, having a facelift, or buying designer clothes makes you feel better about yourself, then launch a gradual self-improvement plan that gets the job done.

Get Good Feedback from Others. Looking your best attracts good feedback, but a more effective way is to be an interesting person. Develop some kind of "entertainment" skill that makes you an important part of any social situation. You might focus on telling tasteful, appropriate jokes, asking interesting questions, being well informed, discussing fascinating topics, or just facilitating conversations for others. All of these skills make you fun to be with and produce positive reactions from others.

Follow the Advice in Chapter 6, "Physical Health and Mental Sharpness." Feeling as strong and healthy as possible helps your self-confidence immensely.

Know What You Want and Ask for It. It's difficult to be self-confident if you feel like a doormat. Study the art of being properly assertive so that you get what you're entitled to without abrogating the rights of others.

Reward Yourself for Succeeding . . . and Even for the Effort You Put Forth. Give yourself compliments and accept them from others. Make note of your little successes and schedule specific ways of celebrating the big ones.

You may be worrying now that these seven confidence builders will go to your head and make you self-centered or egotistical. Actually, true self-confidence produces the opposite characteristics. When you feel good about yourself, you have a quiet ability to appreciate others and make way for their needs. So everyone wins!

WORRY STOPPERS

Worrying is a futile, destructive way to handle anxiety. Here are some ways to break the worry addiction:

- Establish a worry schedule: Book specific times to worry about one problem. For example, "2–2:15, must worry about why Rochelle didn't call this week." If you concentrate on your concern during the scheduled time, you'll either get sick of it or find a solution—or both. In either case, you'll be ready to let it go.
- Write down your worry, then flush or burn it. Symbolically destroying it rids you of the worry and reduces your anger.
- Do just one thing about your worry—make a phone call, write a letter, or do something else—then let it go for four days. Structuring your worries disempowers them and empowers you.
- Let your friends worry for you. Shedding the responsibility temporarily lightens your load, and their fresh point of view might turn up a solution. You might even trade worries with them.

THE DANGERS OF BURYING EMOTIONS

Review now the primary emotions as we've described them: fear, anxiety, anger, hate, sadness, shame, pleasure, and love. As you think about them, try to put your emotions into perspective. Can you think of times when emotions made it difficult for you to think clearly? Can you look back and see progress that you've made in balancing your emotions? Can you think of things you understand now that you didn't earlier in life? Have you purposely stretched yourself to understand and experience better emotional control? Don't be discouraged if you're not a Mother Teresa or Albert Schweitzer. We'll give you some guidelines later, but first, we want to tell you what *not* to do.

When you use faking, pretending, or ignoring to cope with an emotional situation, you are multiplying the strain on your system. Not only are you fogging your thinking process, you're doing harm to your body. The bottom line is that you cannot fully realize your potential for clear thinking when you fly off the handle *or* when you avoid dealing with the emotion.

Posttraumatic stress disorder (PTSD), an emotional problem that combat soldiers sometimes suffer, illustrates dramatically that extreme emotions can impair your thinking. When you have a close call, you experience the same kind of emotional reactions as the soldier who is wounded or who sees a friend killed. Your responses might be at a lower intensity but you feel the same emotions: shock, denial, anxiety, anger, self-doubt, depression, and finally acceptance.

These are normal, healthful responses to unnatural occurrences as diverse as the death of a child or experiencing an earthquake. When we have the opportunity after the trauma to talk about what happened, understand our emotions, and put the matter into perspective, most of us have no severe long-term aftereffects.

Combat soldiers are unable to go through this natural sequence of emotions. They are trained to bypass them. They have learned to ignore their fear and anger. They do what it takes to survive the moment. And if they have no chance later to "process" these experiences with buddies, loved ones, or a counselor or therapist, they develop symptoms of PTSD, several of which directly interfere with thinking. From their examples, we've learned that burying extreme emotions can cause:

- **sleeplessness:** Lack of sleep affects the memory and general mental vitality.
- **flashbacks:** Terrifying memories of the event cause concentration problems and make it difficult to stay in touch with reality.
- **psychic numbing:** Being insensitive to your own feelings causes you to be distant or blunt with loved ones.
- **anger:** Persistent anger causes you to speak and think in hostile, pessimistic ways.
- **hyperalertness:** Being constantly on the alert causes you to think in a guarded way; always prepared for trouble, the mind darts impulsively, making concentration difficult.
- **mental processing problems:** Such problems lead to blocked memory, vertigo, feeling out of it, ineffectiveness under stress, and poor self-image.
- **self-medication:** The need to "feel better" causes you to take too much medication, drink too much alcohol, or overeat.

It is not just serious shocks that can have a deleterious effect on your emotional balance. Long-term, low-level stress produces the same kinds of mental problems. As a result, you burn out. For example, being angry with a colleague at work daily for six years takes its toll on your emotional balance and inevitably interferes with clear thinking. Ignoring burnout and the aftereffects of a traumatic experience inevitably leads to depression, an especially dangerous challenge to emotional balance and clear thinking. It is tied to prolonged arousal of the right brain, and its effects can be seen on a CAT scan.

Depression

All of us feel sad at times and have periods when we just feel down. We're not talking about that kind of depression. We're concerned about clinical depression, the kind that interferes with everyday life. Clinical depression is much more common than most people realize. According to Dr. A. John Rush, professor of psychiatry at the University of Texas Medical Center, many people fail to recognize the symptoms or don't seek help because they fear the stigma of a "mental disorder." He points out that depression is not a personal weakness or moral defect. It can often be treated with minimum medication and short-term therapy, six weeks or less. Dr. Rush and his colleagues have devised a set of guidelines for general practitioners to use in identifying serious depression. It says that if you have any of the following symptoms for two weeks or longer, you may be suffering from something more than garden-variety depression:

1. loss of interest in everything: reading, sex, socializing, working
2. pervasive sadness not connected with any particular loss
3. sleep disturbances—you can't go to sleep, wake up frequently, sleep fitfully, don't feel rested in the morning
4. changes in appetite (you either can't eat or eat all the time) and weight (loss or gain)
5. concentration problems, feeling distracted, poor memory
6. suicidal thoughts
7. feeling physically restless or slowed down

If you are experiencing these signs, see your doctor at once.

COMMON WAYS PEOPLE SEEK EMOTIONAL BALANCE

People vary widely in how strongly they feel and express emotions. For example, anger can range from rage to measured response to a whining complaint. Either extreme on a continuous basis is hard on the body and brain. You want to strive to be in the middle of that continuum for each of the emotions most of the time.

Luckily, there's a natural gravitation or pull to the center. Whether you're aware of it or not, your body and emotions seek homeostasis. Are you aware of how you might keep your emotions between the two extremes? Here are some of the ways people often seek balance—not always successfully.

Finding Your Opposite

A common way we seek (and sometimes find) emotional balance is by choosing a mate, friend, or business partner who has opposite personality characteristics. Type A's seek out Type B's; right-brainers look for left-brainers; extroverts and introverts are drawn to each other. While this drive for balance is natural, in the long term it can present problems.

For example, Phil and Dawn were opposites in almost every way. He was a pessimist, she an optimist. She had a hot temper; he was easygoing. He liked to stay home; she wanted to dance the night away. He was logical and left-brained; she was emotional and right-brained.

When they met, he was taken by her cheerful enthusiasm. He was touched and intrigued when she cried in movies and spoke passionately about civil rights issues. She was impressed by his ability to see through sales scams and to make sense out of appliance instructions. His serene and confident way of handling sticky situations made her feel secure.

After they married, each did what he or she was best at. Phil took on all the paperwork chores, such as balancing the checkbook, paying bills, and planning their future. Dawn decorated their town house, stayed in touch with both their families, and studied child psychology (in preparation for the children she hoped to have). By the third year, he was a financial nag and she lavished her time and attention on matters outside their relationship. On their fourth anniversary, she asked for a divorce. She was bored with him and resented what she thought of as "his attempts to regiment their lives." He was hurt and mystified about what had gone wrong but rather relieved to be out of this entanglement with a "spendthrift."

Getting emotional balance is not like soldiering in the Civil War: You can't pay someone to do it for you. Dawn and Phil encouraged themselves and each other to become more extreme in their emotional approaches to life. They came to resent and finally abhor the very characteristics that had originally brought them together. This kind of polarization often occurs in couples, partnerships, and teams, and it limits the thinking of all parties concerned.

If Phil had taken on some of the shopping and social tasks and Dawn had assumed responsibility for some of the record keeping and home repair tasks, each person's self-confidence would have increased, along with appreciation for the other person's skills.

Folk or Professional Therapy

Talking to a trusted friend or loved one is the most common way to determine when our emotions are out of line and to get suggestions for tempering them.

Although someone you know may give you valuable insights, there's a great difference in the skill levels of a therapist and your best friend. The therapist knows how to listen and empower you to think through situations yourself. Because therapists know what is normal and what is not, they can intervene when you're off the scale in either direction. Finally, therapists are objective: They do not allow their own emotions to color their therapeutic approach. A competent therapist can be helpful, especially at times of crisis.

But even the best of therapists or friendly ears cannot do it for you. Achieving and maintaining emotional balance require a high level of self-awareness and a willingness to make sometimes wrenching changes in attitude and behavior.

Self-medicating

Some people take drugs or medicines to help themselves feel better. This includes everything from occasionally taking pain-killers prescribed for other conditions to total dependence upon alcohol or heroin.

When some people feel mad or nervous, they take a tranquilizer to keep their emotions in check. When they're feeling tired or low, they take a pep pill or have a drink to perk them up. Some people smoke or overeat.

Self-medicating is a risky way to seek a feeling of emotional balance. The chance of addiction is too great. Consider that recent retirees and those who move to retirement communities have increasingly high rates of alcoholism. Even people who never drank early in life find that the boredom of retirement, the depression from losing one's spouse, or living in a "partying" retirement community makes them vulnerable to alcohol abuse. And younger generations are even more tolerant of self-medicating, having grown up on media promises that "there's a pill for every pain."

FOUR SOUND APPROACHES TO EMOTIONAL BALANCE

Matching up with your opposite, trying folk or professional therapy, and turning to drugs or alcohol are common enough ways to seek emotional balance, but as we've seen, they all have their problems. Psychotherapists have come up with four approaches that often have better success. These approaches can help you greatly in your daily struggles with emotional balance. Each school of thought focuses on the problem from a different point of view: the event, the behavior, the belief, or the emotion.

Change the Event

The first approach is based upon the theories of William James and Carl Lange, who saw emotions as purely physiological responses to an event or environment. The physical reactions send your brain sensory messages, which are interpreted as an emotion. Therefore, the psychologists said, if you want to stabilize your emotions, you must control the event or environment.

For example, when you reach into a filing cabinet at work and the divider pinches your thumb, pain messages that produce an angry feeling go to your brain. The environment-oriented solution is to fix the divider or get another job. There are times when this approach is appropriate. But let's go on with this example as the plot thickens:

Change the Behavior

The second approach is related to B. F. Skinner's behavior modification, a system for changing emotions by changing behavior—by punishing or rewarding yourself.

This might sound entirely too simple to be effective, but there is physiological support for it. If you fake a smile, your brain temperature warms, endorphins are released, and your emotions are calmed. When you stiffen your spine, hold your head up, and take a deep breath, you get more oxygen to your brain and thus feel more confident and in control.

It is easy enough to smile or hold your head up, but what behavior can you change to control your anger? Punishment is appropriate in some situations—but not for the file drawer problem. The reward system is best here. Reward yourself for not feeling angry when the divider pinched. Commend yourself: *I didn't curse or blame anyone, even myself, when it happened.* You might add to the reward by allowing yourself to take an unscheduled break or eat an apple.

Obviously, the reward system requires planning and understanding, plus a commitment to using the system when you next encounter an anger-provoking situation. Eventually, though, you can replace your negative reactions with such positive thoughts as *I wonder why this divider is off track. It'll be fun to check it out.*

When the behavior approach works, the Reptilian and Limbic systems are bypassed. The mental processes required to avoid pain and get rewards require some rather intricate thinking, feeling, and planning that use the left and right hemispheres as well as the frontal lobes.

Change Beliefs

The third approach to emotional balance is based upon Albert Ellis's Rational Emotive Theory (RET), which says that since you didn't expect the divider to pinch your finger, your belief about the safety of using the file has been defiled (pun intended). In an effort to explain what happened, you try to place blame: Someone broke it, or it was poorly constructed. Now you have someone to be angry with.

The RET solution is to check reality. Are there signs that the file cabinet was tampered with? Has anyone else used it? Haven't you used it for years without getting hurt? In other words, when you check out the facts, your attitude will change, and thus your anger will come into balance. You don't want to simply squelch the anger. Instead, use it to energize yourself to solve the problem: Fix the filing cabinet or replace it.

You're using both sides of your cerebral cortex with the RET approach: Finding the facts is a left-brain speciality; your hunch that someone broke the divider is from the right brain; comparing the two and deciding which perception is correct uses both sides of your frontal lobes.

Change Emotions

The fourth approach is based upon the Freudian concept that you have buried memories that need to be understood in order to balance your feelings about relationships and events. For example, you unknowingly connect an adult experience with a memory that you were hurt by your brother when you were three and a parent comforted him, not you. The Freudian approach is to talk about it until you can remember and understand why you are so angered by the file divider's pinching your hand. Through this understanding, your anger is dispelled, and you are able to solve your problem with a clear head.

Even though they did not usually consult with therapists, this approach, more than any other, seems to fit the way we've found that balanced elders handle their emotions. The self-understanding they've gained through experience helps them actually change their emotions. They seem to use three mental strategies to achieve this self-awareness:

- They *reframe* the incident, putting it into a different perspective.
- They're willing to take *responsibility* for their part in the incident.
- They can easily *distance* themselves from the situation.

Because of their many life experiences, older people find it easy to *reframe* upsetting incidents. They've lived through similar situations, they are more tolerant of the mistakes of younger people because they realize their own frailties, and they don't have to prove themselves. This broader perspective defuses extreme emotions.

Because they've come to terms with their own self-worth, elders are not afraid to take *responsibility* for their own errors. Besides, they've made mistakes before and they know that being imperfect is not the end of the world.

Because they have thought through their values and beliefs, they find it easier than young people to *distance* themselves from challenges to their ideas. They know what they think and believe and thus feel no need to explain or justify themselves. Their equanimity enables them to dissociate themselves from emotionally charged situations.

This approach involves more brain functions than any other. Your Limbic Brain helps you conjure up memories loaded with feelings. These move to the right brain for emotional expression (I'm angry, sad, happy, and so on), then to the left to figure the whys of the emotion. Your executive brain functions in the frontal lobes enable you to be more tolerant and understanding of others' roles in the event, and eventually to figure out how to look at the event in a practical, yet altruistic, light. All these kinds of thinking are effective in calming your emotions and using them appropriately.

When we talked with black political leader Cecil Reed, now in his eighties, he recalled an experience with "calming emotions" he'd once had when making a speech in Des Moines: "It was in a big fancy hotel, the kind I used to have to enter through the back door. After I got settled, I changed into my jeans and went down to check out the ballroom where I'd be speaking. A lady came up to me and said, 'Move these chairs over there.' I wasn't doing anything, so I moved them for her. Then she said, 'We need another table over here.' I said, 'I don't know where the tables are.' She was plainly irritated and said in kind of a threatening way, 'I'm going to call the manager.' I laughed and said, 'That's a good idea. I don't work here, so I can't help you anymore.' She was really embarrassed."

In earlier days, Cecil might have been annoyed with the haughty woman, but he was amused by the situation and even said he felt a little sorry for her when she discovered he was the featured speaker. A sense of perspective enabled Cecil to find humor in such an experience and to use it to teach the very lessons he communicates to his audiences about the pitfalls of stereotyping. The officious woman had assumed that Cecil was hers to command because he was a casually dressed African-American.

On page 117 is a table that summarizes all we've told you about the four strategies for emotional balance.

Using the Four Approaches to Emotional Balance

Now, how are you going to apply these four approaches when you get kinks in your emotional armor? How can you use them to handle everyday situations that send you up the wall or down the drain?

Think of a recent situation when you've "lost it," and then ask yourself the questions below. They use all four approaches. It is best to write out your answers.

Event
1. What change can I make in my schedule or environment that will prevent this from happening again?

Behavior
2. How have I been *punished* for having an extreme reaction to this situation?
3. How might I be *rewarded* for reacting in a measured way to such an experience?

Four Approaches to Emotional Balance

	Event	Behavior	Beliefs	Emotions
Theorist	James/Lange	Skinner	Ellis	Freud
Theory	physiological responses	behavior modification	RET	psychoanalysis
What you do	change event	change behavior	change belief	change self
How you do it	common sense	reward/ punishment	reality check	reframe; responsibility; distance
Parts of brain	Reptilian; Limbic	left/right frontal; Limbic	left/right frontal	left/right frontal; Reptilian

Beliefs

4. What idea do I have regarding this situation that contributes to my strong feelings? Is it accurate?

Emotions

5. What perspective on this experience would help me feel less negative about it? (*reframe*)
6. What view do I have of myself that makes this experience so stressful? (*responsibility*)
7. In the larger scheme of things, does this situation really matter to me? (*distance*)

To demonstrate how to use these seven questions, here's how they helped Marie Phillips, a fifty-nine-year-old newlywed who doesn't want house pets. Marie's stepdaughter, Barbara, is an animal lover; she and her husband have three cats, two dogs, and no children. When the young couple first visited Marie and Barbara's father in their comfortable two-story home, Barbara declared, ''What you need is a dog.'' Marie wasn't aware that she needed anything other than her new husband and their pleasant life-style, but she smiled benignly and said nothing. Every time they were together during the next three years, Barbara told Marie, "You need a dog." Marie would feel a flame of irritation and a burning desire to blurt out, "I don't tell you that you ought to have children, so butt out." The last time they were together, Marie thought this statement so strongly, she was afraid momentarily that she'd actually said it. Something had to be done before their relationship was permanently damaged.

Here's how answering the seven questions helped Marie deal with her strong emotions:

1. What Change Can I Make in My Schedule or Environment That Will Prevent This from Happening Again? Marie ruefully answered that if she never invited Barbara to visit again, there would be no problem. However, she actually liked Barbara and wanted to keep a good relationship with her. So her real answer was "Barbara apparently feels there's something missing from our lives, so I'll have to look around and try to see what makes her feel this way."

2. How Have I Been *Punished* for Having an Extreme Reaction to This Situation? "I'm increasingly irritated by her comment, and it requires more and more self-control not to say something nasty to her."

3. How Might I Be *Rewarded* for Reacting in a Measured Way to Such an Experience? "She might stop bringing it up if I said, 'I can see that you are very good with animals, but I'm not and I don't like to have them in the house. I know your dad likes cats, but we discussed my aversion to indoor animals before we got married and agreed not to have them.' Even if she continued, I'd feel better for having stated my case."

4. What Idea Do I Have Regarding This Situation That Contributes to My Strong Feelings? Is It Accurate? "I'm afraid she thinks I'm depriving her father of something he's entitled to . . . an animal in the house to pet. She probably does feel that, but she might also be a little defensive because they've decided not to have children."

5. What Perspective on This Experience Would Help Me Feel Less Negative About It? "To see Barbara's comments as unrelated to how happy her father is with me. To see her as an exuberant young woman who loves animals and simply wants others to enjoy them, too."

6. What View Do I Have of Myself That Makes This Experience So Stressful? "In general, I like people to think of me as a warm, loving person, and I especially want Barbara to feel that I'm good to and for her dad."

7. In the Larger Scheme of Things, Does This Situation Really Matter to Me? "Only if I brood about it. By viewing Barbara in a different light and explaining my feelings about indoor animals, I can put this matter to rest. Besides, we have so many good times together, it's not that big a deal.''

Marie acted on the insights she had gained from this exercise. The next time the subject of animals came up, she told Barbara how she felt about them. Barbara asked if her beloved dogs and cats offended Marie, and Marie honestly replied, ''I have no problem with animals in other people's houses where I don't have to tend them.'' Marie showed the questions and her answers to her husband, and the couple confirmed their agreement not to have house pets—at least not in the foreseeable future, ''because we're on the go too much . . . we don't have time for them.'' The last statement shows that once Marie was out of a defensive mode, her feelings about pets softened to the point where she might later reconsider her stand.

You may be tempted to stop after an early question that produces a particularly insightful answer. But it is best to answer all seven of the questions. By doing so you will use all four approaches and experience progressively deeper insights into your emotions. Furthermore, you will come across the one approach that is best for that particular situation. After you've used the seven questions for a while, you'll automatically know which is most appropriate for a given problem. All seven are needed for difficult, ongoing emotional situations or if you have a hair-trigger temperament. By thinking them through each time you lose it, you'll soon be able to stay in emotional balance through most of your trying times.

The situation we referred to above regarding Marie Phillips's problem with her stepdaughter demonstrates how age helps us improve the way we deal with our emotions. Marie confessed that twenty or even ten years earlier she would not have taken any action. ''In fact,'' she mused, ''I'm not sure I would have even been aware that Barbara's attitude was bugging me. I'd probably have just avoided her as much as possible, then exploded one day over something unrelated. By middle age, I would have had a better understanding of my feelings but it's only in the last ten years that I've started looking for ways to deal with my emotions.'' During those ten years, Marie was divorced from her first husband, was unemployed for several months, and remarried. Those experiences forced her to be more introspective, but the normal physical changes that occur in the fifties also contributed significantly to her more thoughtful and successful approach.

MOVING TOWARD BALANCE

There's a definite trend today toward self-understanding and expression. Male bonding seminars abound; there's a support group for every kind of emotional problem; talk shows discuss the most intimate feelings and behavior in detail. Maudlin, you say. Or is it that we've come to a turning point in our society where we must achieve emotional balance to survive? We believe that emotional sensitivity (which psychologist Howard Gardner calls "social intelligence") is growing within us because it helps us adapt to changing times. Primitive people didn't need great awareness of their emotions. In fact, if a caveman had anguished over killing Bambi for dinner, he would not have lasted long.

Today, survival depends upon interacting in a sophisticated, sensitive way with others. To do so, we need to understand their feelings, and thus our own. If we do not understand our own emotions, the strain of keeping them in check during everyday interactions can be overwhelming.

Unlike primitive people, we can be in charge of our emotions and enjoy the comfort of emotional balance.

HOW EMOTIONS CHANGE WITH AGE

It is amazing to realize that four kinds of emotions (Scared, Mad, Sad, and Glad) carry us through every emotional experience of our lives, no matter how minor or major. As we progress in age and experience, though, we use and are used by our emotions in different ways. What frightened you as a child? What frightens you now? You may have the same fear of dogs that you had at two, but you're probably not paralyzed by the fear today. Adults who have unreasonable fears are called phobic and are expected to get help for them, but we know that most two-year-olds will "get over it" with a little reassurance and friendly experience with furry animals.

As we grow older, the way we experience emotions changes in several ways:

Emotions Are More Often Directed Inward than Outward. The young child becomes angry when Mommy won't buy her bubble gum at the check-out counter; the fifty-year-old becomes angry with herself when she forgets an appointment.

The Actions Our Emotions Cause Are More Restrained. Crime statistics alone demonstrate this. We still feel strong emotions, but can express them more quietly and intelligently.

We Have More Strategies for Dealing with Emotions. We consciously seek ways to solve problems; we know how to avoid trouble; we know people who can help in trying times.

Yet it's a myth of aging that fear and anger, love and hate disappear with age. Older people continue to feel emotions deeply. So while the pitch and rhythm of emotions sound different, they actually become richer and softer. The tender emotions are more deeply felt, while the negative ones are easier to deal with because you can put them into perspective. So don't be surprised if you still love life as passionately at seventy-five as you did at seventeen.

Practice your emotional instruments every day of your life. Study your emotions, think about them, feel them, talk about them, so that the symphony of your life will be rich in timbre and vibrato. Start composing today.

BEST BOOKS TO FEEL BY

At your bookstore or library, you will find many books on emotions. Here are some of the best:

The Complete Guide to Your Emotions and Your Health by Emrika Padus. Emmaus, Pa.: Rodale Press, 1986.

The Dance of Anger by Harriet Goldhor Lerner, Ph.D. New York: Harper & Row, 1985.

Feeling Good: The New Mood Therapy by David D. Burns, M.D. New York: Morrow, 1980.

Love Is Letting Go of Fear by Gerald G. Jampolsky, M.D. P.O. Box 635, Tiburon, Calif. 94920, 1988.

Necessary Losses by Judith Viorst. New York: Simon & Schuster, 1986.

The Seasons of a Man's Life by Daniel J. Levinson. New York: Ballantine Books, 1978.

You Just Don't Understand: Women and Men in Conversation by Deborah Tannen, Ph.D. New York: Morrow, 1990.

How to Be Sharper than Ever Before

Sharpening Your Memory

Middle age is when you've met so many people that every new person you meet reminds you of someone else.

—OGDEN NASH

I always have trouble remembering three things: faces, names, and—and—and—I can't remember what the third thing is.

—FRED ALLEN

"**Y**ou're losing it, kid!''

Have you said that to yourself recently? If so, you have lots of company. Most of us fear we're losing it when we suddenly become aware of a cluster of mental lapses such as missing an appointment, losing the car keys, and forgetting the name of a favorite movie star.

When we're young, we call these simple oversights. Later, though, we focus on them and often fear they're the beginning of a dismal slide into senility. The truth is that most of us have memory lapses all our lives.

However, memory does change as we grow older. In most respects, though, it is merely different, not worse, and in some ways memory actually gets better. As we age, our memory's strengths move from the specific to the general—instead of details, the big picture.

HOW EXPERIENCE HELPS

During middle age the ability to quickly retrieve an isolated bit of information begins to slow, but the ability to relate new knowledge to other information increases. An older person has a great deal of experience and can fit information into the context of it.

For example, you read an article about private companies' taking over government services. Later, you remember that you read an article about privatization. You can't recall which magazine it was in, or some of the statistics, but your memory of the main points of the article is rich. First you recall that a form of privatization began during the Nixon administration when the post office shifted to self-financing status, and that it has had its ups and downs since then. Relating the article to other things you know, you form a network of general memories from which you work your way back to the specifics. Eventually, you'll have nearly total recall of the main points of the article, with the additional benefit of knowing their historical context.

One reason people over forty usually have better "whole cloth" memory may be that their motivation for remembering things has changed over the years. Younger people often want to remember information for exterior reasons: tomorrow's test, job advancement, to get a reputation for being smart. As we establish ourselves at work and socially, many of us begin to seek information because we're truly interested. We have internal reasons for wanting to remember who fought in the Battle of Waterloo, which phase of the moon is best for planting corn, or who composed *La Boheme*. We see the facts in a broader and more personal context.

WHAT'S IN IT FOR ME?

When you know specifically *what* you want to remember and *why,* your memory powers zoom. So when you are reading a newspaper story, for example, first ask yourself what is important in the article, then ask why it's important for *you* to remember it. Your answers might be "This article describes the changes in this year's income tax form. One change pertains to selling real estate. Since I'm thinking of selling my house this year, I need to understand and remember that part of it."

Similarly, you recall the look and sound of a word better when you're young, but later in life you can better recall the full meaning of the word and are more apt to use just the right word for any situation. Spelling bees are for the young, but expressive language is for the old.

By hooking memories onto previous experiences, we can compensate for the types of memory that become less keen as we age. For example, visual and auditory memories are sharper in young people. A young person who hears or sees a telephone number once can often dial it from memory. The older person would do better to associate the number with other experiences. If the number is 555-1956, the person might say, "Five-five-five is the prefix of Mary's telephone number (perhaps seeing Mary's face) and 1956 . . . ah yes, that was the year my son was born."

The trick is to add other cues to help reinforce your visual or auditory memory. Seeing Mary's face provides a visual cue for retrieval, and connecting the year to your son's birth provides a verbal one (and possibly an emotional cue).

A study by David Arenberg, at the Gerontology Research Center of Baltimore City Hospitals, clearly demonstrated that the visual recall of older men improved when they were given verbal cues. Dr. Arenberg tested high-school-age boys and a group of men aged fifty-nine to seventy-seven for their recall of geometric designs. They looked at each design for twelve seconds, waited fifteen seconds, then were asked to reproduce it. In the second stage of the study, Dr. Arenberg described the designs while the subjects viewed them. The teenagers did better than the men with and without verbal cues, but the men improved their recall significantly with the descriptions.

Younger people organize facts into categories and commit them to left-brained kinds of abstract structures such as charts. The older person, however, operates better with a less abstract, less structured system such as mind mapping—a right-brained method of recording ideas that begins with the most dramatic thought, then works back and forth until the entire concept is reconstructed.

THE SHIFT IN BEST MEMORY SKILLS

Some memory skills tend to be stronger before sixty, and others come into their own later. The shift occurs gradually, and it happens differently for each person. Still, in general the best memory skills move from short to long term, and from detailed, quick recall to slower, full remembering.

How the Memory Ages

40 > > > 50 > > > 60 > > > 70 > > > 80 > > > 90 > > > (on a continuum)	
Better in forties to early sixties	**Better after sixty**
visual and auditory	elaborative/episodic
verbal	semantic
taxonomic	crystallized
specific	associative

Better in Forties to Early Sixties

visual and auditory memory—retaining something you see for one to two seconds; something you hear, up to three seconds

verbal memory—recall of the look and sound of words you know (but not necessarily their meanings)

taxonomic memory—memory based on an abstract system, such as an outline (You recall key words in each section, then details at each level.)

specific memory—the ability to retrieve quickly an isolated bit of information (Who shot Lincoln? John Wilkes Booth.)

Better After Sixty

elaborative or episodic memory—information stored with mental and emotional tags about where and when you acquired the memory of an event ("I was at the airport, buying *Time* to read on the flight, when I felt a sharp pain. . . .")

semantic memory—relatively permanent memories of words, coded and stored on the basis of their meaning, not just simply recalled. The impact of a weak semantic memory is illustrated by the career of Bela Lugosi, the Hungarian actor who played Count Dracula on stage and screen. Since he did not understand English, he memorized his role phonetically. As a result his performance was wooden and he became typecast for Grade B movies, even though he had been an accomplished actor in Hungary.

crystallized memory—previously acquired knowledge and skills that have been crystallized with experience. How such things as a second language, chemical compounds, and the rules of law, once learned, are remembered.

associative memory—recall by connecting bits of information (John Wilkes Booth, an actor himself, was brother to Edwin Booth, a famous Shakespearean thespian. Neither was related to William Booth, founder of the Salvation Army.)

You can see how all this looks graphically in the table "How the Memory Ages" on page 128.

To take full advantage of the natural changes in your memory, you need to make the most of your developing skills, yet keep your "young memory" skills as supple as possible. Without memory training, the young memory skills gradually become more difficult, and people typically shift to the others. With training and practice, most people can keep their young memory skills, and enhance them with their new strengths.

TRADITIONAL MNEMONICS

Older people with sharp memories aren't just people born with good genes or good luck. In fact, many of them have suffered major health and financial misfortunes, but have stayed sharp and mentally vital because of the ways they challenged their minds. They have some plan for staying sharp, even though they may not have defined it that way.

In a survey of more than a hundred people from fifty to their late nineties who have excellent memories, we found that all of them used most of the standard aids, or mnemonics, taught by memory experts. Some used as many as fourteen different techniques (including those that follow and additional ones). Several said they used only one or two techniques, but when they explained how they remembered things, it was apparent they had used many others.

See how many of these traditional memory aids *you* use regularly:

- **acronyms and acrostics:** choosing certain letter configurations to make ideas memorable (for example, MADD, Mothers Against Drunk Driving)
- **association:** relating new information to something you already know
- **chunking:** breaking a long series of numbers or letters into chunks (such as telephone numbers, social security numbers)
- **the link system:** making up a visually stimulating story to connect one item in a series to the next
- **loci:** associating items or ideas with different locations so they can be reviewed more easily

- **mediators:** using an out-of-place item as a reminder (for example, sticking a piece of paper on the steering wheel as you get out of your car, to remind you that you're running low on gas)
- **patterns:** forming a big picture of the overall material and then fitting the details into that pattern
- **the peg system:** adding to the link system numbers connected to words; for example, *one* is *gun,* *two* is *shoe,* so when you want to recall a list, you always picture a gun with the first item, a shoe with the second (when naming U.S. presidents in order: "George Washington put a gun between his false teeth. John's huge Adam's apple is stuffed in a baby shoe.")
- **phonetics:** connecting words with similar sounds (*One* sounds like *gun* so it's easy to connect the two.)
- **rehearsal:** seeing the upcoming event or activity, setting the stage for your memory to fill in the details easily
- **repetition:** repeating the information to yourself several times (This is the rote system that you probably used in elementary school to learn the multiplication tables—do you remember using flashcards over and over until you got it?)
- **review:** going over in your mind what you've just read or heard, putting it into your own words, and relating it to something you already know
- **rhymes:** using rhymes ("In fourteen hundred and ninety-two, Columbus sailed the ocean blue.")
- **rhythm:** chanting or clapping your hands to a beat as you memorize a sentence (Try this one: "I need to mail the check today." After several chanting or clapping repetitions, you'll have this sentence in your short-term memory.)
- **visualization:** picturing the item (To improve your memory of the previous example, for example, visualize your hand in a lace glove placing the check in a mailbox.)

These memory aids developed over the years of human history. Before written language, a culture's history was passed on orally from generation to generation. Oral history was usually recited in a singsong way, to the beat of drums. The singer would link each past leader of the tribe to the next by telling vivid stories of the heroics and horrendous events of each one's life, sparking visual and emotional reactions that made the long story memorable. The stories were recited over and over again—usually at feasts and dances, which added the memory triggers of sensory stimulation, such as the smell of food and the look of body paint.

The accuracy of a culture's oral history depended on the ability of the historian to link colorful stories and people together. The great Greek and Roman orators refined this system by thinking about abstract thoughts in specific places. To memorize a long speech, they rehearsed the introduction in the vestibule, the first major point in the first room to the right of the vestibule, and so on. Then when they delivered the speech, they'd move mentally from room to room to trigger their memory of each segment of the speech. This system, called loci, Latin for *locations,* is still used effectively by speechmakers today.

Written language gave us symbols to represent our thoughts and enabled us to think more abstractly. As a result, we developed many more ways of remembering, such as acrostics, chunking, and mapping.

Usually when we are exposed to a bit of information, we retain it in sensory memory for one to three seconds. Then it goes to the working memory, where it stays between four to five seconds and two hours. If it seems important to us and is reinforced several times in this short-term-memory stage, it becomes part of long-term memory.

But now we are knee-deep in the Information Age. Even with megabyte-memory computers, we need new ways to focus on essential information and retain it. Advertising research shows that each day the country is bombarded with half a million messages through television, radio, billboards, faxes, mail, and the telephone. Is it any wonder we think we're losing it?

Obviously, we cannot absorb or respond to all of this information, so we forget most of those messages. Advertisers call it perceptual screening. We automatically screen out the unpleasant, the frightening, the irrelevant, the difficult to understand, and the boring. Furthermore, we screen out the unwanted idea that might bring more work or force us to alter an opinion.

Without such screening, our minds would be garbage heaps of ideas and impressions, with useful memories indistinguishable from the useless. Perceptual screening is vital to a good working memory because it keeps the short-term-memory banks from becoming overloaded.

But perceptual screening can be tricky. It works so automatically, we sometimes eliminate useful information without being aware of it. We didn't forget it—we never got it.

LESSONS FROM MADISON AVENUE

In devising new memory aids for these information-heavy times, we've learned much from today's masters of establishing and accessing our collective memory—advertisers. Let's use some of these Madison Avenue lessons for our own purposes.

The most familiar trick advertisers use to break through our mental screening is to repeat themselves numerous times. Advertising research shows that when a company is presenting a new product or service, the typical buyer must be exposed to the name seven times before it sticks. That's why radio commercials repeat names or telephone numbers as many times as possible in one spot. It's also why, during a televised football game, a sponsor might repeat the same commercial three or four times. If you hear it many times, it might drive you bonkers, but you'll remember it!

You are probably already aware of the power of repetition but perhaps are not as well acquainted with the other, more subtle Madison Avenue approaches to making messages memorable:

Cognitive Dissonance. This involves holding two diametrically opposed ideas in one supposedly coherent message. For example, a magazine ad for an airline shows a neat, energetic-looking businessman walking off an airplane. Large, bold type says: FLOWN IN FRESH DAILY. Since "flown in fresh daily" usually refers to fish, most of us will focus on the picture and the headline to try to make sense out of the seeming inconsistency. Then, most of us smile at the clever play on words. They gotcha!

You can use cognitive dissonance by covering your phone with your wife's scarf to remind you to call her. The scarf does not belong there, and so you are jarred into puzzling out what it's doing there.

Emotional Versus Rational Appeals. Although good ads make both emotional and rational appeals, many focus on the emotions because most of us make decisions based on appeals to the right brain. Sex, babies, animals, and power sell because they arouse our emotions. It is the sizzle that sells the steak, not the price, caloric intake, or protein level. So when you want someone to remember the directions you're giving, you should provide logical details, of course, but don't forget the sizzle. For example: "Go north on Niagara to Range Avenue. On the northwest corner, *there's a billboard with a picture of Channel Three's great-looking new anchorperson.* The next three miles will seem like six *because they're bumpy as a teenager's com-*

plexion.'' The billboard with the picture of an attractive anchorperson provokes an emotionally appealing image in your mind. The allusion to a teenager's complexion is not attractive, but it is equally memorable because it's likely to provoke a chuckle or an uncomfortable feeling.

Mental Completion. We all have a need to have thoughts completed, to have circles closed. When you come across a sentence with a   in it, you feel suspense, even anxiety. So you'll focus on it, try to complete it, and therefore *remember* it. You might use the same trick in reading to children. When you come to a key word, pause and allow them to fill it in. This makes the children part of the reading process and more apt to remember the story.

Covert Involvement. A message that touches upon your personal values is very memorable. When your pride is stirred or your sympathy aroused, the message becomes very personal and memorable to you. This is one reason why advertisements that appeal to your pride, sympathy, or sense of altruism are so effective. A stirring example is the Coca-Cola commercial in which a diverse group of people sing about sharing a Coke in "perfect harmony.'' This message has an intense appeal to those of us who believe in cultural diversity and who long for a peaceful world.

These lessons from Madison Avenue suggest many ways of attracting and focusing attention. But once your attention is riveted, a broader approach to memory is needed . . . one that stimulates the whole brain.

The more areas of the brain you use in building a memory, the more complete and instantaneous your recall. Therefore, in the following section we present devices that are visually, verbally, auditorially, and kinesthetically stimulating. *Visual* stimulation refers not only to pictures, photographs, or graphics, but more importantly to mental pictures that are provoked by words, music, and aromas. *Verbal* stimulation excites the language part of the brain through speech, writing, or thought. This stimulation occurs when we repeat, rehearse, reflect, or rephrase. *Auditory* stimulation helps us store memories from listening to lectures, telephone messages, or the radio. It is enhanced by adding music, rhyme, vivid details, outrageous exaggeration, emotional appeals, and unusual voices and pacing. *Kinesthetic* stimulation occurs when mnemonic devices arouse body reactions, such as when a perfumed ad sends your pulse racing and your thoughts to the tropics.

Now that you've thought about the ways the brain works when remembering information, you're ready to learn some new mnemonics—memory secrets for the world of today.

New Mnemonics

From interviewing hundreds of people over forty, and working with thousands of others in communication seminars, we have identified memory aids similar to those used by Madison Avenue marketers to overcome perceptual screening. They also appeal to all parts of the brain.

These new mnemonic devices are particularly successful as we age. They're designed to take full advantage of the aging brain's strengths, while stimulating waning skills.

Because they were developed in the laboratory of life, these memory strategies work amazingly well in today's fast-paced world. Of the multitude of strategies we've investigated, these are the easiest, most amusing, and most useful. Try them, practice them, adapt them. You'll soon notice (and so will others) that instead of losing it, you're sharper than you've ever been before!

They are: See It, Say It, Hear It, and Do It.

See It—The Try-Angle Strategy

"I didn't realize how much I was missing until the Anita Hill–Clarence Thomas hearings," Janet Brown told classmates in a listening and memory class.

"I was at a party the next evening and the topic came up. I'd watched the hearings gavel-to-gavel and plunged into the discussion with details, background, and insightful opinions. It was fun! I was proud of myself for being able to express myself so clearly and back up my ideas with facts.

"Driving home, I realized that I had not been so enthusiastic about a discussion for years. It has been my habit to sit on the sidelines during most such discussions, occasionally offering neutral comments to give the impression that I was with it.

"Why was it different tonight? I wondered. And then I realized that for a long time I'd been afraid to tell a story or describe a magazine article because I was unsure of my ability to remember accurately.

"Many times I'd read several books on a topic but couldn't recall much about it. I'd say, oh yes, I read so-and-so about ergonomics, the Russian Revolution, or the health care crisis. All eyes would fasten on me. I'd begin with enthusiasm to make a cogent point, but couldn't remember any specifics or even the main themes of what I'd read. I'd drift off into generalities and lamely finish up with 'It was really a swell book; I'd be happy to loan it to you. . . . '

"It didn't take many experiences like that to turn me into a sideliner," Janet concluded.

Janet's clear memory of the Hill-Thomas hearings can be partly attributed to her intense emotional interest in the topic. But a more important reason we found is that she is primarily a visual learner. She could have read about the hearings and listened to them on the radio just as extensively and intently, without grasping the details as well as she did through television. Television is the ideal medium for her memory style; Janet's way of thinking is to "see" ideas. Janet learned how to use her natural ability to see thoughts and apply it to remembering data, details, and concepts.

One way to visualize the facts is the Try-Angle approach. Here's how it works. Take whatever you're trying to absorb, divide it into thirds, and then "see" the information or idea on a three-part shape (a triangle, a clock face divided by three hands, nested circles, or a line divided into three segments).

These shapes give you a structure for deciding what information you want to remember and visualizing it. For example, suppose you read this movie review:

A Fun Feminist Goes to War

Linda Voss (Melanie Griffith) is your typical late-model feminist hero-ine—brave, bright, spirited, sassy and clearly overqualified for her sec-retarial job. She is also—what else?—hopelessly in love with her boss, Ed Leland (Michael Douglas). At once distracted and self-absorbed, he can't see why she wants a promotion, and he's a little too casual about their love affair. On the first score he has a point: the job she aspires to is spying. In Berlin. During World War II. Maybe she is a bit too spunky for her own good. But not for the good of *Shining Through*. She's a terrific character, and it's a terrific idea to project her anachronistically back into the kind of improbable melodrama that made home-front life during the war so entertaining. Indeed, Linda borrows some of her best espionage tricks from the Hollywood thrillers to which she's addicted. At a certain point, writer-director David Seltzer, finding himself with too many obli-gations to an overcomplicated plot, forgets to keep up Linda's perky, amusing spirits. But he's a basically lively and knowing guy, and, on balance, *Shining Through* is a cheerfully suspenseful entertainment.

—R.S., *Time*, February 10, 1992

To use the Try-Angle Strategy, first extract from this review three main ideas or bits of information you'd like to remember. Usually, you'd want to remember the stars of the movie (not the roles they play), the movie title, and the gist of the plot. Now, visually plot these facts on a triangle:

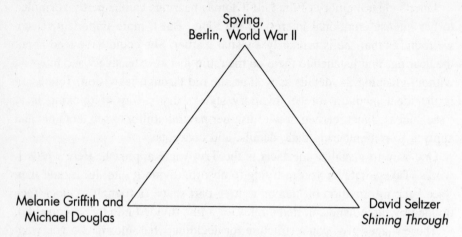

Spying,
Berlin, World War II

Melanie Griffith and
Michael Douglas

David Seltzer
Shining Through

The placement of the facts is meaningful. By placing Melanie Griffith *before* Michael Douglas, you remember that the reviewer thought her role was superb. By "seeing" Berlin during World War II, you have a feel for the intrigue these characters are involved in. And now that you're visualizing, you can picture the title, *Shining Through,* with sparkling seltzer water, and—eureka!—the director's name, David Seltzer, becomes part of your memory mix.

Different individuals prefer different shapes. If you are a triangle person, you may never need to use anything else. Sometimes, however, the situation suggests the best shape. Seminar participants frequently say that the flat line or clock face divided into three sections works well when memorizing sequential or chronological information. They also find that triangles work best for mastering information about relationships, and that the triple circle is ideal for recalling emotional content. The important thing is to find which shape most enhances your recall. So try them all and invent others.

Visualization is one of the skills that deteriorates in elderly people. So if you are in early middle age, the Try-Angle probably will be easy for you. Whatever your age, if it isn't easy, practice the Try-Angle intensely so that you can stimulate the visual parts of your brain.

The Try-Angle Strategy is effective not only because it gives you a way of visualizing information, but also because of the mental process you go through. It stimulates you to analyze the material and do something with it, activating the cognitive and motor parts of your brain. You'll understand how this works more clearly once you have learned and practiced the other memory strategies below.

Say It—The Six R's

The Six R's are memorable in and of themselves because each begins with *re: re*hearse, *re*peat, *re*phrase, *re*view, *re*flect, and *re*inforce. You say on paper, mentally, or aloud, as many times as possible, the material you wish to deposit in your long-term-memory bank. The more repetitions, the greater the payoff.

Rehearse. This means to go through mentally what you expect to encounter ahead of time and put your expectations into words. This strengthens what you already know and provides a framework for inserting new information. Warm up your memory in advance, and it will work better. You'll be more at ease if you're prepared.

For example, Jack, an engineer, and Lisa, his wife, were driving to the annual three-day conference of a professional engineers' group he belonged to. Since they'd attended the previous year, they talked their way through a rehearsal of meeting people they expected to see again this year: "Who was the guy who had hair like Steve Martin and brought his wife and two teenage kids last year?"

"Yes, I remember, it was Sam Cole. What was his wife's name?"

"Connie."

"And remember those three chemical engineers who always sat together at the big round dinner tables? They ended up in a brouhaha with Jerry Jenkins. I guess mining engineers don't mix with chemical engineers."

This conversation helped them set the stage for recalling the people they'd met before. Later, they could easily insert new characters and names into their conference drama. It proved to be valuable in preparing them for encountering a number of people they'd met the year before. They were able to use many names without being reintroduced. People were pleased and amazed. They talked about what terrific memories Jack and Lisa had. This built their self-confidence and encouraged them to continue their efforts.

Repeat. This is simply repeating the information as soon after you hear it as possible. Jack and Lisa, like most of us, usually repeat the name of the person to whom they are being introduced.

Rephrase. This is a way of clarifying and summarizing what you've heard. For instance, when Jack and Lisa were registering at the hotel desk, they saw Sam Cole across the lobby and called out to him by name. He joined them and told them about his plans to stay over after the conference. As they parted, Jack rephrased what he'd heard: "Sounds like this trip is both pleasure and business."

"Yes," Sam replied. "Connie and I haven't had a getaway in years. It's time. And Bryan and Amy are away at school. We're spending ten days here all together. We'll have a chance to see the sights around here, play some golf, and..." He trailed off with a wink and a smile.

You can see that the rewards of rephrasing were *ample*. Jack and Lisa got background information on Sam and his family. Sam used his wife's and children's names as well as the details of their trip.

Review. This is simply going over what you've just heard or read and putting it in context with other information. For example, when Jack and Lisa got on the hotel elevator, they reviewed Sam's wife's name (Connie), their two children's names (Bryan and Amy), and the fact that Sam and Connie would be in the city for ten days.

Reviewing should be done periodically (every hour at a dinner party, or every three to ten pages in a chapter you're reading) so that you can deal with the information in manageable hunks.

Reflect. This is done from afar. As she was bathing that night, Lisa thought about their conversation with Sam. She reflected upon the fact that in spite of his gray hair, Sam didn't look old enough to have teenagers. She thought how nice it was that he and Connie were adding a mini-honeymoon to the end of the conference. Later, Lisa discussed her thoughts with Jack. By this time, they felt they knew the Coles pretty well and were very comfortable with them.

Reinforce. Reinforce a memory at regular intervals for best results. Jack and Lisa felt they really knew the Coles by the time the conference ended. But they'd had only one meeting with the three chemical engineers (who sat together again throughout the entire conference), so back at home Jack read an article about a new development in chemical engineering and mailed it to Hal, the friendliest of the three. On a note, he asked to be remembered to the other two. He was surprised to get a note several weeks later from the third and quietest chemical engineer, saying that Hal had forwarded the article to him. Another reinforcement for Jack!

REINFORCING WITH ANSWERING MACHINES

When you get a piece of vital information at a meeting, call home and leave it on your answering machine. This gives your memory three reinforcements: You heard it from another, you spoke it, and you heard it on your own machine.

Another way to use answering machines is when you're both dashing out the door and you want to remind your spouse that "tonight's our dinner date with the Johnsons." There's no time then for your spouse to write it down, so call his or her office and leave a reminder on the machine.

Hear It—The UFO Strategy

The UFO Strategy is a way of "rehearing" a conversation or situation to clarify what actually happened. It can be immensely helpful in handling problems such as this one:

"My wife and I consistently remember things differently. She'll be at the corner of Fifth and Milwaukee to meet me at one P.M. sharp, and I'll be at First and Milwaukee at five P.M. Of course, that causes some real hassles," Tim Stuart complained at a listening and memory class.

"She claims I never listen to her. But it's not that. We just don't hear the same way. Often we'll listen to a radio newscast when we're driving somewhere and come up with entirely different information. Then we spend fifteen minutes trying to figure out who is correct.

"One time we were driving in a blinding snowstorm on the interstate, and the announcer broadcast which exits were still open. We disagreed on what he'd said and nearly got stranded from staying on the interstate too long. It wasn't just annoying—it was life threatening," Tim emphasized.

Sometimes these conflicts of opinion occur within ourselves. We're not sure what we heard and keep vacillating between two versions. Both situations can be remedied with the UFO Strategy.

UFO is an acronym for *unfocus—focus—onward*. It works this way. First, you step back mentally from the information as you remember it. You try to put yourself back into the situation in which you heard the information and open your mind to the entire scenario. By moving away from the nitty-gritty details and toward the big picture, you defuse the irritation you're feeling with yourself or the person you're disagreeing with. This is important because it's very difficult to have clear recall of anything when you're angry, tense, or frustrated.

Think of putting a wide-angle lens on your mental camera. Once you've opened the lens on your view of the situation, you'll feel more relaxed and will be less apt to misunderstand the information. Relaxing also enables you to replay the mental videotape you have of the original conversation or monologue.

Now you're better able to listen to the message without bias, and you can sort out the details that confused you. Watch for out-of-tune words and gestures that make you feel uncomfortable. Cognitive dissonance is at work. Your mind is saying, *There's something wrong here,* and you are then able to bring back the original scene, full blown. In other words, when something doesn't ring true, your recall is often heightened because both your emotions and your thoughts have been aroused.

Sometimes in such a flashback, you notice subtleties you overlooked the first time. When you first experienced the scene, you were probably in your logical mode of thinking and didn't notice body language and vocal nuances. You were focused on the content, the words. In the unfocused state, you are more attuned to emotional and visual subtleties.

Once you have reviewed the scene and heard the detail you were in doubt about, move on to a point of agreement with your spouse. Don't dwell on who was right or wrong. If it's an inner debate, don't beat yourself up for getting confused.

Replaying your mental videotape will be only as accurate as you are willing to let it be. If you are pessimistic about your ability to recall what you've heard, or if you are angry with someone else, you may not be able to listen in an open way.

Here's an example of how you practice the UFO Strategy: You've heard the sixty-second test of the emergency broadcast system over the radio countless times. Can you remember the words used?

First *un*focus—try to hear the electronic bleep—and then the announcer's voice. Here we are trying to open up to get a broad view. The point is to relax and expand mentally. We are using divergent thinking.

Now *focus* on what is being said. Write it down or repeat it to yourself immediately. Here we are narrowing our perspective; we are turning the focus sharp and down small, using convergent thinking.

Finally, move *onward* to your next thought or task. Don't consider other answers. Statistics show that in most cases where students change answers on a test, they had it correct the first time. So it is with everyday memories.

Furthermore, carrying on an inner debate wears away at your confidence and vitality. Think of someone you know who can wrangle for hours about whether she drove or flew to Grandma Blair's funeral. Or have you caught yourself debating within yourself whether "Jody finished school in 1930 or 1931"? Don't get caught in the trap of debating endlessly over details—focus, unfocus, and then move on.

For another test of the UFO Strategy, you might use it to remember how your mother answers the phone, the wording of a time and temperature recording, Terry Gross's opening on NPR, and so on. Any of these will work for practice.

Do It—The Body Memory Strategy

Seeing, saying, and hearing provide you with three excellent ways of remembering. However, actually *doing* something with the information makes it a part of you, because the memory of the action enhances the memory in the brain.

Children learn by doing—through trial and error. Likewise, most adults learn best through experience.

Doing is effective because it provokes physical reactions, producing a body memory. There are many examples of this happening in your everyday life. If you play bridge, the challenge of playing out a difficult hand can produce an adrenaline rush that will make your hands tremble and your voice quake. You remember forever if you made the right bid and, if not, the mistakes you made. When you read an erotic novel, you can become aroused by the mental pictures the words provoke. The dialogue in that scene may come back to you in toto during your own tender moment. Watching the ups and downs of your favorite football team in a crucial game creates strong emotions and a vivid memory of that game.

When you are able to attach a body memory to something you want to remember, you have the ultimate in reliability.

MEMORY TIPS

Here are some quick visual, auditory, and kinesthetic ways to remember the bits and pieces of information that sometimes elude us:

Elusive Keys

- Buy a Key Finder chain that beeps when you whistle or clap for it.
- Jangle your keys when you take them out of the ignition or put them on the hall table.
- Pat the keys in your pants pocket before you lock the car door, to make sure you're not locking them in.
- Feel the edge of the car key as you remove it from the ignition, then listen to the zipper as you secure it in your purse.
- As you remove the keys from the car or put them on the hall table, mutter or sing to yourself "I have the keys" or "I put the keys on the hall table."

Did I Lock the Door?

- As you lock the door, try to "see" sparks coming off the key and fusing the door shut. Or as you close the garage door, picture it falling with a crash, sending dust and splinters all over.
- As you lock the door, say "Now the house will be safe." Hear the sound of the door snapping closed.
- For a body cue, hold the key or push the garage door opener with a different finger than usual, or use the opposite hand.

Forgetting Where You Parked Your Car
(or If Even You Brought It Today!)

Always park on the same floor of your garage, or in the same part of the lot, so you don't have to remember something new from day to day.

Names and Faces

Shake hands when you are introduced to a new person, so you can get a good look at the face and eyes. However, your look can be intimidating if it is too intense. So after a brief glance, look down at the person's shoulders and add that clue to your memory. (There's an amazing variety in shoulders—sloping, square, big, little, rounded, one lower than the other.) Also notice the feel of the hands—cold, clammy, warm, soft, hard and callused, and so on, and add these clues to your memory.

If you forget your new acquaintance's name, play the waiting game: Listen carefully to hear others mention it, then use it right away.

The Number Game

- For security codes or locker numbers, use combinations of meaningful numbers (birth dates, your house number, and so on).
- When memorizing long numbers, chunk them by putting a price tag on them: Convert "294781964" into "$294.78 is more than $19.64."

Scout's Honor

The Boy Scouts use "Better Be Prepared, Scout" to remember the proper order for administering first aid: breathing, bleeding, poisoning, and shock.

Righty Tighty, Lefty Loosey

Use this ditty to remember which way to turn bolts, bottle caps, or keys. Turn to the *right* to make them *tight* or closed, and *left* to *loosen* or open them. See and feel yourself twisting a white cap to the right while a brown bottle moves in the opposite direction.

You're a CAD

When you want to reboot your computer, you need to push the Control, Alternate (Alt), and Delete keys at the same time. To help you remember this command, say to yourself, *You're a real CAD for wanting to boot up your computer again.*

Phone Conversations

Write notes as you talk with someone on the phone. Notes help you concentrate and tune out distractions, and they help your recall. Finally, the record will jog your memory later.

Why Am I Here?

Are you exhausted at the end of the day from retracing your steps to places where you went to look for something, only to forget what that something was?

- Before you leave on your trip to the kitchen or the file room, jot down on a piece of paper or say out loud why you're making this trip.
- Use the World War II slogan for saving gas by asking yourself, *Is this*

trip really necessary? Thinking about the reason will make it more memorable. Also there's a possibility that the answer will be no, and you'll save yourself a trip!

What Are Your Memory's Strengths?

Now you know some proven ways to improve your memory. But where should you start? Which ones are for you? The following mini-quiz, called the Whole-Brain Memory Map, will tell you the strengths of your memory. Once you know them, you can focus on improving your memory in other areas. You will need a pencil and several sheets of paper to write down the answers, and a clock with a second hand or a one-minute timer. Then relax and enjoy it—that's when your memory works best.

The Whole-Brain Memory Map

1. What is being sold, or what is the sponsoring company, of each of the following radio or television commercials?
   (a) "Reach out, reach out and touch someone."
   (b) "Just do it."
   (c) "You deserve a break today."
   (d) "We bring good things to light."

2. What logos are the following companies known for?
   (a) Orion Studios
   (b) MGM
   (c) Columbia Pictures
   (d) NBC Television

3. Read this sentence: "Improving your recall takes an *U*nderstanding of how your memory works, *S*kills development through practice, and an *A*ttitude that you can do it."
   Without looking back at the sentence, write down the three essentials for improving memory that it mentions.

4. Visualize these political figures: George Bush, Bill Clinton, Albert Gore, and Ross Perot.
   (a) Which one has the darkest hair?
   (b) Which one speaks most quickly?

(c) Which one speaks with the most variation in tone?

(d) The least variation?

5. Think of the faucet handles in a typical American shower. Is the hot on the left or right?

6. *In one minute's time,* write down on your sheet of paper the names of all the birds you can recall.

7. *In one minute's time,* write on your paper as many *actual* numbers as you can retrieve from your memory bank. (Examples: current or former phone and address numbers, birth dates, Social Security numbers, lock combinations, phone access codes.)

8. Read: banana, calendar, photograph, computer, parsley.

Have you heard about the girl who picked up a frog that said, "Kiss me, kiss me and I'll turn into Donald Trump." Instead, she put it into her pocket and walked on.

A friend asked why she hadn't kissed the frog. She replied, "I *know* a talking frog is worth something."

Now, without looking back, write down on your sheet of paper the five items you read before the joke.

9. Circle all the *f*'s and 3's in the following lines, going straight through each line and without looking back:

f r w t q b f j s a f b c p 6 f 6 i 4 & - * f j p q f [g 2 v O o 8 x f z g a l #
p m c q F w 9 3 - f t r e e f g h 3 v x c & 1 p f @ o t w y u g . 1 $ p s f p
s f q f # @ 6 3 - f f x w e * f 7 9 1 h r z 9 f * _ 3 g x f b e s n o p f 9 4
& / u p f n P l F 3 o O n q u a e i , & f r e a m 4 1 r v 3 t c p f f i c d u
f g a s e d 3 t h r e e x # j O w b e 3 f y v o t e

10. Read these paragraphs from a news clipping:

Vacaville, Calif.—Theodore Streleski, convicted of beating his professor to death with a hammer to publicize the plight of graduate students, was freed unconditionally from prison Sunday, without promising not to kill again.

Streleski, 49, who served seven years and 20 days on a second-degree murder conviction, walked through the gate of a chain-link fence to meet more than 60 waiting reporters.

—Associated Press, from *The Denver Post,* September 9, 1985

Now cover the two paragraphs and answer these questions on your paper.

(a) What is the name of the man being released from prison?
(b) How old was he at the time the story was written?
(c) How long a prison term had he served?
(d) How many reporters were waiting for him?
(e) What was his crime?

11. Look at these drawings:

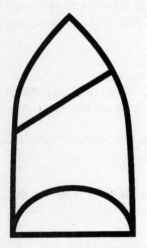
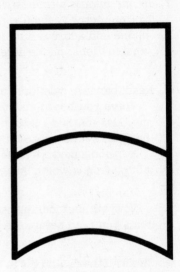

Now, immediately cover these figures and draw them on your answer paper.

On the next page, you can score the Whole-Brain Memory Map.

Scoring for the Whole-Brain Memory Map

Answers	Your Score

1. (a) AT&T, (b) Nike, (c) McDonald's, (d) GE (4 points possible) ____
2. (a) Stars, (b) a growling lion, (c) a woman holding a torch or Lady Columbia, (d) a peacock (4 points possible) ____
3. Understanding, Skills, and Attitude (3 points possible) ____
4. (a) Gore, (b) Perot, (c) Clinton, (d) Gore (4 points possible) ____
5. Hot water is on left (2 points) ____
6. Number of birds you named ____
7. Number of actual dates, codes, and numbers you listed ____
8. Banana, calendar, photograph, computer, parsley (5 points if you listed them all, 6 points if they were in order) ____
9. 25 f's, 2 capital F's, 8 numeral 3's, and 1 spelled-out *three* = 36; divide by 6 to find your score (6 points possible) ____
10. (a) Theodore Streleski (2 points for first and last names, 1 point for either alone) ____
    (b) 49 years old (1 point) ____
    (c) 7 years and 20 days (2 points for both numbers, 1 point for one) ____
    (d) 60 reporters (1 point) ____
    (e) Murdered his professor, second-degree murder, or manslaughter (1 point) ____
11. 3 points for each picture with correct shape and detail *or* 1 point each for correct shape with little or poor detail (6 points possible) ____

TOTAL NUMBER OF POINTS YOU SCORED: ____

It is possible to score 42 points on this test just by giving correct answers to nine of the questions. Your score could go much higher if you listed many birds and numbers in questions 6 and 7. More important than the total number of points you scored on this quiz, however, is the *kind* of memory your score portrays.

What Areas Look Good?

Kind of memory	Measured by questions	Your score
Long term Short term	1, 2, 4, 5, 6, 7 3, 8, 9, 10, 11	
Visual Auditory Kinesthetic	2, 3, 4, 5, 6, 8, 11 1, 2, 4 5, 11	
Attention/focus	3, 8, 9, 10, 11	
Rational/left-brained Emotional/right-brained	3, 7, 8, 10 1, 2, 3, 6, 11	

Long- and Short-Term Memory. Generally, short-term-memory skills decline with age. However, in tandem with the decline, most of us improve our ability to remember long-ago events, both in detail and the "big picture." Bringing up this fuller memory of an event takes longer and often gives the impression that our recall is slower than it really is. Since devising this quiz in 1990 we have administered it to approximately one hundred adults of all ages and found that middle-agers typically have equal scores on the long- and short-term-memory tasks; people in their twenties and thirties have higher scores for short-term memory than long-term; and those past middle age score higher on long-term memory than short-term.

Suggestion: The UFO Strategy is particularly helpful in developing both short- and long-term memory.

Visual, Auditory, and Kinesthetic Memory. When you want to remember a quote, a song, the name of a person you've just met, or directions to a location, do you usually (a) write it down, (b) picture it in your mind, or (c) listen carefully to the speaker and ask him to repeat or clarify? Answer (a) is an example of kinesthetic memory, (b) of visual memory, and (c) of auditory memory. Most of us have a preference for visual, auditory, or kinesthetic memory, but excellent memories come from using all three. Since it is much easier to measure visual skills in a written test than hearing and touch forms of memory, our quiz has more visual questions, and so you probably scored highest on visual no matter what your preference is. A good rule of thumb is that each auditory point is worth two visual points, while each kinesthetic point is worth four.

Body (kinesthetic) memory is best in childhood, when auditory memory is poorest. That's why children learn better by imitation than by being told what to do. In young adulthood, we become skilled at connecting the spoken and written word to a mental picture and rely less on the touch and feel of memories. In old age, the ability to conjure up mental pictures declines, and we use auditory memory more.

Suggestion: Here again the UFO Strategy is helpful, but the Try-Angle adds the ability to "chunk" ideas and see abstractions. Also, diagraming your Try-Angle helps to make it feel solid and tangible.

Attention/Focus. Concentration is essential to having a good memory. Your ability to focus your attention usually improves with age, although medication and emotional shock can interfere.

Suggestion: The Six R's give you different ways of focusing on the material you want to remember. Also, the UFO Strategy gives you practice with manipulating your mind backward and forward in time.

Rational Left-Brained and Emotional Right-Brained Memory. The left and right sides of the brain have different thinking skills and most of us use one side more than the other. The left-brained thinker is skilled at recalling numbers, outlines, and vocabulary, while the right excels in recalling visual details and the emotional content of an event. The right brain's spatial skills help you turn objects in your mind's eye, which is essential in map reading.

When your work or home life change drastically, you might be pushed to using your less preferred brain hemisphere, thereby developing other memory skills.

Suggestion: Use all the strategies and tips we've offered and you'll develop a left-brain/right-brain balanced memory.

Question by Question, What the Quiz Means

The purpose of the quiz is not to come up with a raw memory score, but to help you evaluate the present state of your long- and short-term memory and your ability to focus on new information. Here are the factors that are important in each of the eleven questions:

1. **Four slogans from radio and TV commercials.** While this is a test of your long-term, visual, auditory memory, it may be influenced by how much TV you watch, how much you listen to the radio, and how old you are. Most of these ads are old ones, and may have been used before

your time if you're a young reader. Furthermore, if you don't pay attention to commercials, you may not have "gotten them" to begin with, in spite of their ubiquitous coverage.

2. **Four studio logos.** This one could be skewed by whether you are a movie fan. Like number 1, it uses long-term memory plus visual and auditory recall.

3. **Understanding how the memory works, having memory skills, and maintaining a can-do attitude.** There are several memory aids built into this question. Did you detect the acronym, U.S.A., suggested in the sentence? The first letters of the three words in the acronym were capitalized and italicized. Furthermore, we kept it short and used simple action words as much as possible, appealing to your visual, emotional right brain.

   If you said "practice" instead of skill, you are probably a left-dominant person who reads for comprehension.

4. **Recalling the hair color and speech habits of four political figures.** Those with good visual memory will "see" that Gore has the darkest hair. Your auditory memory is tested by the remaining questions.

5. **Is the hot-water faucet on the left or right?** This one tests your kinesthetic memory. Did you have to close your eyes and "feel" yourself in the shower? It's the same kinesthetic memory you use for typing and driving. Once you have a kinesthetic memory in place, it's very difficult to retrieve it through the left brain. For example, that's why you probably can't tell someone where the *G* is on the typewriter.

6. **Recalling bird names.** Research by the Creative Education Foundation in Buffalo, New York, shows that college-age adults score an average of 8. Older adults in our corporate training classes have done slightly better, with an average score of 10. People who participated in the Whole-Brain Memory Map scored between 8 and 40. Those who scored very high used some system for recall, such as covering one category at a time (for example, raptors or songbirds). Others abbreviated bird names and were thus not so limited by time constraints.

   How did you do? If you are a bird watcher, you probably did very well because of your familiarity with the topic and the system you've no doubt developed for identifying birds. Hunters, hikers, and people who grew up in rural areas might also be above average. If you've never been outside the borders of New York City, doing poorly on this one is no reflection on your mentality or memory. And writing difficulties such as arthritis or a bad ball-point pen might prevent you from writing down as many as you could recall in one minute.

7. **Recalling numbers.** Organized, factual, left-dominant people usually come up with scores of 15 or more, because they like the efficiency numbers bring to their daily lives. They typically recall business phone numbers, contract amounts, or the Dow Jones average on Black Monday.

The more emotional, visual, right-brained person will focus on telephone numbers of friends and family, birthdays of loved ones, and addresses of homes they've lived in. Even though they have the advantage of being able to see the houses and people in their memories, they're sometimes distracted by these pictures. These people typically can score 11 to 13 (some incomplete, as one visualization quickly changes to another).

Individuals we tested with the Whole-Brain Memory Map from 7 to 16 (the 16 was scored by a fifty-four-year-old lawyer who organized them into categories such as nuclear-family birth dates and parents' birth dates, and used ditto marks when listing phone numbers with the same area codes; when listing birds for question 6, he organized the birds into categories, too). As in the preceding question, writing difficulties could affect your score.

This exercise is a measure of long-term memory. Whether you scored 7 or 15 does not say whether you're a left- or right-brained thinker or how smart you are. What matters is *how* you did it. Were you relating one visualization to the next, then interrupting the flow to write a number down (right), or categorizing and writing while moving to the next number (left)? If you used the former approach, you know you can rely on your visual memory and should work on other kinds of memory strategies.

8. **Recalling a list of unrelated words.** This indicates how good your short-term memory is when recalling a list with an intervening distraction, and how good you are at making visual associations in your mind. If you got all the words, were they in the same order? If so, you most likely conjured up a story relating them together. For example: You see yourself trying to use a banana to type out your calendar on a computer. But it turns into a camera that photographs the computer spitting out parsley instead of the calendar.

This visual-story technique comes easily to right-brained people. A more left-brained approach is to put the items in categories and number them, or memorize the first letter of each item and use them as cues.

9. **A block of numbers laced with *f*'s and 3's that tests your ability to focus intently.** As we age and cut out many unimportant events and interruptions, we aren't as easily distracted from tasks. This helps concentration. Did you notice that some *f*'s were capitalized and that a 3 was spelled out? If you saw beyond the seeming rules and got some extra points, congratulations. You showed creative thinking as well as an ability to concentrate.

10. **Recalling details of a news story.** This news story was chosen because of the figures embedded in its very dramatic content. Here again, the nature of your memory depends upon your background as much as on mental alertness. Motivation is also very important. You knew you were going to have some kind of test on these paragraphs, so you probably planned to use a familiar technique for organizing the information. However, the emotionally jarring content of the murder may have blotted out recall of details and facts and skewed the sequence of your thoughts. In such a case, you'd remember the most horrendous parts most clearly and answer the questions with inaccurate details or merely a sigh.

    A person in law enforcement (a police officer, judge, or court bailiff) is most likely to have total recall of the details and to recall them in the order written.

    Journalists might be distracted by the way the item is written and, therefore, not have accurate recall: An editor might think it's too wordy; a writer might dislike the choice of words.

11. **Recreating two geometric figures.** Clear visual recall is a skill we all need because it enables us to remember details as well as generalities. Sketching simple objects from memory is good practice. The UFO and Try-Angle strategies use and improve this valuable skill.

Think about what your scores on the memory quiz tell you about the state of your memory. Is your long-term memory better than your short-term one? Is focusing your attention difficult for you? Do you remember concepts better than data? Use these indicators to direct your efforts to make your memory sharper than it's ever been before.

CROSS-TRAINING YOUR MEMORY

The memory test identifies areas you should work on. Use your strengths as much as possible while you gradually improve your weak areas.

But take small steps. Ensure success at each level so that your confidence will grow with each experience.

Skillful ski instructors structure lessons so that beginners experience success at each step. You first go down a short, gentle slope with your skis parallel and your eyes on the instructor, who's waiting to make sure you can stop at the bottom. You feel a happy little tingle in your stomach. The next step is to go a little higher up on the slope and bring your toes toward the middle in a snowplow. Once your body gets the feel of that, another factor is introduced, another opportunity to boost your self-esteem.

So an important part of creating a better memory is breaking your efforts down into small steps and enjoying success each step of the way. Success is particularly important as we age because of the negative myths we have about memory. Most of us have been programmed to believe we're going to lose it—and the dynamics of that self-fulfilling prophecy are difficult to overcome.

So be gentle with yourself—but not so gentle that you don't practice all the memory skills. To keep a check on yourself, here's a handy workout schedule for your memory. It is designed to reinforce regularly all the strategies you have learned, cross-training all parts of your brain.

Get your calendar. In each of the next six months, write reminders of the schedule below:

The First Monday of Each Month

Warmup: Be visual. Wherever you are, whatever you do, try to see the big picture, the colors, the textures of life around you.
Workout: *Identify* the most recent memory problem you've had and *Try-Angle* it.

The Second Monday of Each Month

Warmup: Commit to focusing on words and saying them. Read headlines aloud; reword them to rhyme or be funny. Find three new words you like and use them often.
Workout: *Identify* the most recent memory slippage you've had and *Six-R* it.

The Third Monday of Each Month

Warmup: Open your ears and notice the language used by your closest friend and your least-admired acquaintance. See how many different ways people have of greeting you. Pay attention to how you conclude telephone calls.

Workout: *Identify* a confusing experience you've had that resulted from your not clearly remembering a situation, and *UFO* it.

The Fourth Monday of Each Month

Warmup: Stay aware all day of how your body moves: freely, painfully, stiffly. Exaggerate all your actions (when no one is watching) by waving your TV remote control wildly, or throwing your head back dramatically when you take a sip of water. Become aware of the feel of everything around you: your place mats, the bath towel, the steering wheel.

Workout: *Identify* an action that, if mastered, would make life much easier for you (operating the VCR, parallel parking) and use *body memory* on it.

You'll find these exercises easier and more fun to do as the months pass, and at the end of six months, you'll have a whole-brained memory for the rest of your life and a great tool for learning, the subject of the next chapter.

Learning How to Learn

Before you sleep, read something that is exquisite, and worth remembering.
—ERASMUS

For the unlearned old age is winter; for the learned it is the season of the harvest.

—THE TALMUD

From the time she was born in 1891, Meta Stone learned the skills and knowledge that have enabled her to survive to this day. She was born a Jew in Germany. Even though her family struggled financially and discrimination was a way of life, her childhood was filled with poetry, the piano, and foreign languages. Her mother taught her to be a seamstress; her father taught her business skills. History taught her foresight.

In the aftermath of World War I, when Meta was a young adult, economic conditions in Germany were desperate. Just when it seemed that matters couldn't get worse, Hitler came upon the scene. Meta began brushing up on her English and looking for sponsors to help her family come to the United States.

Friends and relatives kept disappearing into prisons and concentration camps. One day Meta's husband was arrested. She called the American consul in Stuttgart to explain their peril, and wrote a letter to the police saying her family had the papers necessary to go to the United States. To this day, Meta doesn't know what happened, but her husband was released two weeks later on condition that they leave the country immediately.

While the terror was over when they arrived in the United States, the struggle was not. They had no money and just a handful of acquaintances. But Meta's English and sewing skills landed her a job in a shirt factory.

Eventually, she and her husband were able to buy a small bookstore across from a high school. The first day, business boomed. The second, nothing. She learned that the business was almost totally dependent upon school purchases. So she set about getting to know the school system, text requirements, publishers, and ultimately the neighborhood. The bookstore became a haven for book lovers and throve in the process.

Now more than a hundred years old, Meta stays abreast of the news, watches opera (not the soap variety) on television, and reads the classics (some in German). She delights in an occasional meal out, chatting over orange juice and shortbread, and shopping for conservative suits and colorful blouses.

Meta's long life illustrates not only the value of learning, but the meaning and texture of it. She learned not just from school but from everything and everyone around her, and she was able to use what she learned to survive and, finally, to enrich her life.

Perhaps you will never need to pick your way as carefully through dangerous times as Meta did, but surely you will benefit both practically and emotionally from being able to apply information in an intelligent way.

Learning is more than memory; it is the ability to relate new information to what you already know, so that you derive some broader understanding of the new fact. Memory is the instrument for learning.

When you think of "learning," you may think first of the rapid progress of infants, or of your years in school. But actually, people learn every moment of their lives, although in different ways at different ages. While the very young mind is built for high-speed acquisition of facts, an older mind is built for broad understanding.

Indeed, learning becomes even more important as we age. A habit of learning new things is absolutely essential to staying sharp throughout old age.

Continual learning is vital physiologically because it establishes more and stronger neural pathways, leading to a richer understanding. When you consciously pursue learning, you stimulate the flow of neurotransmitters in the brain, strengthening the connections between axons and dendrites. Without the excitement of new learning, the paths wander off in many directions, often becoming extinct.

In early childhood, we love to learn. In fact, young children cannot be kept from learning. They are eager consumers of all the information in their environment. Unfortunately, many of us lose this enthusiasm in elementary school when we become mere receptacles for the information given us by teachers and parents. Consequently, many of us grow into adults who never take the active role in learning that we need for the years that follow formal schooling. Yet now, as never before, it is vital to be in control of your learning; if you are to keep your toehold socially, financially, and emotionally these days, continual learning is essential.

LEARNING WITH MUNCHIES

Munching while you study enhances learning, according to recent research. But it may be that you have to eat again to recall what you learned—in the same way that students who take "bennies" to cram for an exam must have another benny when they take the test. Scientists call this "state-dependent" learning, and have found that information learned while drinking alcohol or using drugs cannot be retrieved unless the same state is re-created through further alcohol or drug use.

Perhaps this phenomenon accounts for the successes reported with Accelerated Learning, Suggestology, Optimal Learning, and Superlearning, a few of the learning systems popular in the 1980s that relied upon relaxation techniques and sensory arousal.

LEARNING AND THE BRAIN

Fortunately, recent research has yielded new insights into the ways we learn. These discoveries suggest the following techniques for learning more information, more easily.

Excitement Counts

Learning occurs when neurons in the brain are connected. Neurotransmitters prepare the synapses on the sending and receiving ends of neurons for making a connection. When enough neurotransmitters have accumulated on the "pre" side of the synapse, they burst forth, sparking a message across the synapse. On the "post" side, neurotransmitters soften the area and make it receptive. Neurotransmitters are the power behind such connections, but *you* control the transmitters. If you are excited about learning, you can stimulate the free flow of neurotransmitters and keep the synaptic romance alive.

Since excitement counts, find out what excites you mentally, and seek it out to expand your learning.

EXCITING YOUR BRAIN

Here are some ways you can stimulate both the ''pre'' and ''post'' parts of the synapse, thus improving learning.

- Intensify the buildup of neurotransmitters by delaying a learning situation. For example, if you've bought a book, postpone reading it for days. When you finally get to it, you'll be so eager that you'll shut out all other thoughts so you can feast on your mental treasure. Your neurotransmitters will flow.
- To ''soften'' the receiving side, you need constant, low-level stimulation. So surround yourself with reminders; leave the book in full sight and talk about it with friends. Then those receptors will be ready and waiting for you to begin.

Learning Goes Both Ways

Scientists once believed that learning went in only one direction over neural pathways, but they have discovered that the postsynaptic messenger also reaches backward in a general, nonspecific way. Although the outcome of this retrograde phenomenon is still not clearly understood, early theories are that it helps generalize information and connect it to related concepts. It could explain how visualization helps athletes improve their skills in general even when working on just one skill.

Since learning goes forward and backward, push your mind even when you don't think you're ''getting it.''

For example, when working on her master's degree, Jacquelyn had a particularly difficult required course on phenomenology. She went to her condo up in the mountains and sat reading and rereading a subject she really didn't understand. At times, she felt as if she was getting small slices of it, but the overall concept eluded her. She strained and strained to understand it—she even broke out in a sweat from the exertion. After about two hours, it came to her, all in a rush. It was thrilling!

TOUGH LEARN

When you're reading something very technical or foreign to you, make three passes. First read it straight through, skipping words you don't understand, to get a feel for what it's about. The second time, pick out key words and concepts. Look up several words that are repeated and seem to be critical. Rest, then relate the new information to something you already know or a theory you hold. Return then for the third reading, and you'll be amazed at the progress you've made in understanding the topic.

On-Site Learning

Specific thinking skills are located in different areas of the brain. For example, a person with otherwise good language skills who has trouble naming colors may be underdeveloped, or may have a lesion, in the left temporal lobe.

Such specialties in the brain explain why we have certain mental lapses. For instance, saying someone's name is an ability of the left anterior temporal lobe. So if you have problems with connecting names to faces, you may not be accessing the appropriate part of your brain. The best approach is to blitz your brain with a number of ways to remember, so you're sure one of them will work. As with the memory strategies in Chapter 8, stimulate many visual, auditory, verbal, and physical receptors. For example, if you're meeting someone named Nancy, hum the first bar of "Nancy with the Laughing Eyes" as you shake her hand. Yes, she's probably sick of the song by now, but explain that you're trying to make sure her name sticks in your mind. While you're at it, look carefully at her eyes and visualize them laughing.

Since the brain develops and ages unevenly, learn things in a variety of ways to make up for possible "holes" in your capacities.

Practice Does Make a Difference

Practice does make perfect and even changes the shape of the brain. A study by Michael Merzenich at the University of California at San Francisco showed that monkeys' brains increased in size in areas devoted to certain fingers that had been exercised over a three-year period. In the same way, humans who play the piano extensively have larger areas of the cortex committed to the fingers than people who don't play the piano. A seamstress's sewing hand will reflect the same phenomenon. Conclusion: Learning changes the brain.

Since practice actually changes the shape of your brain by strengthening neural pathways, you know that it's the way to deep-seated learning.

LEARN LIKE A KID

Your elementary-school teacher had many ways to involve you in learning facts . . . and some of the ways were fun. Here are some school-day learning techniques that can make grownup learning enjoyable.

- **Flash cards.** Construct flash cards whenever you're trying to remember lots of facts, such as telephone numbers, client names, or computer commands. A few times through and you'll have them down pat.
- **Book reports.** When you've read a book and don't want to forget the essentials, jot the main ideas inside the back cover. Or write a one-page digest with author and title at the top, then deliver it classroom-style to your spouse or roommate. You'll find you not only remember the book better, but also have a new perspective on its overall meaning.
- **Crib notes.** Write key phrases on your hand, on note cards, or on the bathroom mirror. Surround yourself with reminders of the information you're trying to master and soon you'll have absorbed it almost without trying.

BE CONCRETE, BE ACTIVELY INVOLVED

Now that you know the whys of adult learning, here are some rules of thumb for how to go about it.

In general, **go from the concrete to the abstract** as much as possible. The more concrete the concept, the more easily you can master it. Conversely, the more abstract the information, the less is learned. For example, an algebraic formula is more difficult to understand and recall than a newspaper story about highway construction a half mile from your home.

Also, **be as actively involved in learning as possible,** and use as many parts of the brain in the process as possible.

Both these general principles are at work in the rankings, listed below, that educational researcher Edgar Dale has assigned to the effectiveness of various learning methods. As you'll see, more abstract processes such as using language are less effective than dealing physically with objects.

- **Reading is just 10 percent effective.**
- **Hearing is 20 percent effective.** Hearing can double reading's value because voices and sounds are quite stimulating to the right brain, while reading relies mostly on left-brain processes.
- **Seeing still pictures and graphics is 30 percent effective** because it arouses left and right thinking as well as the occipital lobes at the rear of the brain.
- **Combining seeing and hearing is 50 percent effective.** The old-time silent-movie flickers were a step up in effectiveness from stereopticons because they added movement and action. Then, when they turned into "talkies," movies became even more compelling because you had both action and sound. Learning is also greatly enhanced by exhibits and demonstrations for the same reason. Did you notice that we didn't mention television? That's because the television screen has certain characteristics that lull you rightward and interfere with left-brained analysis. To compensate, teachers of children and adults include hands-on and analytic exercises with any television presentations.
- **Speaking or writing about what you hear and see is 70 percent effective** because you're putting what you've learned into your own words, involving many more parts of your brain.

- **Doing** what you've learned **is 90 percent effective.** When you can physically replicate what you've learned, then you understand it completely and will probably never forget it. Soldiers who learn to take their rifles apart and reassemble them blindfolded say they never forget the steps. Actors remember the words, intonations, and gestures of their roles years later, because they used so many parts of the brain to learn them.

We'd add one more level: **Teaching what you've learned is 99 percent effective.** Teaching involves all the other processes, plus now you're thinking of the information from your students' point of view and searching for ways to make it clear to them. Interpreting in this way helps you clarify your own understanding. The 1 percent remaining is for any mistaken ideas you may have—which, as any teacher will testify, will soon be corrected by your students.

RIGHT-BRAINED VIEWING

Have you ever wondered why you can't see mistakes on your word processor? Canadian professor Eric McLuhan tested groups of adult students for their responses to the same educational film presented in different ways. Half saw the film on television, the other half on a movie screen, then all were asked to critique it. The video watchers wrote long, emotional evaluations of the film, while the movie screen watchers described it in the terse, factual language of the left brain. McLuhan believes that the movie screen does not involve the right brain as does the video screen. He points out that computer screens have the same effect as video, lulling you into noncritical right-brained thinking, making it difficult to edit on screen. And so, it is not until you see the hard copy that mistakes jump out at you.

HOW DO YOU LEARN BEST?

Another rule of thumb for adult learning is to **use the approach best suited to your learning style**—at least in the beginning. As we explored in the chapter on memory, there are four ways in which we learn: visual (See It), verbal (Say It), auditory (Hear It), and kinesthetic (Do It).

Visual learners. These people learn best by reading or looking at charts and pictures. They usually like to take notes and copy from chalkboards. They want copies of everything. They doodle, draw pictures, and make outlines and diagrams of what they're learning. To learn from the spoken word, they need language that conjures up pictures; it should be loaded with concrete and colorful terms and lots of examples, the more emotional the better.

Verbal learners. These are the learners who ask and answer questions in class, love to read aloud, and learn best from discussions. Their need to speak often causes them to mumble (subvocalize) what they've heard as they replay it mentally.

Auditory learners. These are the lucky individuals who are so relaxed in lecture halls and college classrooms. No frantic note taking for them! They learn best by listening to tapes, the radio, and the spoken word. Often they "listen" to television, rarely looking at the screen. They "hear" your body language—the rhythm of your breathing, the changes in tone—just as they detect impending motor problems by the hum of an engine.

Kinesthetic learners. These learners are most successful when they "do something." They like to participate in demonstrations and simulations. They'll volunteer to role-play and like hands-on projects. They like educational toys. They like to take things apart and usually succeed in putting them back together.

SHIFTING BRAIN POWER

These simple procedures will stimulate many new areas of your brain:

- Brush your teeth, open doors, and drink beverages with the hand opposite the one you usually use.
- Move your office desk and chair to a different part of the room.
- Sleep on the opposite side of the bed (or in a different room).
- Read your least favorite section of the paper first.
- Move articles off your desk, so that you have to get up and walk across the room each time you use them.
- Wear your watch on the opposite wrist.

In short, do as many things differently as you can. You may feel disoriented at times, but this feeling often precedes creative ideas.

Incorporating All Styles

While it is important to start in your "comfort zone," the more easily you can use all four learning styles, the more you can learn from formal settings as well as everyday life.

The learner who uses only auditory methods is great with theory but often a bumbler when it comes to using the new burglar alarm or fixing a flat tire. The verbal learner talks herself through new or difficult tasks—"Now just be patient, take one step at a time"—and often gives herself positive feedback—"There, you've done the first part. . . ." The strictly visual person learns such practical tasks best from schematic or video instructions. While the kinesthetic-dependent person would feel her way through such a learning problem, she'd have difficulty explaining the process to others or expressing the theory behind such skills. Somewhat like the person who "cooks by feel," the kinesthetic person cannot provide a "recipe" for her skills and so must always do things for herself.

Since most of the situations we encounter in adulthood require all four kinds of skills, it's best to incorporate as many of them as possible into every learning situation. For example, training professionals, who know that adults have many learning styles, use multimedia presentations. While videotapes and flip charts appeal to some, group discussions, music, and hands-on projects engage others.

Using all four learning styles is not as difficult as it might seem. After all, adults have many advantages when it comes to learning, as you'll discover in the next section.

MENTAL WARM-UPS

You can gain an hour or two of sharp, focused thought each day. In the first five to ten minutes upon awakening, sit comfortably and try one of these warm-ups. They'll prime your brain for list making, memory, and word visualization and comprehension.

- Count down from 100 to 1 as quickly as you can.
- Recite the alphabet, giving each letter a word partner (*"A,* apple; *B,* basket. . . "*)*, as quickly as you can.
- Recite twenty men's or women's names as quickly as you can, and number them as you go ("One, Phillip; Two, Joe; Three, Robert. . . ").
- Name ten types of food as quickly as you can, again numbering them ("One, banana; Two, hamburger; Three, Jell-O . . ."*)*.
- Choose one letter of the alphabet and name twenty words that begin with that letter as quickly as you can, numbering them as you go ("One, morning; two, mother; three, massage. . . ").

If your eyes were open during the exercise, that's fine, but close them now. Count to 20, then open them. Your mind is now warmed up and ready for the day.

FOR ADULTS ONLY

Adults have several characteristics that enhance their ability to learn. Here's what they are and how you can use them to improve your ability to absorb and use information.

Adults Learn Because They Want To

Many teachers love working with adult education classes because the students are highly motivated. It is their idea to be there, not the school board's. So look for courses, books, and activities related to your real interests and needs. Explore what it is that you want to know more about. Then stay focused on your interests, since a hodgepodge of learning experiences with no purpose can quickly become discouraging. Know why you're there, and what you expect to get out of the situation.

WHEN YOU'RE SENT TO SCHOOL

Even in adulthood, we are sometimes *sent* to school. The boss assigns us to take some specialized training, or we have to attend a seminar we're not keen on. People who have been business executives or officers in the military, or have occupied other positions of authority, are often very resentful because they hate giving up control in the classroom. They don't want to be told, "Read this, write that, work with this person." If you find it difficult to adjust to being in the student role, think about why. Do you share the "in charge" person's discomfort with being under the control of others? You can overcome this problem and actually enjoy the experience by doing much more than the teacher and curriculum require. By choosing to do more than what is expected, you're getting more out of the class . . . and you're still in control.

Adults Are Building on a Broad Base of Knowledge

Adults learn best when they start with the known and move to the unknown—it's more comfortable. When you're trying to learn some big new field, identify what you know and start there—reviewing, then moving on to the unknown. Watch for signs that your information is dated, so that you don't build on false assumptions.

Educational psychologists say we go through four stages before we really know something. In the first stage, we are unaware that we are lacking the information. In the second, we're aware of the deficit. At the third level, we have the information but don't truly understand it. Finally, at the fourth level, we know it and are aware of all its ramifications. This phenomenon explains why experience counts and how age is often an advantage in learning situations: The more experiences you have had, the better equipped you are to skip over levels one, two, and three. Your awareness and knowledge are already in place, and you need only connect the new information to the broad-based knowledge you already have.

As you go through your busy day, take "learning moments" to connect what you're seeing to what you already know; for example, *Ah, so this strange-looking machine they're using to rout the top layer off this street is one of those new "planers" I read about in the newspaper*. Think, *I'm learning something here—what is it?*

Adults Have Control over Their Learning Environment

Make sure your environment is designed for learning. "The mind can only absorb as much as the bottom can tolerate" is a saying among people who train adults. As a result, smart trainers (teachers of adults) schedule frequent breaks and provide opportunities to move around in the classroom. When you're learning on your own, give yourself a break and get more out of it. Dress comfortably; sit for short periods of time, then move around; have a comfortable study area. If you're in a classroom situation that doesn't provide for breaks, ask for them. And when you get them, go for a walk down the hall, do some limbering exercises in the restroom or outdoors. Move that body!

If you have vision or hearing problems, seat yourself in the spot easiest for you to see or hear. You'll also need more than breaks, and perhaps even a cat nap off in a corner (or out in your car) to refresh yourself.

Focus your learning efforts on one area at a time. Research shows that forgetting increases with the amount of interfering material introduced. For instance, in the Whole-Brain Memory Map, question 8 distracted you with a joke about Donald Trump. But if you must endure interference, the more dissimilar it is to the topic you're learning, the better your comprehension and retention. It's easier for your brain to separate the wheat from the chaff when they are different.

Baby Naps for Better Learning

Research by child psychologists shows that babies who nap immediately after a learning experience learn more, faster. This works for adults, too. So, schedule naps after learning. Focus on the new information mentally as you fall asleep. When you awaken, review the material immediately and think about how it applies to some specific situation in your life.

But first, train yourself to take baby naps. Start at home with a timer set for twenty-five minutes. Get up whether you feel rested or not. Practice these naps until you are able to feel rested and ready to awaken in twenty-five minutes. Then gradually reduce the amount of time to fifteen minutes. Soon, you'll be able to awaken yourself from a fifteen-minute nap and feel refreshed for hours. Eventually, you can take a baby nap wherever you are: on a bus, in the rest room, at your desk, in the car. A quick nap will improve your alertness and mood, and put the curve back into your learning.

Adults Have Broad, Discriminating Vocabularies

Research shows that very little verbal skill is lost in old age. In fact, elders perform better on verbal skills tests than younger people, *except* when they're being timed, according to Carl W. Cotman and Christine Peterson of the University of California, Irvine. This is a real strength that you can use, so it's important to build your vocabulary at every age, and involve yourself in activities that keep you expressing yourself on paper and in speech. Besides, it's a great way to lower stress and develop more reflective ways of thinking. Grow your vocabulary all your life long—and use it daily.

Adults Have a Great Many Opportunities for Learning

Take advantage of all the formal and informal ways that adults learn: through Elderhostels, communication classes, special-interest tours, self-directed travel, book clubs, religious education classes, educated friends, and many others.

For example, Peggy Bliss, a seventy-three-year-old widow, consciously pursues an activity for each kind of learning that is important to her:

- To stay in touch with the community affairs she's always been fond of, she volunteers one Saturday a week at the Humane Society and twice weekly at the elementary school in her neighborhood.
- For competition and comradeship, she plays golf weekly and keeps track of her golf club's tournament scores.
- For cultural interests, she attends movies, plays, and the opera regularly.
- For muscles and flexibility, she takes physical education classes at the community school, currently power lifting and line dancing.
- For exploring the world, she travels at least once a year (recently, a cruise to Alaska and a trip to the Orient).
- For her spiritual needs and interests, she attends church regularly.
- For continuing her professional skills, each winter and spring for three months she rents an office and prepares tax returns, the profession from which she retired.

Early in her marriage, Peggy was the quintessential corporate wife. She enjoyed rearing her children, helping her husband's career along, and performing civic duties. In later years, her husband's kidney disease required daily dialysis. Most people live only two years with such a condition, but Peggy trained for six weeks so that she could administer the dialysis at home, and they had "eight more good years together." This may in part account for Peggy's conscious pursuit of learning. She knows the value of lifelong education.

You may not think of yourself as a lifelong learner, but you are. Every time you figure out how to operate a new automatic bank teller, read the newspaper, or sit in on a meeting, you are learning. So use these tips and strategies. Make the most of your advantages as an adult learner, and use all four approaches to learning: visual, verbal, auditory, and kinesthetic. Whether you ever set foot in a classroom again or not, you are continually learning. Make that learning count.

10

Systems for the Small Stuff

There is more to life than increasing its speed.
—MAHATMA GANDHI

A budget is what you stay within if you go without.
—CLAUDE MCDONALD

M any people today, old and young, feel overwhelmed by the details and complications of life. Elders are often especially afraid that they're getting scattered, out of it. They worry they won't be able to handle the paperwork needed to file health claims or get benefits owed to them. They worry they'll start to lose track of birthdays, phone numbers, important papers. Those in the work force want to make sure they stay on top of things as always.

The truth is that because the world is complex in many ways today, we *all* need to develop better systems to manage the flood of information, the demands on our time, and the myriad of choices. The more good systems you have in place to organize routine matters, the more time, money, and energy you'll have left for making decisions that truly require focused attention (the subject of the next chapter, ''Making Wise Decisions''). So now is the time for you to think about systems that will help you.

As you age, the systems you've put into place will become increasingly valuable to you. They will bring you power and control over your own life. They'll make you feel good about yourself. And they will bring you peace of mind.

In this chapter, you will learn many easy systems for managing time, money, and energy efficiently and automatically. But first, let's explore further why these systems are so crucial in today's world.

THE WORLD OF TOO MUCH

You read two papers a day. You click through sixty different TV offerings morning and night. Your calendar is jammed from dawn through dinner. You worry if your deposit was in time to cover the check you just wrote. You can't remember the last time you hiked with an old friend or played the piano. In other words, you are the average, aware, thinking person. Is it any wonder you feel so out of control? The pressures you face are enormous, but is frantic any way to run your life?

Today, there really *are* more demands upon people's time, money, and energy than ever before: too much to do in too little time, too much information, too many people, too much speed, too much communication, and too many choices. We call these the ''mega-realities.''

Too Much to Do

A day is still twenty-four hours, but it seems to shrink in the face of more to do or greater expectations about what has to be done. Each of us plays many roles in everyday life, each with a separate set of activities. If you are a parent, you are concerned with your children's education, health and safety issues, moral guidance, and entertainment. Likewise, each of our other roles (employee, citizen, spouse, and so on) draws us into a different web of activities and concerns. Without systems for gaining control over them, personal time erodes constantly.

Too Much Information

Today, the enormous volume of new knowledge that is broadcast and published in every field exceeds anyone's ability to keep pace. New discoveries and new bodies of knowledge are available in multimedia: books, radio, television, audiotape, videotape, and soon virtual reality and the Information Superhighway. We need to understand most of this information: frequent flier programs, investments, long-distance telephone service, medical insurance, retirement options. But each day the rules and regulations take longer to read and are harder to comprehend. Before you can fully digest one news story, the focus shifts to another and then another. You're never free from worrying about a terrible crime or crisis somewhere; you find it impossible to stay abreast of new developments in your field or to make sense of it all.

Constant exposure to the media shower and the steady flood of facts leaves each of us incapable of absorbing and synthesizing, let alone applying, the data before tomorrow's downpour drenches us in still more information.

You begin to live in a state of perpetual frustration when the volume of information you believe you need exceeds your ability to absorb and apply it. How does it feel? Professor Marshall McLuhan, the forward-looking communications genius of the seventies, said we're stuck "with an enormous backlog of outdated mental and psychological responses," and are often left

d

  a

    n

      g

        l

          i

            n

              g.

And j a n g l i n g, too. Too much information violates our senses and our ability to think clearly. As you try to take in more information, you feel anxious, stressed, even helpless.

Too Many People

Three out of four households are extended by divorce, remarriage, stepchildren, double sets of in-laws, and half brothers and sisters. In addition to family members, you have relationships with fellow workers, your friends, and the hundreds of people you do business with (the mail carrier, doctor, food server, and so on).

Outside your personal circle, the world population threatens every aspect of the planet and its resources. We have densely packed urban areas where crime and poverty abound. Just getting to and from work becomes a hellish ordeal. The average American commutes 157,600 miles during her working life, six times around the earth. One stalled auto on a highway can make fifteen thousand people sit and suffer for an hour. The frustration even leads to waves of traffic shoot-outs. Many such times we promise ourselves we'll find a simpler, quieter life, but minutes later we're caught up in the same traffic-jam existence.

Too Much Communication

In 1988, 12 billion catalogs were mailed in the United States, up from 5 billion in 1980—equal to fifty catalogs for every man, woman, and child in America. In the last decade, growth in the total volume of regular, third-class bulk mail (junk mail) was thirteen times greater than the growth in the population.

You can shield yourself for stretches from the other, mega-realities, but those piles of paper on your desk and around your home constantly assault your concentration and comfort. Overuse of faxes, voice mail, and such corrupts the quality of the very communication they're designed to improve.

Too Many Choices

In the years between 1978 and 1986, the number of items carried in the average supermarket more than doubled—from 11,767 items to 24,531. More than 45,000 new products were introduced during that time period but failed. Currently, more than 1,260 varieties of shampoo are on the market, 75 kinds of exercise shoes, and more than 2,000 skin care products.

Product proliferation is only one part of our problem with making choices. Minute by minute, all year long, we must select causes, political candidates, careers, recreation, investments, and life-styles, to mention a few choices. Is it any wonder that sometimes you'd rather wear your old clothes than shop for something new?

Too Much Speed

The life-span of the average caveman was nineteen. Life expectancy in Europe circa 1392 was thirty-eight, and it was forty-nine in America by 1892. Today, it is seventy-six for American men, seventy-eight for women, and quickly rising for both sexes. It's ironic that the very technology that helped extend our life span now keeps us from enjoying those extra years. Where natural pauses were built into our days in the past, now time is speeded up. Everything is done fast. Radios, phones, and faxes all send us messages instantaneously. The faster we're able to travel or to gain new information, the further behind we fall. News travels so fast that we have no time to formulate, much less temper, our responses.

After a few years in the vortex of this mega-change, your perception of time becomes warped and your own natural energy flow is disturbed. Time seems to pass very slowly, or quickly without your realizing it. Your energies ebb and flow without your knowing why.

You Know You're Too Busy If...

- If you're too busy to enjoy your life, you're too busy.
- If you're too busy to stay calm, you're too busy.
- If you're too busy to stay in shape, you're too busy.
- If you're too busy to see your friends, you're too busy.
- If you think that someday you'll "catch up" in all these areas, you are living under a delusion.

STRATEGIES FOR DEALING WITH TOO MUCH

The mega-realities consume our time, money, and energy; they often leave us confused and frustrated. We find ourselves starting anew each day trying to wend our way through thousands of details. But there are ways of thinking about your busy life that can help you deal with it.

Realize That You Can't Do Everything

You can't treat every detail of life with intensity, nor do you need to. Abandon the illusion that you can or must keep up with the mountains of information and ideas that surround you. It is comforting to realize that the task is impossible! The sooner you give up the notion that you can do everything if you just try hard enough, the better you'll feel and function.

This is even true of getting organized—set up your systems gradually, so you don't overwhelm yourself with too much, too soon.

Decide What Is Important to You

Most choices come down to the same few issues: career advancement versus a happy home life; income goals versus income needs; and social-, peer-, or employment-induced priorities versus individual wants or needs. Many retired people are swept up in their own conflicts: time to travel versus family time, starting a new career versus relaxing, and so on. Once you clarify your goals, the path to accomplishing them is much clearer.

Spend your time, money, and energy on what matters most to you. Acquire knowledge that supports your needs, not knowledge that you simply happen to ingest or think you should ingest. Spend your time with supportive, interesting people, rather than those who leave you feeling less confident or energetic.

Are your days filled with activity but not the experiences and accomplishments you'd like to enjoy? When you examine the broad canvas of your life, interesting surprises often surface. What you say is important to you isn't on your schedule. What you say you dislike is where you expend energy.

Your life is finite, a fact most of us become more aware of as we age. You can't just settle for living your life in what's left over after each day's onslaught. You alone need to make sensible choices regarding what is best ignored and what merits your attention.

GET CARDED

Once you know what matters to you, write your priorities on several three-by-five cards. Keep these cards in your wallet, appointment book, desk, or car so that you are ever mindful of your goals. Reading your list frequently is invigorating because it gives meaning to what you're doing and helps you eliminate activities that don't contribute to your goals.

Drop the Rest

Avoid that which does not support your goals. Each of us has 168 hours a week. One way or another, they're used up. When you're deciding how to use them, consider this: Any activity that consumes thirty minutes a day, over a typical work life of forty-eight years, consumes one solid year of your life. Think of it! If you spend a half hour a day, from twenty-two until you are seventy, polishing your shoes, you will have used up one entire year on your shoes. It's nice to have shined shoes, but does it matter a whole year's worth to you?

This rather profound realization may help you eliminate activities that do not support the things that matter most to you, or at least help you find ways to limit the time they take.

Dropping an activity is not easy. Old habits, the familiar, what once mattered—all are difficult to give up. Here are some ways to ease the Big Drop:

- Review your priorities list; then, for each item you face, ask, "Does this support my priorities?"
- Temporarily drop something and see if you miss it. Often you will not.
- Ease it out; drop a little of it periodically.
- Ask others whether it's something you need to, want to, or have to keep doing. The feedback may surprise you.
- Go cold turkey (only for the brave!): "XYZ is out of my life." This is not as harsh as it sounds, since the decision usually follows sound reasoning.

Limit the Number of Decisions You Make Each Day

Get in the habit of making only a few thoughtful or reflective decisions a day—the ones that count. Recently retired kidney doctor Dr. Wag Schorr says, "It isn't the number of decisions we must make that is overwhelming, but the fact that we treat all of them as life-and-death matters." When you catch yourself making a low-level decision, ask yourself, *Does this really make a difference?* Low-level decisions (such as what to wear today or which toothpaste to buy) can be part of a system that you employ automatically. For example, develop a specific way of paying your bills or shopping for groceries; you'll save time, energy, and money.

Be selective about when you make choices. Most decisions you could make are of little consequence. Not choosing can be restful, comforting, even refreshing. It can also open up new possibilities: "Honey, you decide where we'll go this evening."

Alvin Toffler, author of *Future Shock,* had it right when he advocated not engaging in low-level decisions. If the same toothbrush is available with a red, blue, yellow, or white handle, and it is all the same to you, just grab the one that is closest or take the one that the clerk hands to you.

This section advocates making thoughtful choices *only* on a few important issues—the ones affecting your emotional, mental, or physical health, or those same aspects in others. It's meant to help you gain control over the small stuff.

Choose when it matters; let go when it doesn't.

In the next chapter, you'll get help making more important decisions.

Manage Your Environment

Do you have a catchall kitchen drawer? One that you can barely open or close because it is overflowing with coupons, small tools, M&M's, rubber bands, traffic tickets, and numerous unidentified objects? Most likely, you didn't consciously commit it to a life of clutter and decay. It just happened. And that's how most of us lose control of our environments.

So take a look at your environments—your office, home, car, and other physical spaces of your life—and *manage* them. Arrange, stock, and maintain such spaces in a manner that helps you conserve your time, money, and energy.

Take your car as an example: Store dimes and quarters for tolls and parking. Put together a small "office box" for the car, with important phone numbers, a pad, a pen, stamps and envelopes, Scotch tape, safety pins, and so on. Last year's phone book is a great help when you forget a street address or want to make a call from your cellular phone.

In a larger box, store such "weather adaptive" items as boots, gloves, and an umbrella. Prepare for emergencies with jumper cables, a gallon of water, a quart of oil, windshield wiper fluid, a shovel, and a blanket.

Contact lens wearers know the value of using multiple stations. It's essential to have saline solution and storage cases at the various stations of your life (such as your desk, car, and locker at the gym), so you are always able to remove or adjust them. Figure out what kinds of supplies you can afford to stash in several places.

Keep a supply of personal items inside your desk at work—your desk is there to support you. Be sure you have personal space at home where you keep your calendar, notes, and other supplies.

What else can be stored at multiple stations, freeing you of having to carry it or be concerned with it? Pens, note pads, calendars? It's your choice. What else is inexpensive, often used, and sorely missed when you're without it?

Manage the Beforehand

Managing the beforehand, as opposed to the aftermath, involves creating space—mentally or physically—in advance of what comes next. Clear out the old and unsupportive, and make room for where you are heading. Managing the beforehand requires anticipation and vision.

When managing the beforehand, you are perpetually turning over files and data. You know that more is coming that will supersede what you're holding, that your interests will change, and that it's psychologically costly to hold on to what you don't use.

Finish What You Start

When you leave tasks or activities uncompleted, the energy you have invested in them is wasted. Finish what you start. If you are working on a long-term project, finish it in stages, and acknowledge your progress as you complete each stage.

Keeping your work space clear is a completion. Eliminating items from your daily activities list is a completion. Quickly scanning and assessing your mail, and tossing most of it, is a major completion!

A variation on gaining completion is not to start activities you don't intend to follow through on. Saying no to what doesn't interest you enables you to say yes to what does interest you. We all tend to say yes to commitments that are off in the future, fantasizing that several weeks or months from now, we'll have more time than we do now. Often, as that future date arrives, we see our commitment as another intrusion. Protect your schedule for now and the future.

Also, say no to the next TV show. Say yes to visualizing how you'd like your day to go.

Seeking completion is a powerful way to gain a sense of control. Achieving completion is energizing because it offers a clean end to activities or even thoughts, and a good beginning for what's next.

YESTERDAY'S COMPLETIONS

Adults enjoy rewards for good behavior as much as children do. So take note of your successes with completions. Each morning, review yesterday's accomplishments. Start by listing three. Not only does this review encourage completions, it gives continuity to your plans for today. And you'll find that when your completions are recorded history, you're motivated to experience that good feeling again and again.

SOMEONE IS WAITING

To increase the probability that you'll deliver on schedule, have someone waiting for your work. Just knowing someone else is seeking
completion prods you onward. A spin-off of this external motivation
approach is to set artificial deadlines on open-ended projects so that
they won't drag on forever.

Choose to Trust Yourself

Trusting yourself enhances your ability to choose based on limited information. Say "I choose to trust my ability to make the right choice," even
without all the data.

You don't need to expose yourself to the daily deluge of the overinfor-
mation era to make appropriate choices. More often than you may realize,
you already have enough information and the tools you need.

Take Responsibility for Control

There are two attitudes that can prevent you from taking control of your life.
One is accepting habits and rituals that are comfortable but unrewarding—
such as opening all the mail you receive. The other is seeing yourself as a
powerless victim (of your boss, spouse, father, mother, kids, in-laws, neighbor, landlord, adviser, or clergy; or the president, governor, newspaper/mag-
azine columnist; or "The devil made me do it!"). Look beyond routine,
ritual, and victimization to ownership and responsibility for what is occurring
in your life.

GETTING STARTED WITH SYSTEMS

If you're not sure whether you're organized enough to survive the mega-
realities, take this short quiz:

1. Do you regularly spend five minutes or more looking for a letter or doc-
   ument?

2. Are week-old newspapers stacked on your desk or kitchen table?
3. Are you planning to get your bookshelves and files organized when you can buy more storage units?
4. Do you lose things by putting them in a special, easy-to-remember location?

If you said yes to any of these questions, you need help. Here's why: (1) Locating letters and documents should take no longer than forty-five to seventy-five seconds, according to efficiency experts. (2) Week-old newspapers are valuable only at the recycling center. (3) Organize things now, and you won't need more shelves. (4) At least you're trying.

If you think getting organized is time-consuming, try disorganization.

The best way to simplify your life is to develop systems to handle routine matters automatically. When you have a reliable way to handle them, you will be free to handle issues that need personal attention.

Organizations use systems for controlling repetitive, predictable functions. For example, they control money through an accounting system. Most of the details that madden us are as predictable as the income and outgo of money in a business. If we can develop ways of handling these predictable details automatically, then we'll have plenty of time, money, and energy left over for solving complex problems and coping with the unpredictable.

The first step in developing a system is to discriminate between those details that can be handled in a systematic way and those that require focus. How do you know which details lend themselves to successful systems? Look for these four system-friendly characteristics:

1. There are repetitive actions or steps.
2. The main elements are predictable enough to be scheduled.
3. The elements can be clearly distinguished from one another.
4. The elements are related primarily to things and facts, not people or feelings.

An example of a situation that is easily turned into a system is to develop a way to make sure you don't miss pickup day for your garbage. The characteristics of the situation are:

1. The wastebaskets must be emptied into the trash bin, which then needs to be rolled to the curb.
2. Pickup day is always Tuesday unless there's an intervening holiday.

3. In the fall and spring there are special pickup times for bundles of tree limbs and bags of leaves.
4. Anyone with the strength of a typical ten-year-old can roll the trash bin to the curb.

A simple agreement among household members as to who should put out the bin and bring it back in works well. It becomes a habit that doesn't waste your time, money, or energy.

How about a more complex situation with characteristics not so easily discernible? Try this one: Your eight-year-old son's teeth are crooked and protruding. You have to decide whether to have orthodontia now, later, or at all. You must find the right dentist, select the procedures, and figure out how to pay for them.

Unless you've been through orthodontia with a child before, these first steps can be lengthy and trying because they involve so many people and feelings, and because the steps are not repetitive. However, after this phase you can develop a system for transporting your son to appointments and paying the bills. These two elements are easy to systematize because they are repetitive and can be scheduled. Getting him to brush and wear his retainer involves his feelings and personality, so you may not be able to turn this aspect into a routine, except in the unlikely event that he is a well-organized, routine-loving eight-year-old. There is one consolation: If you have numerous children with orthodontic problems, you'll know the basic routine the next time through.

CALENDAR POWER

At seventy, Jerry, a retired accountant, continues to keep a daily calendar as well as a monthly and yearly planner. But now he uses his calendar to schedule time for exercise, volunteer work, and visits with his granddaughter, who lives out of state. Maintaining a close relationship with her is a high priority, so he carefully plans quarterly trips to visit her. His well-developed talent for scheduling serves Jerry well in his retirement years.

Some Great Systems

Organizing Paper

Put Everything in Its Pile. If you face a stack of paper, without sentiment or hesitation, allocate each item to one of four locations—an "Urgent" pile, an "Important" pile, an "Interesting" pile, or the recycling bin (wastebasket). Caution: Do not attempt this when you are tired or not fully alert, because the process will seem overwhelming.

If you are unsure of any particular item, you may place it at the bottom of the large stack, but only *once* for each item. On the second encounter, you have to classify it.

Within thirty minutes, the mess will be gone.

Whenever you find folders and tasks mounting up on all sides, remember how they got there, and that you are in charge of them, not vice versa.

Start a Beforehand Pile. Start a file called "Review in One Month," "Hold for More Information," or "Temporary Hold." Allow for what you know or suspect is coming, so when it does, you're in control.

The holding file takes the place of strewing things inconveniently about your office or home: "I don't know what to do with this, so I'll just park it here (. . . and hope the organizing fairy comes by and does something with it)."

Tear Through Catalogs. When you get a catalog, tear out the pages you are interested in, and stuff them into the catalog's mailing envelope. Throw the rest away. Then if you want to order something, it's easy to do.

Turn Off Junk Mail. The ideal number of times to handle most of your mail is zero, by not receiving it in the first place! Direct mailers send you more than double what you received in 1978. In an era in which each piece of mail adds to environmental glut, it's a civic duty, as well as an effective technique for controlling your life, to reduce the amount of junk mail you receive. You can eliminate 40 percent of your junk mail with one letter to:

Mail Preference Service
Direct Marketing Association
11 West 42nd Street
P.O. Box 3861
New York, NY 10163-3861

Write, "I would like my name removed from your direct-mail lists."

Cure Packratitis. Faced with bulging filing cabinets, ask these questions:

- Have I used this information in the last year?
- Will there be any dire consequences of tossing it?
- Can it help me, my family, my job, or my community?
- Is the information irreplaceable?

A pattern of nos is enough to put an item on your exit list. If you suffer from terminal packratism, you're probably in a lot of pain. So take these antidotes:

- Find a good home for your castoffs to reduce separation anxiety.
- With each reduction in treasures, think how many more items you have room for.
- At least quarterly, reexamine everything you own and practice creative trashing. This will get easier and go faster each time you do it.

Say, "Off with Its Head!" Clear the in boxes of your mind and your desk with the royal approach: Regard each piece of paper that enters your personal kingdom as a potential mutineer, rebel, or disloyal subject. Each piece of paper has to earn its keep to remain inside the palace gates. Were it to speak, it would have to convey an important message to you in a royal minute (fifteen seconds). Otherwise, "Off to the shredder!"

Organizing the Media Flow

Touch That Dial. To be well informed and stay sane, you need to tune in selectively. Instead of being buffeted by news coverage that skips around the world and changes topics at the speed of "And now this," have a listening plan. For ever-changing headline news, you can listen to your car radio, skim the front page of your daily newspaper, or watch the first few minutes of your local TV news broadcast.

For information you need to fully understand and remember, tune instead to more focused news shows and specials that treat subjects in depth. They offer you a way to ensure that such important information goes into your long-term memory bank.

Close the Switchboard. Turn off your information receptors for several hours each day. Do not let new information invade your being if it doesn't relate to you, your family, your community, or any area of your life, or if it comes after hours.

Organizing the Phone

Stop Playing Telephone Tag. Telephone tag—that endless cycle of returning calls only to find that the caller is unavailable—is the most virulent communication disease we have today. It cannot be stamped out entirely because there are so many careless carriers. However, here's what you can do to help:

- Assume that whomever you call will not be able to speak with you. Therefore, have a message in mind to leave on an answering machine that will clearly state your business, with instructions for answering you so that "his machine can talk to your machine."
- Determine which of the people you talk to really are unavailable. Some people use telephone tag to avoid certain conversations, and others gain a sense of importance from having a string of calls to return. Check your own motives in this regard to make sure you're not guilty of "tag abuse."
- Before you initiate a conversation, ask yourself, *Is this call really necessary?* Could you find the information more quickly yourself?

Keep Calls Short. When you're returning a phone call to a real talker— or you're simply short of time—make the call ten minutes before a scheduled appointment. Open the conversation with this statement: "I've got an appointment in ten minutes, but I really wanted to talk to you now." Focus on one topic for six minutes, then sum up with "It's almost time for my appointment, so I need to wind it up."

For this system to work, you need to have the opening and closing statements clearly in mind, keep your eye on the clock, and stay with your plan. Don't commit to "finish up later" in an added phone call. *Do* commit to a meeting sometime in the future if you want or need to be with this person. If not, continue the limited phone call approach until he finds another listener.

There are additional benefits to this system: While you're watching the clock, you might find that you're part of the problem. You might be rambling yourself or asking open-ended questions that keep the other person talking.

Work the Phones. Portable, cellular, and speaker phones; answering machines and voice mail; faxes and E-mail. The advances in telecommunication grow daily. Are you using them fully? Review the technology you have now and see if you can find new ways to control your time, money, and energy by working your phones.

Organizing Your Home

Clear the Decks. The more you are able to keep flat surfaces clear—the dining room table, your desk, small tables—the greater your ability to manage the flow of items in your life, deal with them capably, and move on. You will experience a wonderful sense of control.

Avoid leaving things at inappropriate outposts. If an item belongs in the den, take it to the den. If it belongs in the closet, go to the closet. When you fail to take items to their end destinations, you create double and triple work for yourself. And you feel overwhelmed.

Organizing Consumer Choices

Analyze the Gadgets That Getcha. VCRs, CD players, camcorders, exotic telephone systems, cameras, fax machines, security systems, automatic coffee makers, microwave ovens, and upgraded computer software can improve the quality of your life tremendously. But they involve details—lots of them.

Awareness, purchase, consumption, and maintenance of these products are draining, to say nothing of the mental energy it takes to learn how to use them. Every new gadget pilfers a portion of your life by taking time, money, and energy. Think how many impossible VCR-type manuals you have struggled through and finally abandoned.

To avoid such expensive, ego-deflating experiences, consider two points before you purchase that next gadget: (1) What are the intended benefits? (2) How easily can you understand, receive, and enjoy those benefits? If you're not comfortable with the answers, don't buy the gadget now.

Map Out a Supermarket Strategy. No matter how many items the supermarket stocks, you can continue to buy what you have always bought, tuning out the rest. You like to try new things? Then on each trip to the supermarket, make a goal of exploring one new area. It could be in the meats, fruits, cheeses, frozen foods—whatever.

Be a Selective Giver. Being selective in the causes you support pays off for both you and the organization of your choice. There is little utility in resonating with all the world's challenges and problems. Contributing fifteen dollars each to five organizations accomplishes nothing other than covering the costs of sending their mailings to you. Instead, pick one cause or one issue, and support it fully. In addition to contributing money, take some kind of action outside your home. Action is invigorating, as is seeing the results of your support.

Organizing Energy

Don't Say, "I'll Do It This Weekend." Do you let errands pile up and then spend your entire weekend completing them? Come Monday morning you feel unrested and resentful that you didn't enjoy your weekend. Avoid this painful syndrome by designating one evening a week as Errand Night. Set time limits and plan to eat fast food that night to stay in your efficiency mode.

Batch Chores. Handling tasks in groups saves time, energy, and money. In one trip, take all your repairs to the tailor, your clothes to the cleaners, and your giveaways to the thrift shop. Return phone calls in batches, making sure you have all the information at hand that you need to complete each call successfully. Pay your bills for a given time span at one sitting. When you can afford it, pay for a month in advance (you'll save lots of money doing this with your mortgage payments). Have a specific time to press and repair the clothes you'll wear during the coming week. Shop for groceries or toiletries once a week, and buy in quantity. Think in "units" to consolidate and conquer the little time wasters.

Learn Small but Mighty Skills. Many of the details of life can be quickly and easily handled with one specific skill. For instance, say the lining of your jacket droops down. If you have the bare minimum of sewing skills, you can tack it in place in a matter of seconds. If you don't, you suffer an array of inconveniences: finding something else to wear that day, getting the garment to and from a tailor or seamstress, paying for the repair, and being without the garment for four or five days. So look around your life and see what small skills would make your life easier. Can you program your VCR? Hang a picture? Get instructions from a magazine article, a friend, or appliance directions. Once you get a mental toehold, you'll probably find that your brain is ready to develop further expertise in that area. Sewing on a button is one small step past tacking up the lining in your suit jacket.

Know When to Call a Pro. To save your time, money, and energy, there are tasks you *should* hire others to do. Face it—some chores are beyond your abilities: renovating your priceless antique chair, for example. Botching the job is costly and makes you feel foolish.

There are other tasks that you can probably do pretty well, such as cleaning out your closet or fixing a flat tire. However, you can learn a lot about your wardrobe by having a wardrobe organizer manage that task for you. And repairing a flat takes special tools and energy you may not have. Experts can do these jobs in one-quarter the time you'd take, leaving you time to do what *you're* best at.

Also, sometimes your time is worth more than the few dollars you could pay to someone else to handle tasks. Okay, so it feels like a lot of out-of-pocket dollars. You're worth it!

How do you find these experts? In any urban or suburban area today, if you peruse the classified ads, shoppers' newsletters, and library and community bulletin boards, you can find nearly every service conceivable. Take a few minutes soon to acquaint yourself with your telephone book and any other directories you have on hand.

Buy Time-Saving Tools. Whether or not your organization will pick up the tab, what is it, right now, that you know will increase your efficiency? A modem? A pocket dictionary? A desktop copier? A laser printer?

Rule of thumb: Any item that saves you one hour per week for a minimum of one year and costs a thousand dollars or less is an excellent buy.

Rule of forefinger: It doesn't matter whether or not you purchase the latest or fastest model; there will always be later and faster models.

Fight Back at Traffic. There are many ways to mitigate the frustration of traffic snarls: Distract yourself with tapes; busy yourself by making lists and solving problems; relax yourself with stretching and deep breathing; avoid the jam by changing routes or your schedule. But have you considered an all-out assault on the jam thing? Think about moving closer to your job, changing jobs, starting your own at-home business, getting out-stationed from your current job, or retiring. These measures may sound draconian, but maybe they'll shock your brain into producing a creative alternative to that daily commute. (Figure it out: Two hours a day on the road means you'll spend more than a year of your life commuting during a twenty-year career.)

Organizing Your Time

Make a Back-to-Front Calendar. Use your personal calendar to achieve your priorities by first entering the deadline by which a goal is to be completed. Then, plot the subtasks and activities that you need to undertake from the due date back to the present day. This helps you establish realistic interim dates that reflect available resources, vacations, holidays, weekends and other off-hours, and reasonable output levels.

Estimate Durations. Listing tasks and appointments in your calendar can be more useful if you estimate how long each activity will take to complete. Specify beginning and ending times for such events as a meeting, your dentist appointment, and gathering materials for your night class. These specifics help you to avoid overscheduling and enable you to stay on time. You'll have time to get from one appointment to another without breaking the speed limit, plus some breathing room to review what you've done and preview what you will do next. A long-term benefit can be that you will develop a better sense of time and clearer view of where you're lacking in efficiency. The short-term payoff is the good feeling you get when you put an X through each item you've completed. And if you finish early, you'll feel even better.

Envision Your Day. Tomorrow morning, while getting ready for your day, rather than switching on the radio or TV, quietly envision how you would like your day to be. Include everything that's important to you. Mentally see your activities and interactions with others, from the start to the finish of the day. With this exercise alone, you'll begin to feel a greater sense of control over aspects of your life that you may have considered uncontrollable.

Take a Transition Minute. You say you don't have a moment to relax; every part of your day is taken? Linger an extra minute at lunch, in the restroom, and at the start and close of each day. Allowing yourself to have transitions between activities decreases your feeling of being rushed and improves thinking.

Take this transition minute to recall a pleasant experience or time when you felt particularly relaxed or calm. Take several deep breaths; drink a sip of water. You'll return to your tasks a little calmer, a little stronger, and a lot more motivated.

It's easy to feel swamped by all the details of your daily existence. Each day, keep watch to make sure the small stuff doesn't start to dominate you. Whether you are besieged with paper or trying to cut through the clutter of your closet, think about what you want from this life at this time or this year. Then create systems to tame the small stuff, and save your mental and physical energy for the big decisions—the topic that comes next.

11

Making Wise Decisions

The test of a first-rate intelligence is the ability to hold two opposed ideas in the mind at the same time, and still retain the ability to function.
—F. SCOTT FITZGERALD

Once he makes up his mind, he's full of indecision.
—OSCAR LEVANT, ON DWIGHT D. EISENHOWER

Should you retire early and move to Arizona, or stay in the town where you've always lived? Take that trip to China, or keep the money to enhance your financial security? Buy a new car, or keep this one until it dies? Call that man you met, or wait for him to call you?

Life is full of decisions, not only for the young, but for elders as well. In fact, many of the most significant ones have to be made around the time of retirement (or nonretirement!).

Many people worry that they aren't up to these important decisions, the ones that require thoughtful reflection. And they worry that, as they age, they'll be even less able to make valid choices.

The reality is that the ability to make good decisions actually improves with age. This chapter will help you appreciate, and take full advantage of, your potential for making timely, sound decisions.

Why Older Is Wiser

The Value of Experience

One reason decision making improves with age is that accumulated experiences tell us what alternatives are available. Then, our more measured way of thinking helps us evaluate their value, risks, and odds.

Part of making good decisions *is* being a good odds maker. Randy, a young, inexperienced bridge player, was partnered with Sam, a seasoned player and gambler, in a betting game of one-quarter cent a point. Sam kept a poker face throughout the game, even though his partner's impetuous bidding led them to eventual losses of nearly a hundred dollars. After the game, Sam invited Randy to a drink at the bar and some friendly advice: "Don't ever play bridge for money, and, for the sake of our friendship, don't ever be my bridge partner again."

You need to be a good odds maker to make the renowned "educated guess." Such foresight, processed primarily in the frontal lobes, evolves with age.

Also with age we develop reflective thinking, the ability to weigh options and to put them into context. Reflective thinking is, in part, born out of the slower reaction time most of us experience with age. And both foresight and reflective thinking help us grow wiser in decision making.

The Evolution of Decision Making

As we age, more and more layers and lobes of the brain take part in the decision-making process. An older person has access to many more thinking skills than the newborn or even the well-educated middle-ager.

When we're infants, we make decisions reflexively, in the Reptilian Brain. We cry when we're hungry, wet, or frightened. We gurgle and sleep when we're content.

During the preschool years, decision making starts to take into account society's rules: We share a piece of chocolate with little sister, but not because we've rationally decided it's the honorable thing to do. We share primarily because it gets us praise and gratitude from Mommy. The Limbic Brain has kicked in by this time; we like Mommy a lot and want to please her so she'll like us. We might also like little sister, but it is several brain layers later that we share for the good of the other person.

In the following years, we share because we recognize that sharing is one of the rules of society that we must live by. The sharing rule is difficult for us at first, but by five or six we are quite taken by rules. We even make up our own and, as a consequence, become bossy. The bossy stage often persists throughout early elementary school, when children develop leaders and followers in their play groups.

As we move through childhood, we become able to hold two different points of view—for example, an emotional response from the right brain and a rational response from the left. Now we can compare the two opinions and hypothesize about outcomes ("If I ride my bike past the Greens' house, Mom will get mad and ground me for a week"). This is the beginning of reflective thinking and foresight.

During the teen years, we unconsciously experiment with extreme ways of thinking; one moment we decide to go to X College because it has the curriculum we need, and the next, we're going to Y College because Suzy's enrolled there.

Once we reach adulthood, most of our decisions are made by the left brain, but often in uneasy compromise with the right. The process often starts in the emotional right side of the cerebral cortex. The right side sends its feelings and responses to the left side to be processed into language. When the left brain receives such urges, it compares them to the facts it knows, and then chooses what to say or think. Sometimes the left brain completely distorts the right brain's message and tells itself, *I'm not angry; I'm spanking my child to make him behave.* Occasionally, the left overrides the right brain's command. The right may want to cheat at cards, but the left says, *I'll get caught if I do, and I'll be completely humiliated.* Other times there is a clear difference between left and right perceptions of a situation. The right feels the salesperson is lying, but the left hears "This fifty percent discount is only good until five P.M. today." The decision is put on hold as the two debate.

At times, the left brain is distracted or tired and may allow a right-brain message to seep through and trigger an embarrassing decision. Picture an already-late woman who gets in the supermarket's fast lane behind three people. The fast lane slows as the clerk chats amiably with a woman who's writing a check in spite of a sign that says CASH ONLY. To quell her anxiety and anger, the impatient woman at the end of the line glances at the tabloid headline on the stand in front of her and tries to figure out what it means:

GRANDMOTHER GIVES BIRTH TO FOUR-YEAR-OLD FROM OUTER SPACE. Another checkout lane opens, and the clerk calls to the woman and the man in front of her, "I can take you two over here." The woman at the end blurts out, "Only if I can go first." Her right brain's message of *me first* slipped by her left's editing process and embarrassed them both.

The left brain usually edits our feelings for public consumption, but sometimes they slip by. This is the source of Freudian slips, too.

By incorporating both rational and emotional factors in decision making, adults have taken a gigantic step forward. But the most exciting skills develop last and are interrelated: foresight and reflective thinking. Foresight, the ability to look ahead, predict, and plan, develops in most of us by middle adulthood, even though we still often jump to flawed conclusions. Our foresight is only as good as our reflective thinking, which allows us to retrieve successful past experiences and match them to present problems or situations.

Both these skills are the result of changes in the brain itself: With age our reaction time slows, our emotions are more in balance, and the neural pathways of long-term memory strengthen. Our perspective shifts from present circumstances to the long view. The extra time it takes elders to weigh choices enables them also to put the situation into context. The greater experience of older people aids this process, because the left brain can base the choice on actual experience rather than theory or personal bias.

However, these developments are not automatic. Many of us gain foresight in our thirties; some never have it. Many of us use our slowed reaction time to become more reflective, and some of us simply get slower. It's up to you to use your brain's changes to best advantage. Luckily, making sound decisions is a skill that can be improved with practice.

STYLES OF MAKING DECISIONS

As adults incorporate rational and emotional factors into decision making, they tend to use one of three styles: Lawful, Waffle, or Aweful. Each of us uses all of these styles, but we tend to use one more than the others. Each is valuable when used at the right time, but each can create problems when used every time, regardless of the kind of decision we're making.

Lawful

Lawful decision makers want to know what is legal and socially accepted. They decide by the rules, and stay with the tried and true ways. They list the important factors, rank them, then follow the rules to a tee. These people are good to have around in situations where life, limb, and freedom are at stake because they rarely throw caution to the winds. When involved in a dangerous situation, they apply logical thinking.

The downside is that Lawfuls may miss opportunities by underestimating the value and possibilities of the situation. They can throw cold water on stimulating ideas and adventures.

Lawfuls often base decisions on the values of their culture: Work hard; speak the language; get an education; be moral and kind; turn the other cheek; follow the Golden Rule.

Jean Barr has been successful because she has followed a rule of an earlier time. She grew the button import business she started on a pool table in her basement into a multimillion-dollar international operation while following this dictum: "Never borrow money to expand. There's too much worry involved, too much risk; it's not worth the grief." Most of us forget that there was a time when there was no plastic money, no charge accounts, no time payment plans. Jean's approach may seem old-fashioned to today's high rollers, but it worked for her business. Now in her seventies, she travels worldwide about 50 percent of the time and her business is expanding.

Waffle

Waffle decision makers easily understand both the rational and emotional sides of a situation. They listen to all points of view when they're making a decision and want everyone to win or, at least, no one to lose. For every chance they take, they try to counter it with the guarantee of a gain.

Wafflers often value the counsel of others, seeking input from mentors, employers, teachers, parents, and sometimes political or religious leaders. They gather opinions, then weigh their decisions carefully. They sometimes feel inner conflict, although the decision-making process can help them grow intellectually.

The Waffle style can be frustrating when you want a definitive, timely decision. The balancing act prolongs decision making, and sometimes even after they reach a decision, Wafflers remain ambivalent.

However, Wafflers rarely lose everything, making this style ideal for investing when you can't afford to lose. Wafflers won't make a million overnight, but they also won't lose everything, as the Aweful might.

Aweful

Aweful decision makers see situations in extreme ways. They are awed by possibilities, whether negative or positive. They view situations as being awfully good or awfully bad.

The Aweful's reckless style is not good for investing or betting unless it is a "sure thing," but Awefuls are wonderful salespeople and campaigners because they see only the advantages of the product or cause. On the other hand, seeing only the bad, they often can't find their way out of a negative situation.

They make decisions quickly and emotionally, and thus seem very decisive. They sometimes have more influence than their knowledge warrants, because they seem so sure of themselves.

Awefuls tend to just go ahead and do things without thinking much about the outcome—in some cases because they want to, sometimes because they feel they have no choice.

Like the other styles, the Aweful approach can be the right one when it's used at the right time. Consider the career of Billie King. As a teen, she was frustrated because her family couldn't afford to give her the clothes and entertainment money she wanted. So she impetuously decided to start her own dance band at the age of fifteen, and she continued it in her young adult years. It was an exciting and profitable way to earn a living. Later, when she was married and a mother, she gave up the band because it wasn't in the best interests of her young family. She then applied her energies and abilities to her husband's business. Now, at eighty-six, she lives in a retirement complex and heads a band of residents who play for charity functions. She handles the bookings, plays her beloved horn, and leads the band. Her Aweful decision as a teen still enriches her life, although she was wise not to let it disrupt crucial years for herself and her family.

Matching Style to Situation

Here's a story that shows the three decision-making styles in action, and also shows how important it can be to use the right one for the situation.

Seven seasoned skiers nearly died in a high-country ski trip during the 1993 ski season, which by February had already claimed nineteen lives through avalanches. Even during such a hazardous year, skiers who stay with groomed ski runs are in little danger from avalanches. But four women and three men embarked on an out-of-bounds ski trip near Aspen, Colorado, in spite of storm and avalanche warnings. They constantly heard the rumblings of snow slides all around them and finally lost their way when a subzero blizzard overwhelmed them.

One couple retraced their steps and found their way back the next day. A second couple walked uphill to get a better view and discovered a familiar landmark in the distance. They took longer but also made their way back. The remaining three debated what to do for a while, then finally fought their way to an old trading post where they were found by a search party after five days in the white wilderness.

You probably detected the Aweful style in the couple who went uphill for a better view and then struck out on their own course. The Waffle style is not quite so apparent because decisions are rarely clear with the Waffler. In this case it appeared in the threesome who debated their approach.

The couple who followed standard rules for survival, retracing their steps, showed the Lawful approach in finding their way back to safety. However, the true Lawful would never have embarked upon the trip to begin with. If the trip had been uneventful, the others would have pitied the Lawfuls who stayed behind for missing the good times. As it turned out, the adventuresome seven almost had a $250,000 contract for rights to their story. In the end, the media agents' ardor cooled, possibly because of some public squabbles among the three Wafflers. The public's intense interest in their welfare quickly faded, then turned to disenchantment when the press reported how many lives had been endangered by the rescue effort and how much money it had cost. In the end, the seven were left with extensive medical bills, the loss of some fingers and toes from frostbite, and a moral obligation to pay something toward the rescue costs of $60,000 at last count and growing.

When you can't afford to take risks, financially or physically, then the Lawful way is best. In other situations, the other two ways can be better.

Which style best describes your usual approach to decision making? You may be reluctant to claim any but the Lawful style after reading the skiers' story, but remember that the key to making effective decisions lies in matching style to situation.

You may well find that your preferred style changes throughout your life. Consider the story of Richard, the kind of guy who, as they say, pulled himself up by his own bootstraps. Born in Iowa to vagabond parents, he moved often and worked his way through Harvard by clerking in a grocery store. He often felt like an outsider. He looked forward to the time when he could be "a member of the club."

Early in his career, Richard was a Lawful. He wanted to live the gentleman's life. Although he was a manager in a shipping company down on the waterfront, he wore a shirt and Harvard tie, a navy blazer, and flannel pants each day. Other middle managers wore work pants and sports shirts to work, but Richard felt he'd earned the right to dress more formally and was determined to do so. After a while, the men began to tease Richard about his style of dress. He decided that if he ignored them, they'd soon stop. They did not. In fact, they became more strident in their teasing and things reached the point of harassment. One day, Richard even got into a fist fight with one particularly obnoxious taunter. But he persisted because he felt his standards were correct. Finally, one tormentor implied that Richard dressed as he did because he was not all man: "We all like women, but we're not too sure about you," he charged.

Richard was shocked. He was tired of this silly battle with unthinking people. He faced reality. If the way he dressed was causing him so much trouble, it was time to change. So he decided to adapt his way of dressing, and wait for another day to dress like a gentleman.

A short time later he met a beautiful, wealthy, aristocratic lady. They were married and went to France to live. They led the life of privilege that Richard had admired from afar. He had gained the financial security to live comfortably, but he yearned for missions to accomplish, goals to reach. He decided he'd have to move back to the United States to get a job. When he booked passage for the entire family to the United States, his wife seemed to acquiesce; however, she didn't show up for the departure. After intense agonizing, he left his wife and children behind and built a career back in the United States. Two of the children came to live with him about two years later.

Later, he held a post in the Department of Navy, then worked for the CIA. He eventually started a business buying and selling surplus war commodities such as motor oil, tanks, and jeeps. He became financially able to live in a very comfortable, but not ostentatious life-style.

In his seventies, he began attending exercise classes. At eighty, he entered the California Senior Games as a runner, in part because "I like to win and there's not much competition in the eighty-year-old category." Richard never remarried but has had several long-term relationships. Today he lives by himself in a classy parkside condominium complex where he is a popular companion to people of many age groups, mostly women, who live there. Last fall we saw him coming out of the movie *Ballroom Dancing*. He was waltzing and whirling down the sidewalk with a lovely woman, and looking very sharp in his navy blazer and Harvard tie.

Richard began his adult life as a strict Lawful. A little later when he met the love of his life, he impulsively married her on her terms (à la Aweful). However, achieving his dream of aristocracy started an inner debate that turned him into a Waffler. All of this occurred early enough in Richard's life so that he could become adept at shifting easily into the decision-making style that best fit the prevailing circumstances in later years. Working for the Department of Navy he was comfortable following extensive rules and regulations. Then when he lost his position through downsizing, he moved to his risk-taking, adventurous side, buying and selling commodities. And having experienced how paralyzing continual inner debating could be, he knew how to set limits on this mental process.

FOUR STEPS TO EFFECTIVE DECISIONS

Let's say you are faced with a decision. How do you begin to sort it all out? Here's a four-step process that will help you make good decisions, taking into account both the emotional and rational factors. Many of these techniques came out of our interviews with wise elders.

1. First you must define the problem and write it down. Ask yourself such questions as "What do I really want out of this situation?," "What's really bugging me?," and "Whose problem is it really?" Sometimes it helps to divide the problem into pieces, then tackle each one separately.
2. The next step is to develop options. You can brainstorm a list of possibilities, as businesspeople in industries such as advertising often do. Check with your mentors. See what your competitors are doing. Follow hunches. Sleep on it.
3. The third step is to predict outcomes. You do this informally when you ask "what if" about all your options. What are the best-case/worst-case scenarios? Reflect on similar situations, and relate this decision to others you have made. Predict, prioritize, pray.
4. The final step is to compare these choices—a monumental task when there are multiple choices, each with several possible outcomes. Yet a decision does have to be made. One of the elders we talked to advised, "Just decide—the only regret is when you don't take charge."

SLEEP ON IT

Did you ever notice that sometimes you wake up with a problem solved? Sleep allows the feelings of the right brain to come out and enables the brain to perceive patterns and solutions. Your brain puts the pieces of the puzzle together while you sleep.

THE DECISION TABLE

We've designed a "Decision Table" to help you work your way through complex choices. Here's how one couple used the table to make a major decision.

Anne and Gabe lived in Vail, Colorado, with their two school-age children. He was a general practitioner who earned about ninety thousand dollars per year. He applied for a fellowship to become a specialist in pulmonary medicine, and had just learned that he'd been accepted for a three-year program in Utah. Now he was having great difficulty deciding whether to go. The move would disrupt the entire family's way of life. They all loved the outdoor activities available to them in this warm, comfortable community. Plus, their extended families were only three hours' drive away.

In part Gabe had applied for the fellowship because his father, also a doctor, had been a specialist. But primarily he thought of specializing because it is a common way for young doctors to earn more money and gain recognition in their field. However, with the country's health care situation in a state of flux, Gabe realized that specialization may no longer be a sure track to advancement. Another unknown was Anne's career as a hydraulic engineer. Her chances for employment might be better in Utah.

There were so many emotional and practical factors involved in this decision that Gabe, normally a calm and decisive person, finally threw up his hands in exasperation and claimed, "Deciding to get married was much easier than this." The fact is, he shouldn't have been surprised at the difficulty he and Anne were having. After all, there were many more people, money, and issues involved in this decision than in getting married.

Anne and Gabe made their decision after using the Decision Table. You can see below how it worked for them. Read along and see if you can predict what their decision was.

Their first step was to list all the factors they needed to consider. It was easy to think of these factors, but not so easy to put them into words. However, Anne and Gabe found that concentrating them into as few words as possible helped clarify the important elements in the situation. The couple defined these points together because, as in any joint decision, both points of view needed representation. Then they listed them on the table below.

Important factors	No.	1	2	3	4	5	6	7
Like life-style	1							
Good environment	2							
Income decrease	3							
Training value	4							
Family tradition	5							
Wife's professional ops	6							
Families' proximity	7							

Each of them filled out a table based on these factors, but we'll just show you Gabe's to demonstrate the process. His next step was to compare each of the seven factors to one another and then decide which one was more important in each pair (comparing 1 to 2, 1 to 3, 1 to 4, and so on). Each time he compared one factor to another, he listed the preferred factor's number on the chart below.

Its structure is like that of a mileage chart, the handy guide for determining the mileage between cities that you find included in good road maps and atlases. But in the Decision Table, you are writing in the number of the preferred factor at the junction of the two factors you're comparing. For example, Gabe felt that a good family environment (2) was more important to him than keeping the fun-filled life-style (1) they were comfortable with, so he put a 2 in the box on the Decision Table where the 1 column and the 2 row meet:

Important factors	No.	1	2	3	4	5	6	7
Like life-style	1							
Good environment	2	2						

Next Gabe compared factor 1 to 3, an immediate income decrease, and decided that the latter was more important. Therefore, he put a 3 in the 1 column.

Important factors	No.	1	2	3	4	5	6	7
Like life-style	1							
Good environment	2	2						
Income decrease	3	3						

Gabe then completed the process of comparing factor 1 to the remaining factors: 4, 5, 6, and 7. You can see below that he felt that current life-style (1) was more important than the value of specialized training (4), family tradition (5), and being close to their extended families (7), but less important than a good long-term environment for his family (2), an immediate income decrease (3), and his wife's professional opportunities (6).

Important factors	No.	1	2	3	4	5	6	7
Like life-stlye	1							
Good environment	2	2						
Income decrease	3	3						
Training value	4	1						
Family tradition	5	1						
Wife's professional ops	6	6						
Families' proximity	7	1						

The next step was to compare factor 2 to the remaining factors: 3, 4, 5, 6, and 7. You can see below that Gabe regarded factor 2, a good long-term environment, as more important than all of them except an immediate income decrease (3).

Important factors	No.	1	2	3	4	5	6	7
Like life-style	1							
Good environment	2	2						
Income decrease	3	3	3					
Training value	4	1	2					
Family tradition	5	1	2					
Wife's professional ops	6	6	2					
Families' proximity	7	1	2					

Next Gabe compared 3, an immediate income decrease, with 4, 5, 6, and 7. Then factor 4 with 5, 6, and 7. He continued this process until each factor had been compared to all the others on the list. Here's how the chart looked when he was finished:

Important factors	No.	1	2	3	4	5	6	7
Like life-style	1							
Good environment	2	2						
Income decrease	3	3	3					
Training value	4	1	2	3				
Family tradition	5	1	2	3	4			
Wife's professional ops	6	6	2	3	6	6		
Families' proximity	7	1	2	3	4	5	6	

Once all possible comparisons had been charted, Gabe counted the number of times each factor had been a "winner" *in any column* and recorded the total in the appropriate box at the bottom of the chart. Then from the totals he ranked each factor in the "Rank" column at the right of the chart. You can see that the rankings are figured with the highest total (income decrease, with 6) having first place and the lowest total (families' proximity, with 0) coming in last.

Important factors	No.	1	2	3	4	5	6	7	Rank
Like life-style	1								4th place
Good environment	2	2							2nd place
Income decrease	3	3	3						1st place
Training value	4	1	2	3					5th place
Family tradition	5	1	2	3	4				6th place
Wife's professional ops	6	6	2	3	6	6			3rd place
Families' proximity	7	1	2	3	4	5	6		7th place
TOTAL		3	5	6	2	1	4	0	

Now there's one more step. To the right of "Rank" in the table below is another column in which you can list whether the factor was an emotional or practical one by writing an E for emotional or a P for practical. This step in the Decision Table helps you know whether you are making a decision based entirely on emotions or practicality. Any complex matter needs input from both your logical, left-brained kind of thinking and your right brain's intuitive thinking. As you can see below, Gabe quite correctly felt that the "training value" factor was both. Although emotional factors outweighed practical in number, it's clear that Gabe did consider the practical side of the decision and gave practical factors high priority.

Important factors	No.	1	2	3	4	5	6	7	Rank	E&P
Like life-style	1								4th place	E
Good environment	2	2							2nd place	E
Income decrease	3	3	3						1st place	P
Training value	4	1	2	3					5th place	E, P
Family tradition	5	1	2	3	4				6th place	E
Wife's professional ops	6	6	2	3	6	6			3rd place	P
Families' proximity	7	1	2	3	4	5	6		7th place	E
TOTAL		3	5	6	2	1	4	0		

The analytical, left-brained reader will want to further quantify these results by totaling the P and E ranks and dividing them by something or other to get a proper weighting of ranks, and a *definitive answer* to whether P outweighed E! Such a left-brain-preferred outcome will not occur in this case, since P and E are roughly equal in weight. However, the left-brained reader will have had a satisfying workout.

Right-brained readers will be pleased that emotional factors balanced practical considerations for Gabe. They'll also be relieved that all this quantifying and weighting is finished.

As for Anne and Gabe, they were delighted with the insights they gained from using the Decision Table. The first step, defining the factors, revealed a lot: It helped them define together what they were really concerned about. Furthermore, they realized that some of the issues were rather murky because of lack of information. It became obvious that they needed to know more about

Anne's employment possibilities in Utah and also what kind of family environment they might find there. As a result, they researched the school system and employment prospects in Utah and found that both were very promising.

Gabe was relieved to realize that the change of environment might actually be an advantage in the long run. By comparing emotional and practical rankings he saw that items related to the future welfare of the family were most important to him. When Anne saw how high he ranked her professional opportunities, she was touched, and her interest in her own career was renewed. Anne completed her own Decision Table, and they could see at a glance where they differed and agreed upon factors.

Then they projected forward three years and found that the move would mean challenge and growth for all of the family members. As for Gabe's quandary about whether specialization would continue to be a money and prestige builder, he decided that he really wanted to improve his medical knowledge and skills whether or not it brought in more money. Once they'd gone through their Decision Tables, they easily agreed to move.

But the table does seem like a lot of trouble, doesn't it? So give yourself a pat on the back for working your way through the explanation. Declare a My Brain Appreciation Week. While you're at it, give yourself credit for going through similar steps unconsciously even when you're making a simple decision such as which flavor of frozen yogurt to buy. It is no small accomplishment, in several seconds, to clarify what decision you're trying to make, predict the outcome of various options, and weigh all the emotional and practical factors. Is it any wonder you never know what you want when it's your turn to order?

You go through this complex process automatically and rather haphazardly—which is fine for everyday decisions. But when you are faced with tormenting problems that intertwine love, money, ethics, and authority, the Decision Table can be immensely helpful.

Try it the next time you're agonizing over a decision. Simply copy the blank Decision Table below and follow the directions given above. Notice that it allows space for ten factors. If you have more than that, review them and make sure each is a separate and clear issue, not one merged with another. For example, Anne and Gabe originally listed ''Kids' welfare'' as an eighth factor. Then they realized that *all* of the factors involved the welfare of their children and that they needed to be more specific. If you can't winnow your list down to ten, you may have several major decisions mixed together. In such a case, use several Decision Tables. After the first time through, you'll realize how easy and useful the table is.

Decision Table

Important factors No.	1	2	3	4	5	6	7	8	9	10	Rank	E&P
1												
2												
3												
4												
5												
6												
7												
8												
9												
10												
TOTAL												

Practice Making Decisions

People get better at making decisions the more they do it. In contrast, people who are not allowed to make their own decisions often lose the will and skill to do so. Long-term prisoners cannot cope with the many choices they must make ''on the outside.'' Most people in formerly Communist countries are having trouble making decisions about careers and life-style in a freer world.

What is your comfort level with decision making? Do you rely almost totally on your lawyer, doctor, or spouse to make decisions about your financial future? Do you rather automatically adopt the opinions of friends, colleagues, or a political party? A yes to any of these questions is a warning that you need to begin now to think for yourself. While it is good to consult with others, taking responsibility for doing your own research and for developing a true understanding of financial and social issues strengthens you at each step. At the same time, it strengthens your self-confidence and makes you a more competent decision maker.

Whatever your age, commit yourself to exercising decision skills that involve the most advanced functions of your brain. Use that brain to its full potential, and you'll find yourself gaining confidence and zest for life.

12

Opening Your Mind to Change

No pleasure endures unseasoned by variety.
—PUBLILIUS SYRUS

It's hard for me to get used to these changing times. I can remember when the air was clean and sex was dirty.
—GEORGE BURNS

Copper Canyon in Mexico, four times larger than the Grand Canyon, is remote and unexplored. Drug dealers camp in its recesses; scorpions and snakes slither through it; the paths abruptly descend ten thousand feet. The Tarahumara, a Native American tribe, live here and keep to the old ways. They are famous for their ability to run incredibly long distances, easily covering more than a hundred miles a day in sandals, up and down the canyon walls.

It was spring in Creel, Mexico, and twelve frustrated American tourists waited to begin their trek through Copper Canyon. They'd been packed and dressed in their hiking gear since 7:30 that morning. Noon approached and still their Tarahumara guides had not loaded the burros. Exasperated, one of the Americans wondered aloud, "When do you think we'll ever get going?" Another replied, "Well, we're on Tarahumara time here, and I think that only the Tarahumara know the answer to that question."

Eventually the burros did get loaded, and the group was able to begin its trip.

But this was only the beginning of continuous frustration and misunderstanding throughout the twelve-day, one-hundred-mile trip. Once, when the group came to a large river, the Tarahumara left inexplicably with their burros. The tourists finally learned from the American expedition leaders that the Tarahumara believed there were spirits in the river who would pull their souls from them. Because of these beliefs they would not cross the river. So the Americans sat there waiting until new guides and burros were found on the other side of the stream. They then forged their way across and continued the trip.

Spanish was the only language that the Americans and the Tarahumara had in common, and even it was spoken by only the two American leaders and the Tarahumara leader. The other five guides spoke only Tarahumara, the twelve tourists only English. This meant that communicating even the simplest message, such as "Is the coffee ready?," was a major chore. Once, the tourists were led to believe that by afternoon they'd pass through some beautiful scenery and end the day at a lovely campsite with lots of water. Neither happened, and the tourists never learned whether the explanation was a difference in definitions of what is "beautiful" and "lots of water," whether the translations were poor, whether it just didn't matter to the Tarahumara, or whether the American leaders didn't really know the terrain as well as they claimed.

When they had such unsettling experiences, the tourists worried whether they'd wasted their money and precious vacation time on a really unpleasant trip. Then they would discuss among themselves what they could do to pin their leaders down and get back some control. Then they'd arrive at some conclusion about how to bring more certainty to the venture. The last of these was a decision to insist on knowing "what time we will leave each morning and just how far we'll go each day."

The Tarahumara did not change, but eventually the group learned to adapt to Tarahumara ways and look for what was positive about the experience. The tourists finally accepted the limitations of their power to control their environment—and adapted to it. This was the most intelligent course of action. Some members of the group adapted early on, and some, less flexible, changed only grudgingly at the very end.

When discussing the trip with them some months later, we were amazed to hear that all of the tourists believed they'd had choices about how to handle the trip, and so ultimately felt in control of the situation.

Being open-minded—seeing multiple viewpoints and realizing the diversity of available options—gives you power and control. On a practical level, an open mind can help you deal with the small and large changes you face every day.

You have much more control over those changes than you think. Gathering information, discussing the change with others, and trying new things can open you up to the excitement—indeed the adventure—of change.

This chapter is about the value of being able to shift your point of view, to "change your mind" intelligently, whether the challenge is dealing with changes you didn't anticipate, solving problems that are new to you, or listening with empathy to those with different points of view. We'll focus on three ways of responding to an unknown or novel (often disagreeable) situation: adapting to it, shaping it into a better situation, and selecting another situation.

In the Tarahumara situation, adapting was the only feasible approach for the group as a whole. Selecting a new environment by starting off on their own or replacing the leaders and guides would have threatened the tourists' chances of getting back to civilization. Trying to call in a helicopter was considered, but dropped because no one had a radio. And because of the communication problem and lack of understanding of the culture, the group could do little to reshape the situation. So they quite intelligently chose to adapt.

Most of us, in a hit-or-miss manner, use these three approaches to solve everyday problems. By using them more consciously, you can improve the flexibility of your thinking.

As the world becomes more complex and fast changing, we all increasingly find ourselves struggling to reach a balance between the old beliefs and new realities. If you always stick with the old, your thinking can become rigid. On the other hand, if you always jump to the new, your thinking can become scattered and lack focus. If you balance the two, you can have the benefit of both the old ways' concrete knowledge and the new ways' possibilities.

WHY IT'S HARD TO BE FLEXIBLE

If flexibility is so good for us, why do we cling tenaciously to old ideas and points of view? There are several answers to that question, and some words of wisdom from elders who have found their own ways around these common problems.

Fixed Ideas Go Way Back

You have many *fixed ideas* that go all the way back to day one. For example, if you grew up in a family that stressed "There's one right way to do things,'' diverging from your usual way of doing things threatens a strongly held belief.

Changing your mind can be a wrenching experience when it forces you to give up long-held beliefs. You've lost a piece of certainty, and there's not much of that around these days. With age, the problem increases because we've accumulated so many more of these fixed ideas.

The danger of the fixed idea is clearly and easily seen in the creative process. For example, have you ever thought of a phrase or line for a letter, report, or poem that you were absolutely in love with? Something like ''They lived in splendid isolation.'' Then you spent hours trying to write around the phrase and find a way to use it. The fixed idea can make life unnecessarily difficult and actually quash your creative output.

Charlotte Conover, an artist in her nineties, does not allow fixed ideas to hem her in. She explained, ''I have to be flexible. I can begin painting a canvas knowing what I want to paint, but there's an undefined goal also in my mind that keeps modifying the picture in response to the unexpected colors and shapes that emerge on the canvas. And I end with a finished work that probably will not resemble anything I started out with.''

Next time you find yourself frustrated from trying to make your actions fit a ''fixed idea,'' modify them to respond to the unexpected, the way Charlotte does.

Change Is Uncomfortable

Trying on a new idea is an *uncomfortable* experience. It is as though you have the old point of view and the new point of view side by side in your mind, each one vying for dominance. Most of us grow weary of the struggle and capitulate to the entrenched point of view. It usually takes many assaults on the old idea before a new one is accepted.

One way to increase your comfort is to be on the watch for small changes within your comfort range. With experience, you will grow more comfortable with change.

Dr. Miles Markley, an eighty-eight-year-old dentist, inventor, and mentor of many young men and women in the field of dental health, has always been on the lookout for new ideas, and thus is extremely comfortable with change. He says, ''I'm always sucking in ideas like a sponge, whether I'm watching TV, eating, talking to someone, traveling, looking at other people's work, whatever. I'm constantly filling up my memory bank in order to improve our profession.''

By searching constantly for new ideas, you can take an active role in changes rather than a passive one, and thus feel more comfortable with change.

Change Can Threaten Self-image

We're often shaken when someone disagrees with us or dislikes something we admire. Differing viewpoints threaten our *self-image,* making it difficult to stay open to new ideas.

Donald R. Seawell, the 82-year-old founder and chairman of the Denver Center for the Performing Arts, points out that performing artists are no less resistant to criticism than the rest of us. In fact, he remarks, "Take Noël Coward for example. Noël was the most complete man of the theater— composer, lyricist, playwright, director, actor, singer, dancer, et cetera. He ignored all criticism from the press. When working with Noël, you could get him to make a change only by suggestions so subtly made that he thought the ideas his own." However, Seawell says, "In putting together something as complicated as a theatrical production, flexibility in the creative process is essential. No play or musical ever sprang full grown from an author's head or any combination of heads involved in the production process. But there does come a time when it is necessary to 'freeze it.' That comes before the dress rehearsal." And living life is at *least* as complicated as a theatrical production. Flexibility is essential, and taking a stand or making a decision is also essential.

On the other hand, many people welcome criticism as a way of getting more information. These individuals realize that each person's view is just that—an individual opinion, a subjective view.

The value of welcoming such subjectivity is twofold. First, it enables one to access a broad range of views so that we can choose the best among them or combine several. Second, it provides us with greater psychological freedom to accept or reject the opinions of others as well as our own. It helps us to become more open and flexible."

Seasoned writers have a similar point of view. They welcome the reader's questioning of their material. How else do they know if they're making their intended point?

So if someone questions your point of view or a change affects you negatively, think of yourself as a professional communicator who needs others' input, not as someone whose value is in question. Welcome the other opinion but keep in mind that it is just one person's judgment and, even though it has some value to you, is no reflection on your character or abilities.

An eighty-six-year-old anthropologist, author, and researcher, Ruth Thone, tells how flexibility helped her research: "One of the greatest strengths of my research was the feedback I received from others. People who represented a variety of opinions and backgrounds helped keep me flexible. Some of my reviewers, who ranged in age from twenty-eight to eighty-eight, had little anthropological experience. Others were talented professionals. But all the people gave me useful feedback. When I asked for input and advice, I got specific answers that could make an improvement in my research. Because these contributions have been so positive for me, I constantly work to try to maintain my flexibility."

Fear of Experiencing Regret

Another factor that sometimes keeps us locked into a point of view is the fear that we'll regret the years and energy we've already spent clinging to an old idea. Other times we refuse to give up on a career or marriage that isn't working because we don't want to live with regretting missed opportunities, what might have been if we'd only made the change years ago.

Scientists often invest many years in researching one minor point only to find there was no validity in it whatsoever. While they'd rather make quick breakthroughs with each experiment, they don't feel regret, because they learn something from each experience. As Thomas Edison said, "You don't fail, you just learn what doesn't work!"

Rather than regretting your mistakes, learn from them, by keeping an open mind.

The Realization That All Change Involves Loss

Finally, each change we experience is a *loss,* even if it is a positive change. For example, if you've always believed that you're not "management material" and you're promoted to management, you might be unaccountably unhappy. Your view of reality has just been challenged. You've lost the comfort of your old point of view, and now must give it up. Sometimes people in this position find it easier to sabotage their prospects by goofing up; witness the rookie football quarterback Marlin Briscoe, who was caught shoplifting right after it was announced that he'd be in the starting position the next Sunday.

As an eight-year-old boy said after a soccer game, "Losing sucks." At any age, I think we'd agree that losing tends to be difficult and painful. But it is generally through our losses that we become fully developed human beings.

It is easier to understand why a negative change is more difficult to adjust to than a positive one. A case in point: An assumption most of us make is that we will not outlive our children. So when an "out of order" death occurs, we are devastated. David Campbell, codeveloper of the Strong-Campbell Interest Inventory, a career-direction tool, said about the death of one of his three sons, "This was the greatest challenge I've ever had to undertake, living with the death of my young son. Thank God for the support of friends and acquaintances, many of whom had gone through a similar tragedy. They told me of the small, everyday things they did to help them deal with such an overwhelming loss. It really did help, though at the time I didn't think anything would. And I tried to remember how, earlier in life, I gained insight from difficult situations. I still try to understand what I can learn from this experience."

Campbell is more aware than most that the human thought process is intricate. His description of how he copes with this tragedy shows clearly how to handle loss through flexibility. He sought and found support from many outside areas and finally looked within for strength.

WHAT DOES MENTAL FLEXIBILITY LOOK LIKE?

Here are some characteristics of flexible people:

- Flexible people like variety in friends, entertainment, and ideas.
- They really listen and give careful thought to the opinions of others.
- They're open to feedback from others, whether it's negative or positive.
- They seek critiques as well as praise.
- They're aware of and sensitive to differences in opinions and changing times.
- They entertain the possibility that new information might necessitate a change in their point of view.
- They reevaluate their ideas regularly and eliminate outmoded ones.
- They add new facts to their store of knowledge.
- They're able to entertain several points of view.
- They stay on the lookout for strategies that no longer work.

- They look for new ways to define problems.
- They redefine insoluble problems, then start anew.

Can you think of a person you know who exhibits many of these behaviors? Do you? Now that you know what flexible thinking looks like, you can watch for it in others and add some of its characteristics to your own repertoire of thinking skills. Start by consciously adding one of the points listed above to your approach to life. For example, try consciously seeking negative as well as positive feedback to your ideas and plans.

Building on the work of Yale University's Dr. Robert Sternberg, we have found three main strategies that can help you increase your flexibility: adapting, shaping, and selecting. Let's look at these through one of the most fascinating flexibility stories we've ever heard, that of Dr. Walo von Greyerz.

Adapting

At the age of four, Walo was sent from Sweden to Point Loma, California, to be tutored by a modern religious sect called Theosophy. This intriguing group was formed in the nineteenth century to be a "School for Future Leaders of the World." Children taken to the sect's school were taught that life must be an act of pure sacrifice, and that suffering is good because it increases the chances you will do better in your next incarnation. Under these circumstances, it is remarkable that during his childhood there, Walo was able to develop a philosophy of his own that disagreed in many ways with Theosophy. To have such insights and still be able to function in an environment that ran counter to them demonstrated a high level of adaptability.

Shaping

Walo took advantage of his inability to gain weight, his cough, and his pale complexion to shape the rules of the school, allowing him to leave. Using his poor health and the fear of a tuberculosis epidemic at the school as reasons to be sent home, he arrived at his home in Stockholm unannounced. He was sixteen, weak, and unable to speak or understand Swedish. His parents had saved and scrimped and sent every extra penny to the school. They were so disappointed. He felt it was his fault he had not fulfilled their dreams and become "a world leader." He began hiking by himself to avoid family conversations. Even though he was in poor health, his love for the mountains pushed him onward. He found that he could "climb with his brain," which propelled his legs. In a year, his Swedish still poor, he began leading climbing trips in Switzerland. As he gained confidence in his ability to hike and to lead others, others who couldn't speak Swedish either, his confidence spread to other areas. He had successfully *shaped* himself by building on his strengths and moving to an area where the impact of his weakness, his poor Swedish, was minimized. Walo says, "I found that I could learn things that I thought were impossible. I got a great feeling of self-confidence. I could handle things."

Selecting

Walo wanted to set up a civil defense system for all of Sweden. In order to get funding for such a broad plan, he decided to take another risk. In 1938, many Swedish medical professionals were afraid of Hitler. They wanted Sweden to have a master plan of civil defense that included sophisticated bomb shelters, but they did not know how or where to build them. Walo volunteered to find out. In order to make his information compelling and to be sure he was heard, he decided he "must speak from reality, not just theory." So he initiated a plan, an absolutely new approach that would dramatize the difference between the needs of civilians and soldiers for aid. Much was known about the needs of those in the trenches, but not about the needs of thousands of civilians dislocated by mass bombings.

To discover the principles of a civil defense system for Sweden, he had to go where the action was. So in 1942 he went to England, which had already set up bomb shelters and civil defense systems to deal with the constant air attacks of the Nazis. "I went each night into the streets of Liverpool, Bath, or Southampton to be bombed, and if I survived I knew I would go to my apartment only to be bombed again. For three months I thought that every night would be my last. From a medical point of view, we were all in shock. *Pity* was a word we did not use—we just made decisions, focusing our attention on who will live and blocking out those we believed would not. The happiness I felt when I found someone alive in the debris is indescribable. During that period of my life I had a feeling of absoluteness. What is, is what exists right now! I had the exquisite feeling of being alive in every sense, and I felt love for all mankind. I now know that living is giving and giving only. That is my philosophy of life. How lucky for me to have discovered this gift for living in my young adulthood." In the horrifying scenes of death he found a life more purposeful than any he could have imagined, a life of helping others.

After medical school, Walo began a practice in family medicine that today is more than fifty years old, spanning three generations of patients. He lectures on family medicine to medical students across the United States and internationally. Recently a third-year medical student at the University of Colorado described him as a fabulous person, as well as a skilled and knowledgeable instructor and teacher. She remarked, "He is so emotionally engaged as he teaches. He brings us along with him." His teaching has shaped many present and future physicians.

Walo first *adapted* to the school of Theosophy. He then *shaped* his environment by creating a way to leave the school, and *shaped* himself by finding ways to regain confidence and skills. Finally, he took the necessary risks to *select* a new environment, first in the bomb shelters of England and then as chief medical officer of civil defense for Sweden.

Although Walo's life has presented him with quite dramatic challenges requiring unusual flexibility, your life no doubt has presented you with some whoppers, too. Or it will in the future—you can be sure of that.

Here are some ways you can increase your abilities to adapt, shape, or select.

Adapting for Successful Change

You might think that adapting is a passive approach, but in reality it requires mental action. To adapt not as a victim, but as a manager of your own life, you need to take charge and decide that adapting is the best thing to do at this time, a way to get through a rough period.

A few winters ago, in her early fifties, Jacquelyn found herself challenged by a quite sudden change. Jacquelyn broke her neck in a skiing accident, which slowed down her life. She had a metal halo screwed into her head and couldn't fly for nine months, stopping her usually energetic schedule. With no choice but to remain immobile, she had to adapt. But there is passive adapting and active adapting, and she did the latter. *This is different,* she remembers thinking. *What can I make out of* this?

She jumped off the lecture circuit and went back to school to earn a Ph.D. And to her surprise, she found a sense of peace in a calmer life. As she considered the situation, she realized that for the first time in her life, she was free of responsibilities to work, to care for others, even to engage in sports and other recreational activities. Her only job was to get well. She loved her usually busy schedule but thought a break would be good. She began to enjoy the luxury of "doing nothing" for a while. She read the books that had been piling up, and she used the time as a hiatus from normal life. She reflected, looked inward for a change, and discovered how beautiful quiet living could be. Without the adrenaline rush from being constantly on the edge, overbooked, and overscheduled, freed from scrambling to stay current in many fields, she discovered the joy of fully experiencing fewer things, whether a book, a field of study, or a relationship. Because she chose to adapt, she passed through the time with pleasure, rather than frustration and bitterness.

Successful adapting requires a positive choice. If you merely try to avoid the situation, or put off thinking about it, you aren't adapting. One reason people often freeze up when they see a change coming is that the situation looks too hard and confusing. Here's how to adapt with ease.

Make Sure the First Step Is an Easy One. Select an action you're already good at and don't mind doing. For Jacquelyn it was reading at leisure. Then choose steps that are the *right size* for addressing the change—not too small or too large. For Jacquelyn that meant talking to her business clients by telephone once a month instead of meeting with them every week or ten days.

For a physical example, consider a tennis player adapting her game from a hard surface to a clay court. An easy first step might be changing the type of shoes she wears. Then she can adapt her best stroke, say the forehand, to the slower surface. Later, she can work on other strokes, and on strategies used by opponents.

To take another example, if your boss or spouse is time oriented and you're not, easy first steps you could take to adapt include wearing a watch, putting a clock in each room at home and in a prominent place at your office, or setting timers. Another small step might be to test yourself when walking or talking with another to determine if you can tell how much time has gone by. After jotting down your guess at the amount of time, check your watch. Make it a goal to accurately gauge ten minutes, thirty minutes, and an hour. This small step will help you to view time in a new way.

Reframe the Situation. Reframing is seeing things, problems, situations, or people in new ways. Jacquelyn could reframe her injury as a gift of time. The tennis player can reframe by seeing the new court surface as interesting rather than irritating. If you're learning to be time oriented, it can be reframed as a puzzle or a game instead of an obligation. Other examples: If your taxes go up, see it as the benefit of an improved property value. If your child isn't accepted into an accelerated program, see it as a chance to work individually with him or her.

Broaden Your Range. Look wider and further when thinking about what you really want. Jacquelyn could allow dreams and intuitive thoughts to guide her to new ways of living. An aging or injured tennis player might try playing doubles instead of singles. The person learning to be time oriented might study biorhythms or astrology, or learn views of time in other cultures, or the difference between *chronos* and *kairos*. An increase in taxes might signal a time to sell or to talk to real-estate agents and neighbors. By doing this you might find out about condos on a golf course or retirement options that broaden your range of choices.

SHAPING THE SITUATION

Whereas adapting requires one to fit into the environment, shaping involves fitting the environment to oneself.

If the tennis player feels a match is getting away from her, she can change the pace by slowing her walk from court to court, or by slowly stretching at each court change. A person in a time-oriented office can change his hours to start and end earlier (so no one really knows what time schedule he is on) or bring in information from management books stressing the correlation between business effectiveness and individuals' working at their own time orientation. A school's rejection of your child might encourage you to look at alternative preschools or to start one yourself. Shaping requires:

Setting a Goal or Outcome You Want to Achieve. "I may not win this match (or job, or race), but I do want to win at least three games (or have an interesting interview, or complete the full five miles)."

Discovering the Other Person's World Through Listening. Stephen Covey, author of *The Seven Habits of Highly Effective People*, says, "Seek first to understand, then to be understood." In shaping changes that involve differences with others, start by looking for the other person's point of view. Practice considering another point of view while putting yours on hold. Visualize your opinion as a finger held behind your back for a minute.

The next time you have a disagreement or misunderstanding, consciously try to imagine and understand the other person's reality first. As a therapist friend says, "You don't have to lose your position by simply listening and understanding another."

Keeping that other perspective in mind, you can gently guide and shape the situation. For example, a client entered the office of his physical therapist furious, stewing, and red in the face. All he could say was how mad he was because he had just been given a traffic ticket. Mary, the therapist, first gained rapport by empathizing with his concern, but just could not calm the patient down. So finally she led him to another view through questions. She asked, "So you saw the lights of the police car in your rearview mirror?" The man said, "Yes." "What did the police officer look like? Was it a man or a woman?" As he described the situation, he moved from an emotional to a thoughtful perspective. Mary shaped the situation by moving him from his feeling mode to his visual mode. By doing so, she gained flexibility for herself and her client. She empathized with him and then moved the client through shaping in order to hold the physical therapy session effectively.

Leading Through Mirroring. When you're trying to establish rapport, imitate the expression, intensity, gestures, and stance of the other person. When you're in sync, start altering your movements bit by bit. Usually the other person will unconsciously mirror your behavior. This works well when you're trying to soften another person's attitude toward you.

Shaping can help change situations. A psychologist used some gentle shaping to help a ninety-three-year-old former engineer named Julian whose move into a residential care home had caused him to feel great anxiety and to withdraw from his interests. Through his discussions with Julian, the psychologist drew out the things that were really important to him—care and privacy, but above all, interaction with others. Julian concluded, rightly, that he was exactly where he wanted to be; the move had really been his choice. With this realization his voice resumed its former powerful tone and his interest in the worlds of politics and sports returned with a vengeance. His family members were amazed by the change. When Julian admitted that he was having more good discussions and more interesting company there than he used to in his own house, they all agreed with him that "I sure picked the best place."

SELECTING NEW SITUATIONS THROUGH PROGRESSIVE RISK TAKING

While adaptation to change entails fitting yourself to the new situation and shaping involves fitting the environment to you, there are times when neither of these approaches works. Then you may choose, or select, a new job, home, partner, or environment.

Selecting new situations involves risk—usually one of four kinds, first described to us by David Campbell:

Physical Risk. The first and most obvious type of risk is physical. People who are avid participants in such activities as motorcycling, skiing, scuba diving, mountain climbing, parachuting, or auto racing usually enjoy the others or, at least, are willing to think about doing them. Their limbs are always on the line.

The benefits of physical risk taking, when successful, include the thrill of meeting a challenge and succeeding, the camaraderie that grows within a group of daredevils, and the increased self-confidence that comes from knowing you can handle yourself in sticky situations. It can also help you gain a new perspective. The author Frederick Forsyth commented, "Whenever I am stuck, when ideas or words just don't come, I go skydiving. Why? Because I fear heights more than anything, and the fear, excitement, and sheer challenge of the physical activity—the need to focus completely on what I am doing—clears the blocks, it gets me unstuck, and I am once again able to write."

Outward Bound was formed after the Second World War when it was discovered that older sailors cast adrift at sea survived much better than younger, seemingly healthier ones. When interviewed, the older sailors said that they had survived other similar, tough situations, and so they felt sure they could survive this one. Learning how to handle risky physical situations generally transfers to the ability to deal comfortably with difficulty in other walks of life.

Financial Risk. Financial risk taking is gambling with your money or, more generally, your career, as in changing jobs or expanding your responsibilities. By doing so, you are putting your bank account, current and contemplated, on the line.

The benefit of financial risk taking, when successful, can be vastly increased financial assets with all the freedom that money can buy, as well as the exhilaration of success in mastering a new system. A successful job change inevitably increases your talents and assets, which means you can attempt even larger risks in the future.

Intellectual Risks. If you don't take a chance now and then, you stand still—and then you begin to slide backward. The benefits of intellectual risks include the invigoration of fresh thinking, the ability to adapt to rapidly changing conditions, and the ability to survive and even thrive in different cultures. It sometimes feels threatening because there is the pain of inferiority if your idea later appears stupid, and the insecurity that may come from leaving your traditional values to embrace new beliefs.

Empirical research shows again and again that an individual's intellect is strengthened by expressing well-formed opinions and beliefs, by publicly supporting an unknown cause or person, or by discussing an unpopular or new view.

Interpersonal Risk. This means opening up to another person—telling new acquaintances that you admire them, enjoy being around them, and would like to spend more time with them. This seldom happens in our society, or at least happens very slowly, because we are so afraid of rejection.

The benefits of success include expanding your group of friends and intimate acquaintances, building a social circle for you to share your joys and sorrows with, and perhaps the stimulation of finding someone else on your wavelength. Virginia Woolf vividly described the zing that comes when two new friends meet. "Habits that had seemed durable as stone went down like shadows at the touch of another mind, and left behind a naked sky with fresh stars twinkling in it." This is perhaps what an acquaintance of ours named Lynn meant when she remarked about her growing friendship with Janet, a lesbian: "After years of believing lesbians were strange, difficult to work with, and so different from me that we'd have nothing in common, knowing Janet is like discovering a foreign country! She has opened my eyes to a whole new world of thoughts, feelings, and values."

Once you leave your family group, risk taking is one of the few ways that love will come into your life, because opening oneself to love always involves that dangerous feeling of losing control.

Taking Risks Gradually

Attempt small risks, with small penalties for failure, first. If the results turn out well, your increased self-confidence will help you take on bigger risks. Not all risks have happy endings, of course, so going slowly also gives you the opportunity to stop the process if you can no longer afford an unsuccessful outcome.

You can control the outcome of your risks by being prepared and well informed. To attempt to climb Mount Everest as an absolute novice would be foolish in the extreme; you would not survive. But to work up to it by studying and practicing climbing techniques, by carefully planning your logistics and strategy, and by joining talented teammates would improve your odds immeasurably.

A similar strategy is good for less dramatic settings, too. The more experienced and better equipped you are, the more likely that your risk will succeed, and that you can continue on to bigger ones with the larger payoffs that come from success. But start slow—in the area where you feel most comfortable. Soon you will feel comfortable in more areas than you might imagine.

Also, you may find that the searing failures that once terrified you no longer seem so catastrophic. The loss of one's job is less threatening after you have successfully changed jobs two or three times and know that it can be done. The loss of a thousand dollars in the stock market is destructive only if it's the last thousand dollars you have. If you have accumulated five or six thousand dollars in the past, however, and know that it can be done again, then the loss of a thousand is placed in a different perspective. The same process operates in the other areas of risk taking as well. Small risks lead to information and perhaps small successes, which lead to medium risks, which lead to medium successes. And it all leads to comfort with change and flexibility.

Failure will threaten progress, but keep in mind that cautious risks will keep you even or at your current level, not really drop you back.

If you want to expand your life, you have to take risks, and as we grow older, that takes more determination. As one of America's most prominent psychologists, John Gardner, wrote in his book *Self-renewal:*

Learning is a risky business, and we do not like failure. . . . By middle age most of us carry in our heads a tremendous catalogue of things we have no intention of trying again because we tried them once and failed. . . .We pay a heavy price for our fear of failure. It is a powerful obstacle to growth. It assures the progressive narrowing of the personality and prevents exploration and experimentation. There is no learning without some difficulty and fumbling. If you want to keep on learning, you must keep on risking failure—all your life. It's as simple as that.

Some Other Strategies for Increasing Your Risk Taking

Confront Your Fears. If you don't, you'll never break through your mental barriers to risk taking. Everyone experiences fear—it's as normal as breathing. But almost always, the fear is worse than reality. By facing it, you take away its power. Ask yourself, *What is the worst thing that would happen if someone said no to me or laughed at me? Would life be over if I lost my job? It might just be the kick in the pants that I need to take a necessary risk.* When you can deal with your worst-case scenario, you're home free. Facing your fears puts you in charge and gives you back your power.

Remember That the Biggest Risk May Be Not Risking Anything. Don't make your life a testimony to the road not taken. Do a *risk analysis,* and take into account not only what you can lose by taking a risk but also what you can lose by passing up a potential opportunity.

Ask for Help. The next time you need help with your career, for example, don't wait for someone to come to your rescue. Think of some people who might be able to offer good advice—contact them. What have you got to lose? If they don't get back to you or aren't willing to help, you'll be no worse off than you are right now. The future belongs to those who are bold.

Be Honest and Direct in Your Dealings with All People. The next time you are dissatisfied with goods or services that you've purchased, take a risk and say something about it.

Take a Risk Every Week. Start small. By simply taking one risk a week, and recording it in a notebook, you'll gain the confidence you need to act more flexibly. Here are some examples. *Physical risk:* Plan a hike to the nearest park, take a bicycle ride for three miles, or investigate the options at an athletic club. *Financial risk:* Place a wager on a current tournament or game in your community or buy a lottery ticket. *Intellectual risk:* Sign up for a book club or Toastmaster International; attend a political caucus or a lecture on the environment or the economy. *Interpersonal risk:* Try telling your son or daughter what you'd like to learn from him or her. Say you're sorry to a neighbor; reveal your fears of loneliness or your need for privacy to your roommate or spouse.

Remember That Even Failure Brings Benefits. Even if you do make a mistake, you'll learn what doesn't work, which gives you the opportunity to try new approaches. You'll also realize that life goes on despite your failures. And finally you'll learn to sharpen your risk analysis skills, so you're less likely to fail again.

As we talked with elders, we found many amazing examples of people who had faced change with courage and inventiveness throughout their lives, by choosing to adapt, to find ways to shape the change, and, occasionally, to embrace the excitement of selecting a new course.

Joanna is an inspiring example of adapting and shaping her environment. At the age of eighty-six, she had a stroke on the left side of her brain, paralyzing the right side of her body and leaving her unable to speak. After three months, however, her doctors were amazed at how well she was doing. They speculated that because she had always played the piano, she had developed speech backup centers in the right side of the brain. Although her words are still few, she is shaping her environment by going out on the screened porch of her nursing home each day to be with visitors. Once when the director of the home said, "Joanna, I'm sorry, I just can't understand you," and started to walk away, Jo burst out, "Wait a minute!" The director smiled and returned. When her family started talking about moving her from Florida, her home state for twenty-five years, she sat up very straight in her wheelchair, opened her eyes wide, and started shaking her head no. She let it be known that she wanted to stay where she was.

Yet she was later faced with the need to adapt to a change of home in another way. Nervously, reluctantly, sadly, her son had to tell her that in order to stay in the nursing home, she would have to give up her lovely apartment. At first she didn't respond. Some hours later, she very intently looked at him and was able to form the words "I can accept it." What a wonderful example of adapting, and what a great relief he felt at hearing those words.

Another woman we interviewed, Betty, has shown by her life the power of selection. At the age of fifty, she lost her husband to a stroke. He died with modest savings and no life insurance, as he had just changed jobs and had not yet taken the company's physical exam. Betty would need to supplement her income. Though she'd held clerical jobs earlier in her life, she was not working outside of the home at the time. Making her job search more difficult was the fact that she had never driven a car, and the family had recently moved to a suburb without public transportation. Betty wanted a job to support herself, and the best one she could get was a purchasing position in a university thirty-five miles away. As she signed the forms accepting the position, she knew she was taking a chance. She was betting that she'd learn to drive in time.

She did. At first her daughters gave her driving lessons, but they were uncomfortable correcting their mother, and not clear about how best to teach her. Then her son-in-law patiently trained and practiced with her. But his availability was not always in sync with hers. Finally she scheduled a series of lessons with a driving school. After many mishaps she passed her driving test, and with faithful practice each day, she arrived for her first day of work twenty minutes early.

Betty had taken risk and changed the situation. Besides helping her keep a pleasant job, learning to drive reduced other restrictions on her life. Now eighty, Betty continues to enjoy her freedom and flexibility as well as the small university pension she now receives.

Life will present you with many changes, too—some great and some small—and the more flexible you are, and the more techniques you can learn for managing change, the more you can make those changes work for you.

13

Finding Your Passions

A bird does not sing because it has an answer. It sings because it has a song.

—CHINESE PROVERB

The time you enjoyed wasting is not wasted time.

—SÖREN KIERKEGAARD

Passion is the spark plug that keeps your engine revving along. When many people think of "passion," they think only of romantic and sexual passion between a couple, but the word also encompasses intense feelings and zeal for ideas, art, work, projects, interests, causes, and much more. A passionate person is vehement, eager, enthusiastic, intense, fascinated, dedicated, animated, vital.

Passion of this kind is a motivating force that can bring happiness and purpose to people at any age, but it is especially important in later years, for passion helps keep the mind sharp and developing, and the senses tuned up high.

Jacquelyn recently experienced the boundless energy of passion as she participated in Explore, a week of seminars, star viewing, photography, creative writing, and fly fishing in the Rocky Mountains for "active and inquisitive mature adults." She arrived at the ski resort as the opening banquet was getting under way and joined five other participants, all in their seventies. The conversation crackled. They connected, women and men discussing topics with boundless enthusiasm. It felt glorious to be around them.

The week gave many examples of their passions: the wonder and mystery of the stars seen through a mountain telescope. The sensuality of writing and hearing each other's creative thoughts. Fly fishing at dawn, photography at dusk. There was peace and serenity along with effort and energy.

In the workshops, Robert Parker, seventy-one, an archaeologist, talked of mystical burying places and glacier remains. Arthur Feldman, fifty-eight, shared his knowledge of history and sang songs until everyone laughed and joined in, feeling they'd all gone back in time. Joan Brett, fifty-two, a cooking-school teacher, sensually fondled, chopped, and caressed her tools and ingredients as she cooked. John Fielder, forty-eight, a photographer, helped the group see the mountains with new ideas.

To have such passions is a great gift, for passion brings a love of life, and the love of others.

Living Your Passion

Maud Morgan, the artist now in her nineties, says, "The love of life I feel makes me feel wonderful!" and indeed she is.

As many people do, she discovered the great passion of her life by accident. One day when she was twenty-four, an artist she was meeting for lunch was too absorbed in his work to leave the studio. He stuck a brush in Maud's hand and suggested she paint a picture while she was waiting for him to finish. "I don't know how," she replied. "It's simple," he said. "Just mix blue and yellow and you get green. Paint that." He pointed to a small pottery vase filled with anemones—blue, yellow, fuchsia, and red. Maud recalls, "I squeezed the tubes, mixed the colors, stared at the flowers, then I made some strokes. What fun! More strokes—it looked like flowers! More tubes, more colors, off with my skirt. Now I had a lovely lavender backdrop—and hours later I'd had no lunch, but what a painting! Those flowers were more appealing than the real ones. I was so excited. When the painting was finished, I realized I had discovered my life's work—art."

Success came early for her. A year later, she had her first show and sold twelve paintings. Later her work hung in New York at the Metropolitan Museum and the Museum of Modern Art, and in the Boston Museum of Fine Arts. For a long time, though, she felt uncomfortable with her success, as if there must be some mistake. "When I had the first inklings of my calling I expected a gentle, continuous confirmation of my talent, not a bolt of lightning!"

Finally she accepted her talent. And as she has grown older, Maud's art has become freer. She believes that the artist's challenge is to transform materials into the sphere of the spirit. She wants to make art that sings. In her nineties, her laugh is throaty, guttural, loud, sexy. She is so sensual— big eyes, exotic dress.

"Passion," Maud Morgan proclaims, "comes from finding and living your calling," or as Joseph Campbell stated, "Follow your bliss."

"But Maud is somewhat right-brained; 'the artist type,' " the left-brained reader might say. "What does passion have to do with me?" In our interviews, we found that passionate pursuits are not limited to one kind of thinking, career, or personality; rather, they seem to take a direction suited to one's talents (open-ended and flowing for the right-brained; definitive and specific for the left). A good example of the latter is Colonel Lloyd Wayne, a math professor, whose lifelong passion was Civil War history. When he was a teenager, he avidly read fact and fiction about the war. Soldiering in World War II taught him a lot about military strategies and equipment. He was severely wounded in the war and spent several years in hospitals, during which time he began to read about the causes and costs of the Civil War. When he was able to resume teaching, he developed a network of friends who shared his interests. In late life, the colonel collected art, rare books, and furniture related to southern history, carefully researching and cataloging each item. Until he died at eighty-eight, he was sought out by his peers, young people, and family members because his passionate pursuits made him an interesting person to be with. He was an able math teacher into his early eighties, when caring for his wife required his full-time attention at home.

Strong, longtime passionate pursuits help keep the brain vital. In neurological terms, the traveling, reading, writing, and discussing that the colonel did in connection with his passion developed a sizable network of memories in his brain. The experience of learning and cataloging information about his passion offered him a pleasurable way of refining his systematic thinking skills and passing this information on to his children. His knowledge made him stimulating to be around. His clever investments in art and antiques allowed him and his wife to have more than enough money during their last years and to leave behind a sizable estate.

By following his passionate interest, the colonel unknowingly stimulated brain processes that helped him be sharper longer.

People often think of passions as frivolous. Be responsible, keep your nose to the grindstone, earn a living, we say. But passion can have some very practical benefits—even though it sometimes takes a while to find them. Witness the case of Victor, the watch repairman who loved clocks and watches so much he couldn't stop talking about them. Instead of keeping to the backroom repair area, he was always darting out front to discuss watches that interested him with their owners. Furthermore, he always had a new marketing scheme to suggest to his employers: countdown sales to increase traffic during slow times, and lifetime watch-repair certificates to show the store's confidence in its top lines. But Victor's enthusiasm was not infectious, merely irritating to his employers. Watch repairmen were not supposed to be enthusiastic, just reliable. Consequently, Victor kept getting fired from one store after another.

Throughout his years as a technician, Victor accumulated a huge collection of watches. Some he bought at garage sales and at close-out prices; others were broken watches given to him by friends who knew of his passion. He repaired and shined all of them, displaying them in a large cabinet in his apartment. Finally, when he was once again unemployed and at rock bottom financially, he began selling his collection just to survive. Much to his surprise, they sold quickly and for phenomenally high prices. Victor realized he could run a profitable business based on his passion. Now he owns a million-dollar business buying and selling old watches and jewelry . . . and he says, "I've never been so happy in my whole life."

Passions also help you continue to find new friends and associates throughout your life. One ninety-five-year-old liked to reminisce about World War I, but he said, "All the people I used to discuss it with are gone now." Then he established a friendship with a young librarian, a World War I buff who loved to talk history with him. Soon he was the center of a group of younger people, eager to hear his war stories.

People aren't born with passions; they "grow" them—and you can, too.

The Evolution of Passion

Why and how do we experience feelings of pleasure in such diverse activities as reading a book, watching a movie, eating a pizza, and hiking through the woods? Why are our brains built to secrete "pleasure hormones" when we're involved in certain pursuits? The answer may lie in understanding what motivated our predecessors.

Lionel Tiger, the witty anthropologist and social thinker, theorized in his book *The Pursuit of Pleasure* that our ancestors' pursuit of pleasure helped them survive. We believe that similar passions still help people survive. Here are four kinds of pleasure that primitive people—and modern people—experienced.

Physical Pleasure. Running, throwing, fornicating, and eating were physical pleasures necessary to the survival of prehistoric humans. Some of today's physical pleasures retain a tinge of the primitive: eating smoked meat at an outdoor barbecue, candlelight dinners, moonlight walks, and perfumes that imitate outdoor fragrances.

Social Pleasure. Our ancestors' brains were designed to experience pleasure in the company of others. As a result, they hunted and gathered in groups, which served to protect them from their common enemies and to produce food, clothing, and other necessities efficiently. Currently we experience social pleasure by watching TV with the family, going to church, hanging out at the neighborhood bar, participating in group activities, and building attachments to co-workers.

Emotional Pleasure. Hunters and gatherers needed love to procreate and survive, so they developed family roles and emotional ties. They needed leaders to strategize better ways of stalking their prey and finding foods that were safe to eat. Some of them found pleasure in leading and some found pleasure in admiring and following these leaders. A status system and rituals institutionalized such "psychological" pleasures.

Today, some of us belong to secret societies; others follow sports teams. Politicians, executives, entertainers, academics, and theologians are accorded status for their leadership. As individuals, we enjoy achieving status on the job or in the community, or in seeing the accomplishments of someone we've mentored. But the bulk of our emotional pleasure—and pain—results from more personal attachments. Most of our energies and resources are spent pursuing the image we have of ourselves in the eyes of family, mate, friends, and associates. When we think the image is a good one, we're happy; when it seems negative, we work at self-improvement to change it.

Mental Pleasure. Prehistoric humans gained comfort and confidence from inventing a fire starter and clay pots to carry it in. When they moved from hands-on invention to painting pictures on their caves' walls, they were making a great step toward symbolic thinking, a complex process that requires many parts of the cerebral cortex.

Today, we express our ideas abstractly through art, speaking, and writing. We express our ideas concretely by inventing machines, activities, businesses, and institutions. Often the concrete and abstract expressions are part and parcel of the ''work'' we do. That's why loving your work is the ultimate high.

Our modern pursuits stimulate higher levels of thinking and thus raise the limits of human intelligence. The next time you get a tingle when you solve a problem or write a poem, double your pleasure with the knowledge that you're also helping your species advance!

Passionate Pursuits and the Brain

How is your brain helped when you follow your passionate pursuits?

According to Carl W. Cotman at the University of California, Irvine, specific brain neurons are stimulated when you engage in physical, social, emotional, and mental pursuits. In the laboratory, scientists can differentiate between the area stimulated and adjacent areas. Stimulation ''irritates'' the receptors, making them more responsive to the neurotransmitter.

Pursuing one's passions produces an overall feeling of well-being by increasing the activity of neurotransmitters. Pleasure stimulates cells scattered throughout the brain, making us feel good. (Drugs like cocaine have a similar effect on specific brain cells.)

You connect the pleasurable activity with the good feeling, and, like Pavlov's dogs, you mentally salivate every time you think of your passion. The resulting flow of neurotransmitters keeps your brain operating at full throttle so each cell is well fed and supple.

Pursuing passions also helps your right brain get equal time, thereby balancing conflicts between your two sides. Since the left side controls the expression of your thoughts through language, the right side needs a compensatory mechanism, passion, to express itself. For instance, the left brain will say to the would-be gardener: ''Did you know that the average home gardener spends three dollars a pound to grow tomatoes? And think how your knees will hurt tomorrow.''

But your passion for gardening inspires your right brain to respond: ''I feel great when I'm out here digging in the dirt. My mind clears, I sing to myself, and I think happy thoughts.''

Research indicates that constantly squelching right-brain urges causes stress that saps your energy and increases risk of illness. For example, a study of the illnesses supposedly cured at Lourdes (a town in France where the Virgin Mary is said to have spoken to a peasant girl) shows that most of them occurred on the left side of the body. Since the left side is controlled by the right brain and the illnesses were hysterical in nature, a good case can be made that a repressed right brain expresses itself by producing physical problems. A converse indicator is that individuals whose occupations allow them full expression of their passions (example, symphony conductors) live long and healthful lives.

The bottom line: Pursuing your passions is good for you physically. Constantly squashing urges to express your passions causes stress that can sap your energy and increase risk of minor and eventually major diseases.

THE ROLE PLAYED BY OTHERS

In talking with elders, we found that some people who have pursued lifelong passions were encouraged early in life. Told that their original thinking was worthwhile, and encouraged with resources and sometimes role models as well, they developed confidence in themselves and their ideas.

Some had the opposite experience. For example, they loved to read, but were forbidden to do so until their chores were done—and the chores were never finished. Sometimes their pursuit was completely outside their family's awareness. There were no books or magazines, no discussion to feed their interest; they came upon their desire without encouragement or role model. For some people, this lack of support merely whetted their appetites. For example, Jane wanted to be an architect but her family did not value professional education for girls, especially not for a man's profession, like architecture. She eventually became an interior decorator, allowing her to pursue her passionate interest in art, structure, and design.

While such delayed gratification doesn't always pay off, it is often the factor that gets the creative juices flowing. Sometimes having to postpone the moment when you can sit down and write, or go to the easel and paint, builds up such a longing to get at it that your energy level is high. This sparks a "rush" that brings disparate ideas into a coherent form. And the pleasure you feel makes all the striving worthwhile.

The human brain, once freed, can carry you into physical, mental, and emotional rapture. That's what happens when you get into a creative state.

Passions Benefit Others, Too

Not only does pursuing a passion benefit you, but it may help others as well. The passion allows you to give the best of yourself to the world.

In college, Walter Oliver was a track star. He enjoyed running, but he saw it as a means to an end. Walter was a poor black living in southern Illinois, a hotbed of the Ku Klux Klan at that time. He used his athletic ability to get a scholarship so that he could pursue his real passion, education. Later he became superintendent of elementary schools in Denver, supervised a school busing plan mandated by the courts, and wrote textbooks on teaching children to read.

Walter's wife, Edna, shares his passion for educating children. Always known as a "teacher's teacher" and a children's advocate, she was a major resource when the Head Start program was instituted in Denver. In fact, an existing center is named in her honor. Even though she was nearing eighty at the time of her interview, she plopped down cross-legged on the floor—a habit she had developed while teaching. "That's the best way to communicate with young children—down on the floor where you can be eye-to-eye with them," she explained. Throughout her interview she enthusiastically sang songs and recited poems she'd written for her classes and leaped up agilely to demonstrate other aspects of her approach to teaching.

Jean Yancey used her training as an actress to become a dynamic speaker and business consultant. Over the years she became a model for women in business. At seventy-nine, her greatest thrill is to see how far women have come since she made her first breakthrough in business leadership. As she pursued her career and passion, she was both an observer and participant in a significant social movement.

Fritz Benedict is an eighty-five-year-old visionary who developed the Aspen Institute for Humanistic Studies in addition to many commercial enterprises. The institute might never have gotten off the ground were it not for his confidence and decisiveness, and the resources and dynamic personality of the blue-eyed Elizabeth Paepke. It seemed "pie in the sky" at the time, but Fritz's assured manner persuaded others that it was a viable concept. His knowhow and leadership were key in the institute's founding and development. Today the institute is an international think tank where the likes of Margaret Thatcher and Carl Sagan hold forth on global problems and opportunities. What a legacy!

With passion, people never lose their ability to be excited about the activities, causes, and ideas that they care about.

KEEPING AN OPEN MIND

A potential pitfall of passion is becoming such an "expert" on your topic that you let new developments pass you by. You may come to believe so strongly that your ideas and passions are correct that you don't keep a lookout for new discoveries and points of view.

Even Albert Einstein allowed his passion to cloud his thinking in his later years. At sixteen, he fantasized a physics concept that was the germ of his theory of relativity; in his twenties, he experienced a sudden insight about photoelectric effects, and a few weeks later an equation, $E = MC^2$, appeared in front of him. But this easy success of his creative right brain was not matched in his later years, when he struggled to develop another concept, the unified field theory. He never made a breakthrough in this area, in part because he was not open to new ideas. He did not like the irregularity and vagueness of such concepts as indeterminacy, probability, and chaos proposed by Niels Bohr, Werner Heisenberg, and Max Born.

It's ironic that Einstein clung to old ideas and ways; in his youth he had been a rebel in both ideas and thinking style. His ideas had diverged greatly from accepted theory and he regularly used visualization and intuitive thinking to solve problems.

After his death, research on his brain tissue indicated a high level of the glial cells that "feed" the brain, so it's doubtful that his declining creativity was related to brain loss. Although there is some research indicating that the ability to visualize declines with age, the more likely explanation is attitude.

Einstein's self-limitation offers several good lessons. For one, relying too much on information from the past and believing that we have "the only answer" diminish our creativity. On the other hand, his decline in creativity did not quell his passion for discovery, only his ability. Luckily he had many other interests—such as music, sailing, and writing humorous quatrains—that filled his life.

No doubt Einstein's continuing pursuit of ideas added zest to his last years that he would not have had otherwise. He continued to enjoy the admiration, almost worship, of people around the world.

Pursuing your passions into old age will help draw others to you, too.

WHAT TURNS YOU ON?

Are you aware of an idea, a person, a project, or a physical accomplishment that really gets your juices flowing? What would you do or learn if you had no financial or time constraints? Is there anything you do, any topic you study, for the pure pleasure of it? If not, don't worry; we're now going to tell you how to get serious about fun.

The first step in developing a passionate pursuit is to respect your own interests. Have you ever longed for a long, uninterrupted time to read, write, build, work, or play? Children in Montessori schools are given that kind of time in order to lengthen their attention span and improve concentration skills. As far as the children are concerned, they're just pursuing a passion; however, it is a Montessori technique for classroom management to interrupt the child who is misbehaving but not the child who is avidly involved in a project, topic, or activity. Respect that intensity. Allow the inner child the privacy and concentration essential to problem solving. Respect *your* interests and give them time to grow.

Next, think about these questions:

1. During the past week, what has made you feel excited? What activity have you been engaged in that you didn't want to stop, that you had to tear yourself away from?
2. What kinds of news stories leap out at you? What types of movies, plays, television programs, or books do you like?
3. What hobbies or interests do you enjoy?
4. What is missing from your life? Is there a physical, mental, or emotional need you have that you ache to fulfill?
5. What are your fondest remembrances of school? Do you feel any derivative interests today?
6. What are you doing when time flows by quickly and pleasantly without your being aware of it?

Is there a pattern to your answers? If so, there's a good chance this is a passion you should pursue, if you're not already doing so. Give yourself permission to pursue it. Be a little selfish: Spend time each day thinking or doing something with it. Spend some money on it. Collect associated newspaper clippings; get a related book out of the library; attend a meeting on the subject. Know that it is good for you *and* those in your life to pursue a passion.

Whatever your age—start now. It's never too late or too early to explore—to acquire a passionate pursuit. And it always makes a valuable contribution to your life, and often to others' as well.

14

An Empowering Vision of Your Future

> I have found very few better lives than that of a former president. Once the pain is gone, once peace and acceptance arrive, the opportunities for fulfillment and satisfaction are wonderfully unlimited.
> —JIMMY CARTER'S ADVICE TO GEORGE BUSH IN *McCALL'S*

We've talked about learning and memory, about physical and emotional health, about organizing and decision making, and about developing flexibility and your passions. Each of these areas is important to know about and to cultivate, but in the years ahead some will be more important for you personally than others. You will need to focus more on some than others. There may even be one area that is the key to your future happiness.

In thinking about where to put your greatest energies, you have to consider the person you want to be someday. Ask yourself the question you always heard as a child: What do you want to achieve in your life? How would you like to be remembered? There are three places to look for answers: in self-reflection, in role models, and in seeing the choices available to you.

WHO ARE YOU?

The first place to look for the future is in the present. Clues to where you are headed can be found in who you are now. As we age, we become more truly ourselves. Research in adult development and neuropsychology has shown that core strengths and weaknesses become more pronounced over time. If you are strong-willed in your thirties, you may become domineering in your sixties. If you are accommodating in your forties, you may be flexible in your seventies.

Consider your current physical, emotional, and mental strengths. Do you get out of breath when you run to catch a bus? Are you known to be moody on a *good* day? Do you ever say about yourself, "I'm so scatterbrained"? Do you resist learning new games, skills, ideas? What would you do if you had to retire from your present career—be it homemaker or head honcho of a company? Do you need to have the final say? Over the years have you developed some habits or systems that work beautifully for you? Are love, joy, and passion in your life right now?

Make lists of the characteristics you like most about yourself, and those you want to change before they become more distilled and dominant with the years. Return to the parts of this book about the characteristics you want to develop in a different way, and change the person you will someday be. The good news is that you are not doomed to fulfill the negative myths about aging, but can shape an old age that will be enjoyable and satisfying.

Role Models

After looking within for answers, look without. Look for someone who is doing something better than you are, then model yourself after that person. When we're children, we tend to envy someone who can hit the ball better or make higher grades than we can. When you're comfortable with your own worth as an adult, you can admire others, strive to be like them, and ask for their advice.

Whether they are acknowledged or not, there are role models all around you: a neighbor, a father, a teacher, a writer, an actress, an activist. A role model does not have to be someone you want to emulate in all ways; you may admire some things about the person but not others. Learn from the strengths you see in the many different role models you find.

A role model can be old or young; for example, a twenty-five-year-old daughter who reads widely on nutrition research and shops in health food stores has much to teach about healthful eating.

Likewise, we have met many people past sixty who are inspiring role models for aging well. Some have a vast store of knowledge that they can apply to almost any problem. Some are fascinating storytellers. One can fix *anything*. Some are witty. Some always see the positive side. Some are so gentle and serene they seem almost holy. Some are irascible and strong, and have made us see things from a different point of view.

Some role models have taught us about the value of assertiveness and taking action; others have shared the joy of sitting back, reflecting, and watching things and people grow—a child, a savings account, petunias. Others talked of trusting their instincts more and the crowd less. Whether it's hemlines or politics, the majority no longer rules them. There is much we can learn from those who are going before us.

THE BONUS OF A PRACTICED MIND

From our experiences in writing this book, we discovered an attribute that seems to come in a cumulative way with the practiced, honed mind—the generous spirit. Many elders develop a spirit, a persona, that makes them self-confident and attractive, engaged and engaging, involved and content. While such grace and kindness are often attributed to a formal religion or ethical training, we believe that the truly empowered spirit emanates from personal serenity, whatever its source. Only when you are content with yourself can you be generous with others.

The elders who have this sanguine, loving spirit that makes them tolerant and caring of others often talked about reappraising themselves throughout life. Periodically they thought about how their lives were going, reviewed the past, and decided how they wanted the future to go. They made a science out of living well. Just as scientists devise theories and test them out, these elders thought about how they were living their lives, and then tested many different approaches. Some did this formally by setting goals and timetables for achieving those goals, while others were less grounded in left-brained logic—they followed their hunches, watched for opportunities, and celebrated the serendipity of life.

To be such a thinking person who can get more out of life—and give more to others—periodically ask yourself, *What did I learn from this experience? What do I want or need to learn now?* With this approach, by the time you reach your late seventies, you'll have such a wealth of experiences (successes and failures) that you will rarely be thrown off-stride. So look around now for the choices in your life and make them.

Discovering Your Many Choices

When you were a child, you may have thought your possibilities were infinite. Then you "grew up" and learned limits. As you age, you need to *un*learn the limits.

During your thirties and forties you could follow thousands of paths, but like most people you were probably too busy to choose at all. With age, you have the time, ability, and opportunity to choose. All ways to live are available at all ages. You can have nine, ten, or twenty lives—different loves, different views, and new adventures.

B. F. Skinner once wrote, "Look at aging as a trip to a new country. Find out all you can about old age so you can get excited about it—and so you can see all the choices you have."

Find a vision of who *you* want to be at fifty, sixty, seventy, eighty, or ninety, and put your energies and power behind it. Then for you, the best years *will* lie ahead.

APPENDIX A: THE BRAINMARKERS FOLLOW-UP

Now that you have read *The Forever Mind,* we're providing a copy of the Brainmarker tests that appeared in Chapter 2 so that you can retake them. In fact, you might want to make several copies to reassess yourself periodically.

Remember how it goes? You just evaluate your present level of awareness, attitude, and activity for each Brainmarker on a scale of 1 to 10 (with 1 meaning not at all and 10 meaning fully):

Brainmarker 1—Body Wisdom

awareness: I know a lot about how health affects thinking.
  low 1 2 3 4 5 6 7 8 9 10 high

attitude: I really want to adopt healthful habits.
  low 1 2 3 4 5 6 7 8 9 10 high

activity: I practice healthful habits daily.
  low 1 2 3 4 5 6 7 8 9 10 high
                    Divide your total by 3 to determine Brainmarker 1: ___

Brainmarker 2—Emotional Balance

awareness: I am aware of my emotional triggers and how to deal with them.

low 1 2 3 4 5 6 7 8 9 10 high

attitude: I want to understand my emotions and those of others.

low 1 2 3 4 5 6 7 8 9 10 high

activity: I express my emotions and try to improve the way I do so.

low 1 2 3 4 5 6 7 8 9 10 high

Divide your total by 3 to determine Brainmarker 2: ____

Brainmarker 3—Memory

awareness: I have a good memory.

low 1 2 3 4 5 6 7 8 9 10 high

attitude: I want to continue developing my memory skills.

low 1 2 3 4 5 6 7 8 9 10 high

activity: I use strategies for remembering things.

low 1 2 3 4 5 6 7 8 9 10 high

Divide by 3 to determine Brainmarker 3: ____

Brainmarker 4—Learning

awareness: I learn quickly and comprehensively.

low 1 2 3 4 5 6 7 8 9 10 high

attitude: Learning enriches my life, and I want to improve my skills continually.

low 1 2 3 4 5 6 7 8 9 10 high

activity: In the last year, I have consciously tried to add to my store of knowledge through reading, formal and informal classes, discussions, and trying new things.

low 1 2 3 4 5 6 7 8 9 10 high

Divide your total by 3 to determine Brainmarker 4: ____

Brainmarker 5—Systems for Control

awareness: I know that I need systems in my life.

low 1 2 3 4 5 6 7 8 9 10 high

attitude: I know that list making, scheduling, and organizing are worth the effort.

low 1 2 3 4 5 6 7 8 9 10 high

activity: I reassess old ways of doing things and try to systematize wherever I can.
   low 1 2 3 4 5 6 7 8 9 10 high
                    Divide your total by 3 to determine Brainmarker 5: ____

Brainmarker 6—Decision Making

awareness: I notice when I and others make wise decisions.
   low 1 2 3 4 5 6 7 8 9 10 high

attitude: I truly want to be logical, caring, and successful in making decisions.
   low 1 2 3 4 5 6 7 8 9 10 high

activity: I review my decisions, analyze why they were good or bad, and seek to improve my skills.
   low 1 2 3 4 5 6 7 8 9 10 high
                    Divide your total by 3 to determine Brainmarker 6: ____

Brainmarker 7—Openness to Change

awareness: I am aware of how differently I feel about change that I initiate versus change that's dumped on me.
   low 1 2 3 4 5 6 7 8 9 10 high

attitude: Doing things in a new way appeals to me.
   low 1 2 3 4 5 6 7 8 9 10 high

activity: I try new approaches when I am faced with change.
   low 1 2 3 4 5 6 7 8 9 10 high
                    Divide your total by 3 to determine Brainmarker 7: ____

Brainmarker 8—Passion

awareness: When I think about a certain idea or project, I'm excited.
   low 1 2 3 4 5 6 7 8 9 10 high

attitude: I believe pursuing a passion is too valuable to be postponed.
   low 1 2 3 4 5 6 7 8 9 10 high

activity: I have a passion that grows stronger with age.
   low 1 2 3 4 5 6 7 8 9 10 high
                    Divide your total by 3 to determine Brainmarker 8: ____

Now record your self-ratings on the table below. It will help you determine which of the eight skills vital to mental sharpness you have developed most fully.

	1	2	3	4	5	6	7	8	9	10
Body wisdom										
Emotional balance										
Memory										
Learning										
Systems for control										
Decision making										
Openness to change										
Passion										

Check back now and see how much progress you've made since you completed the Brainmarker evaluation the first time. Repeating this evaluation every few months, or even just once a year, will help you keep focused on the areas you wish to improve, as well as providing a gauge of how well you're doing with your Forever Mind. Good luck!

Appendix B: Design and Conduct of the Excellent Elder Interviews

The protocol for our interviews with the fifty-eight excellent elders described in this book went through an evolutionary process that was both rigorous and rewarding. Our challenge was to discover how we and our readers could stay healthy, happy, and sharp throughout life.

We decided at the outset to exclude "celebrity" interviews because we wanted experiences that were replicable by ordinary people leading everyday lives. We began by looking at what was being written about aging and mental capacities. What did the experts think comprised the ingredients of a Forever Mind? We made a list of descriptive terms used in this literature, added a few of our own, and then polled people in our seminars to further define each description. Next we surveyed forty-two adults to make sure the list had left-brain/right-brain balance. Then we winnowed it to the list at the end of this Appendix.

We used this list to solicit candidates from "professional interviewers," individuals who by the nature of their work, talents, and lives were in contact with a number of older people whose mental abilities they could easily discern. We asked the professional interviewers (counselors, journalists, lawyers, therapists, doctors, educators, personnel managers, and others) in their forties and fifties to nominate the sharpest person they knew who was at least seventy years old.

Our next step was to devise an interview approach that would elicit the information we wanted—what had these sharp elderly people done during their lifetimes that made them so mentally acute, so involved, and so much in demand in old age? We had already chosen specific questions to cover the mental, physical, and emotional categories found in our study of the literature. We first tested the questions on younger people and a sampling of elders. There were unplanned benefits from this pilot group; for example, we noted a clear contrast between the answers of different age groups, plus we became comfortable with the interview instrument and were able to ask the questions in a conversational way.

We also needed a way of organizing and analyzing the data that we would gain from the interviews. We found a method for conducting qualitative research called the Ethnograph. It seemed ideal for our purposes because the Ethnograph helps the researcher convert data from recorded interviews into quantifiable form by identifying and counting key words or responses to specific questions.

Thus, from our taped interviews we detected certain commonalities in the responses that enabled us to draw the broad conclusions upon which this book is based. We found that these elders shared many approaches to living: They had led physically active and mentally stimulating lives; they had "worked at" maintaining good memories and emotionally satisfying environments; they had developed methods for making decisions and simplifying everyday activities; they had stayed flexible in their attitudes—learning and growing from change; and finally, they'd had fun in life—chasing rainbows, whether in their work, their hobbies, their social life, or their art.

We had established specific procedures for conducting the interviews, such as the opening dialogue, order of questions, and time limits, but as we worked our way through the interviews we had to reconsider our approach. We found that many interviews took several days, rather than the several hours we'd prescribed. We started with six categories of expected answers to watch for but had to add several more. Furthermore, we discovered that we could not control the direction of the interviews—each took on a life of its own.

We agonized over these defections from our original protocol and ultimately decided that we preferred the richness of the information we got from freewheeling interviews. Compiling data from such interviews was more dif-

ficult, but infinitely worthwhile because of the quality of the ideas they elic-
ited. In addition, many of these "out of control" interviews developed into
abiding friendships.

The outcome of this evolved protocol, we believe, is a valid response to
the question: What can I do now to stay mentally sharp all life long?

WHOLE-LIFE-THINKING CHECKLIST

Below are traits typical of elderly people who live life to the fullest. Please think of someone seventy or older whom you admire and circle no more than ten terms that clearly describe that person. We've left space on the facing page for you to add any other words or phrases.

flexible
good posture
powerful
independent
well informed
reflective
charming
fun loving
energetic
analytical
enthusiastic
creative
content
fluent thinker
competent
experienced
stable
philosophical
reliable
self-aware
adventurous
agile
feisty
forgetful
realistic
emotional
restless
accommodating

fit
disorganized
good memory
self-sufficient
lifelong learner
courageous
organized
involved
intelligent
indomitable
persevering
no-nonsense
knowing
equitable
responsible
adaptable
tightfisted
mature
open-minded
sharp
impatient
candid
confident
biased
misinformed
intuitive
gentle
romantic

passionate
reliable
industrious
vigorous
contemplative
good listener
manipulative
detached
repetitious
frugal
available
professional
exasperating
fragile
decisive
aware
healthy
sociable
curious
honest
optimistic
cagey
eccentric
active
witty
giving
sensitive
capable

headstrong	tolerant	prominent
honest	enlightened	altruistic
humorous	receptive	

Add any other words or phrases not listed:

BIBLIOGRAPHY

CHAPTER 1—REASSURING REALITIES

Agree, E. M. *A Portrait of Older Americans*. Washington, D.C.: American Association of Retired Persons, 1987.

Berman, P. *The Courage to Grow Old*. New York: Ballantine Books, 1989.

Berman, P., and C. Goldman, eds. *The Ageless Spirit*. New York: Ballantine Books, 1992.

Borg, W. R., and M. D. Gall. *Educational Research: An Introduction*. New York: Longman Books, 1989.

Bronte, L. *The Longevity Factor: The New Reality of Long Careers and How It Can Lead to Richer Lives*. New York: HarperCollins, 1993.

Cole, T., and S. Gadow, eds. *What Does It Mean to Grow Old?* Durham, N.C.: Duke University Press, 1986.

Etheredge, L. "An Aging Society and the Federal Government." *Statistics on Aging: The Millbank Memorial Fund Quarterly* 4, 1984.

Kidder, Tracy. *Old Friends*. Boston: Houghton Mifflin, 1993.

CHAPTER 2—THE BRAINMARKERS

Beck, Samuel J., and Herman B. Molish. *Reflexes to Intelligences*. New York: Free Press, 1959.

Corsini, Raymond J., ed. *Encyclopedia of Psychology*. New York: Wiley, 1984.

Gazzaniga, Michael S. *Psychology*. New York: Harper & Row, 1980.

Kagan, Jerome. *Psychology: An Introduction*. Harcourt Brace Jovanovich, 1972.

Loehr, James E., and Peter J. McLaughlin. *Mentally Tough: The Principles of Winning at Sports Applied to Winning in Business*. New York: Evans, 1986.

Population Reference Bureau. *Aging America: Trends and Projections*. Washington, D.C.: U.S. Department of Health and Human Services, 1988.

Walford, R. *Maximum Lifespan: The 120–140 Limit*. Boston: Houghton Mifflin, 1983.

CHAPTER 3—BREAKING THROUGH THE MYTHS ABOUT AGING

Billig, N. *Growing Older and Wiser: Coping with Expectations, Challenges and Change in the Later Years*. New York: Lexington Books, 1993.

Blurton Jones, N., and R. H. Woodson. "Describing Behavior: The Ethologists' Perspective." *Social Interaction Analysis: Methodological Issues*. Madison, Wis.: University of Wisconsin Press, 1979.

Butler, R. N. *Why Survive? Being Old in America*. New York: Harper & Row, 1975.

Charlesworth, W. "Ethology: Its Relevance for Observational Studies of Human Adaptation." *Observing Behavior* 1, 1978.

Henig, R. M. *The Myth of Senility: Misconceptions About the Brain and Aging*. Garden City, N.Y.: Anchor Press/Doubleday, 1981.

Linden, E. "A Curious Kinship: Apes and Humans." *National Geographic* 181, Mar. 1992.

Montagu, A. *On Being Human*. New York: Ballantine Books, 1966.

Nachbar, J. H. *The Evolution of Cooperation*. Boston: Houghton Mifflin, 1989.

Nishida, T. "Myths of the Wild." *National Geographic* 213, Feb. 1992.

Opie, I. and P. *The Classic Fairy Tales*. New York: Oxford University Press, 1992.

Rosenthal, S. *Education and the Self-fulfilling Prophecy*. Cambridge, Mass.: Harvard University Press, 1982.

Tan, Amy. *The Joy Luck Club*. New York: Putnam, 1989.

Tan, Amy. *The Kitchen God's Wife*. New York: Random House, 1991.

CHAPTER 4—WHAT HAPPENS WHEN THE BRAIN AGES

Bromley, D. B. *Behavioural Gerontology: Central Issues in the Psychology of Aging.* New York: Wiley, 1990.

Friedan, Betty. *The Fountain of Age.* New York: Simon & Schuster, 1993.

Grzimek, Bernard. *The Encyclopedia of Ethology.* New York: Van Nostrand Reinhold, 1976.

Restak, R. *The Brain: The Last Frontier.* New York: Warner Books, 1979.

Restak, R. *The Mind.* New York: Bantam Books, 1988.

Rybash, John M., William J. Hoyer, and Paul A. Roodin. *Adult Cognition and Aging: Developmental Changes in Processing, Knowing and Thinking.* New York: Pergamon Press, 1986.

Whitbourne, S. K. *Adult Development.* New York: Praeger, 1986.

Wonder, Jacquelyn, and Priscilla Donovan. *Whole-Brain Thinking.* New York: Quill, 1992.

CHAPTER 5—GOOD NEWS

Furst, Charles. *Origins of the Mind: Mind-Brain Connections.* Englewood Cliffs, N.J.: Prentice Hall, 1979.

Gardner, Howard. *The Shattered Mind.* New York: Knopf, 1976.

Gregory, Richard L., ed. *The Oxford Companion to the Mind.* New York: Oxford University Press, 1987.

Hudson, Frederic M. *The Adult Years: Mastering the Art of Self-renewal.* San Francisco: Jossey-Bass, 1991.

Sacks, Oliver. *The Man Who Mistook His Wife for a Hat.* New York: Summit Books, 1985.

CHAPTER 6—PHYSICAL HEALTH AND MENTAL SHARPNESS

Ackerman, Diane. *A Natural History of the Senses.* New York: Random House, 1990.

Becker, Robert O., and Gary Selden. *The Body Electric: Electromagnetism and the Foundation of Life.* New York: Morrow, 1985.

Dychtwald, K., and J. Flower. *Age Wave: The Challenges and Opportunities of Aging America.* Los Angeles: Tarcher, 1989.

Evans, William, Ph.D., and Irwin H. Rosenberg, M.D., with Jacqueline Thompson. *Biomarkers: The 10 Determinants of Aging You Can Control.* New York: Simon & Schuster, 1991.

Fallows, J. *More like Us.* Boston: Houghton Mifflin, 1989.

Fries, James, and Lawrence Crapo. *Vitality and Aging: Implications of the Rectangular Curve.* New York: Knopf, 1981.

Keeton, K. *Longevity: The Science of Staying Young.* New York: Viking Penguin, 1992.

CHAPTER 7—EMOTIONAL BALANCE AND MENTAL SHARPNESS

Benson, Herbert, and Eileen Stuart. *The Wellness Book: The Comprehensive Guide to Maintaining Health and Treating Stress-Related Illness.* Boston: Birch Lane, 1993.

Bergland, Richard, M.D. *The Fabric of Mind.* New York: Viking, 1985.

Bernard, Michael E. *Staying Rational in an Irrational World.* St. Louis: McCulloch Publishing, 1986.

Bortz, Walter M., II. *We Live Too Short and Die Too Long.* New York: Bantam Books, 1991.

Bradshaw, John. *Healing the Shame That Binds You.* Deerfield Beach, Fla.: Health Communications, 1988.

Burns, David D., M.D. *Feeling Good: The New Mood Therapy.* New York: Morrow, 1980.

Dienstfrey, Harris. *Where the Mind Meets the Body.* New York: HarperCollins, 1991.

Harrington, Anne. *Medicine, Mind, and the Double Brain.* Princeton, N.J.: Princeton University Press, 1987.

Jung, C. G. *The Portable Jung,* trans. R. F. C. Hull and ed. J. Campbell. New York: Penguin, 1971.

Lerner, Harriet Goldhor, Ph.D. *The Dance of Anger.* New York: Harper & Row, 1985.

Levinson, Daniel J. *The Seasons of a Man's Life.* New York: Ballantine Books, 1978.

Minsky, Marvin. *The Society of Mind.* New York: Simon & Schuster, 1985.

Reber, A. *Dictionary of Psychology.* New York: Penguin, 1985.

Reed, Cecil, with Priscilla Donovan. *Fly in the Buttermilk.* Iowa City: University of Iowa Press, 1993.

Scarf, Maggie. *Unfinished Business: Pressure Points in the Lives of Women.* New York: Ballantine Books, 1980.

Tannen, Deborah, Ph.D. *You Just Don't Understand: Women and Men in Conversation*. New York: Morrow, 1990.

Viorst, Judith. *Necessary Losses*. New York: Simon & Schuster, 1986.

CHAPTER 8—SHARPENING YOUR MEMORY

Festinger, Leon. *A Theory of Cognitive Dissonance*. Stanford, Calif.: Stanford University Press, 1957.

Fitzgerald, Joseph M., and Renee Lawrence. "Autobiographical Memory Across the Life-span." *Journal of Gerontology* 39, no. 6, 1984.

Maitland, D. J. *Aging: A Time for New Learning*. Atlanta: John Knox Press, 1987.

Mark, Vernon H., M.D., with Jeffrey P. Mark. *Brain Power*. Boston: Houghton Mifflin, 1989.

McCarthy, Michael J. *Mastering the Information Age*. Los Angeles: Tarcher, 1991.

Minninger, Joan, Ph.D. *Total Recall: How to Boost Your Memory Power*. New York: Pocket Books, 1984.

Rossi, Ernest Lawrence, Ph.D., with David Nimmons. *The 20-Minute Break*. Los Angeles: Tarcher, 1991.

CHAPTER 9—LEARNING HOW TO LEARN

Baldwin, A. Y. "Tests Do Underpredict." *Phi Delta Kappan,* 1977.

Biklen, S., and R. Bogdan. *Qualitative Research for Education,* 2nd ed. Boston: Allyn & Bacon, 1992.

Caine, G., and R. Caine. *Making Connections: Teaching and the Human Brain*. Alexandria, Va.: Association for Supervision and Curriculum Development, 1991.

Chase, Marilyn. "Mapping the Mind." *Wall Street Journal,* Sept. 29 and 30, Oct. 5 and 12, 1993.

Kidd, J. R. *How Adults Learn*. Englewood Cliffs, N.J.: Prentice Hall, 1978.

Maslow, A. H. *The Farther Reaches of Human Nature*. New York: Viking, 1971.

McCrone, John. *The Ape That Spoke: Language and the Evolution of the Human Mind*. New York: Morrow, 1992.

McLuhan, Eric. *Coping with the Subliminal Effects of VDTS*. Toronto: McLuhan & Davies Communications, 1986.

Ostrander, Sheila, and Lynn Schroeder. *Superlearning*. New York: Dell, 1979.

CHAPTER 10—SYSTEMS FOR THE SMALL STUFF

Davidson, J. *Breathing Space*. New York: MasterMedia, 1991.

Hait, P., and D. Hunt, Ph.D. *The Tao of Time*. New York: Simon & Schuster, 1990.

Keyes, R. *Timelock*. New York: Ballantine Books, 1991.

Waldman, S. "The Tyranny of Choice." *New Republic*, January 27, 1992.

CHAPTER 11—MAKING WISE DECISIONS

Erdmann, Erika, and David Stover. *Beyond a World Divided: Human Values in the Brain-Mind Science of Roger Sperry*. Boston and London: Shambhala, 1991.

Gordon, J. J. *Synectics*. London: Collier-Macmillan, 1961.

Heirs, Ben, with Peter Farrell. *The Professional Decision-Thinker: America's New Management and Education Priority*. New York: Dodd, Mead, 1988.

Lewis, David, and James Greene. *Thinking Better*. New York: Rawson Wade, 1982.

Luthans, Fred. *Organizational Behavior*. New York: McGraw-Hill, 1973.

Matheny, Philip R. *Critical Path Hiring*. Lexington, Mass.: Lexington Books, 1986.

O'Dell, William F. *Effective Business Decision Making and the Educated Guess*. Lincolnwood, Ill.: NTC Publishing Group, 1991.

Ohmae, Kenichi. *The Mind of the Strategist: The Art of Japanese Business*. New York: McGraw-Hill, 1982.

CHAPTER 12—OPENING YOUR MIND TO CHANGE

Barzun, J. *Television and the Child*. Chicago: University of Chicago Press, 1991.

Bridges, W. *Transitions: Making Sense of Life's Changes*. Reading, Mass.: Addison-Wesley, 1980.

Campbell, D. *Take the Road to Creativity and Get Off Your Dead End*. Allen, Tex.: Argus Communications, 1977.

Crichton, M. *Jurassic Park*. New York: Ballantine Books, 1990.

Fallows, J. *More like Us*. Boston: Houghton Mifflin, 1989.

Gardner, Howard. *Frames of Mind: The Theory of Multiple Intelligences*. New York: Basic Books, 1985.

Garner, J. D., and S. O. Mercer. *Women as They Age: Challenge, Opportunity, and Triumph*. New York: Haworth Press, 1989.

Kanter, Rosabeth Moss. *Change Masters*. New York: Touchstone Books, 1985.

Kuhn, T. *The Structure of Scientific Revolutions*. Chicago: University of Chicago Press, 1962.

Levine, S. L. *Promoting Adult Growth in Schools*. Boston: Allyn & Bacon, 1989.

Peters, Tom. *Thriving on Chaos*. New York: Knopf, 1987.

Simon, Sidney B. *Getting Unstuck: Breaking Through the Barriers*. New York: Warner Books, 1988.

Sternberg, R. J. "Toward a Triarchic Theory of Human Intelligence." *Behavioral and Brain Sciences* 7, 1985.

Sternberg, R. J. *Beyond IQ*. Cambridge, England: Cambridge University Press, 1985.

Wonder, Jacquelyn, and Priscilla Donovan. *The Flexibility Factor*. New York: Ballantine Books, 1989.

Woodward, Harry, and Steve Buchholz. *Aftershock: Helping People Through Corporate Change*. New York: Wiley, 1988.

CHAPTER 13—FINDING YOUR PASSIONS

Arieti, S. *Creativity: The Magic Synthesis*. New York: Basic Books, 1976.

Barron, F. "Putting Creativity to Work." In R. J. Sternberg, ed., *The Nature of Creativity: Contemporary Psychological Perspectives*. New York: Cambridge University Press, 1988.

Calvin, William H. *The Ascent of Mind: Ice Age Climates and the Evolution of Intelligence*. New York: Bantam Books, 1990.

Ehrenwald, Jan, M.D. *Anatomy of Genius: Split Brains and Global Minds*. New York: Human Sciences Press, 1984.

Erikson, Erik H. and Joan M., and Helen Q. Kevnick. *Vital Involvement in Old Age*. New York: Norton, 1986.

Goodnow, Jacqueline. *Children Drawing*. Cambridge, Mass.: Harvard University Press, 1977.

Harman, Willis, Ph.D., and Howard Rheingold. *Higher Creativity: Liberating the Unconscious for Breakthrough Insights*. Los Angeles: Tarcher, 1984.

Jacobs, R., Ph.D. *Be an Outrageous Older Woman—A R*A*S*P*. Manchester, Conn.: Knowledge, Ideas & Trends, 1991.

Johnson, E. W. *Older and Wiser: Wit, Wisdom and Spirited Advice from the Older Generation*. New York: Walker, 1986.

Levinson, Harold N. *A Solution to the Riddle of Dyslexia*. New York: Springer-Verlag, 1980.

Siegel, G., B. Agranoff, and R. W. Albers, eds. *Basic Neurochemistry*. New York: Raven Press, 1989.

Simonton, D. K. "You're Never Too Old to Be Creative." *The Gerontologist*, 1990.

Tiger, Lionel. *The Pursuit of Pleasure*. Boston: Little, Brown, 1992.

CHAPTER 14—AN EMPOWERING VISION OF YOUR FUTURE

Epstein, R. "Generativity Theory and Creativity." In A. Runco and R. S. Albert, eds., *Theories of Creativity*. London: Sage, 1990.

Martz, Sandra, ed. *When I Am an Old Woman I Shall Wear Purple*. Watsonville, Calif.: Papier-Mache Press, 1987.

Nietzsche, F. *Beyond Good and Evil: Prelude to a Philosophy of the Future*. New York: Vintage, 1966.

Tournier, Paul. *Learn to Grow Old*. Louisville, Ky.: Westminster/John Knox Press, 1972.

INDEX

AARP (American Association of Retired
Persons), 40, 93
acetylcholine, 71
acronyms, 129, 150
acrostics, 129, 131
acting, 10
activities, Brainmarker:
body wisdom and, 25–26, 243
decision making and, 32, 245
emotions and, 27, 244
learning and, 29, 30, 244
memory and, 28, 244
mental skills and, 24
openness to change and, 34, 245
passion and, 35, 245
system for control and, 31, 245
adolescents:
emotions of, 26
flexibility of, 33
hormone levels of, 105
adrenaline, 102–103, 105, 141
advertising, 74, 131–133
aging:
attitude toward, 37–45
brain and, 19–22, 23, 49–65, 94,
159
emotions and, 120–121

exercise and, 86–90, 198
learning and, 156–157, 159
memory and, 37, 41, 43, 45, 127–129
myths about, 20, 37–45
negative attitudes toward, 38–39
normal, 83
positive attitudes toward, 39–40
self-fulfilling prophecies about,
43
AIDS, 71
alcohol, 55, 69, 80, 95, 109, 112
Alcoholics Anonymous, 93
alcoholism, 68, 73, 75, 92–93, 112
Allen, Fred, 125
Allen, Gracie, 42
aluminum, 70
Alzheimer's disease:
age and, 68, 70
causes of, 70–72, 73
diagnosis of, 68–72
medications for, 71, 72, 78
memory loss and, 67, 68–69
mental functions disturbed by, 20
"picture profile" of, 98
signs of, 67, 68–69
American Association of Retired Persons
(AARP), 40, 93